EXPLANATION
AND POWER

EXPLANATION AND POWER
The Control of Human Behavior

Morse Peckham

A CONTINUUM BOOK
THE SEABURY PRESS · NEW YORK

1979
The Seabury Press
815 Second Avenue
New York, N.Y. 10017

Printed in the United States of America

Library of Congress Cataloging in Publication Data
Peckham, Morse.   Explanation and power.
(A Continuum book)
1. Meaning (Psychology) 2. Psycholinguistics. 3. Personality.
4. Culture. 5. Social institutions. I. Title.
BF455.P354   401   78-17604   ISBN 0-8164-9352-9

For Robert L. Stewart

I thought of turning honest — what a dream!
Robert Browning

Why does a man write? Because he does not
possess enough character not to write.
Karl Kraus

CONTENTS

PREFACE

This book got itself written because I was told to write it, and like everyone else I usually do what I am told to do. Some years ago my friend and colleague, Robert L. Stewart, Professor of Sociology, University of South Carolina, told me that my writing through 1970 pointed directly toward a general theory of human behavior and that I must write such a book. I was astonished, and to a considerable degree I remain astonished. Through nearly a decade of discussions Professor Stewart has encouraged me and urged me forward; not the least of his services is that his acute and demanding mind has not let me get away with anything that could not meet his rigorous intellectual requirements.

It is also a pleasure to offer my thanks to Professor Leo Daugherty, of The Evergreen State College, who probably knows my work better than I do. He read the manuscript, gave me enthusiastic encouragement, and offered to edit it. His extensive labor freed it of innumerable infelicities, syntactical tangles, and confusions in my argument.

Both of these friends have struggled manfully against my natural impatience, carelessness, and indifference to what I write once I have written it. And I am also grateful to colleagues, students, and other friends who have listened to me, argued with me, encouraged me, and read the manuscript, offering their encouragement and their help. It is a particular pleasure to name them: Beate Bennett, George Buelow, Robert Combs, Daniel Fineman, Judith and Lee Friedman, John Gagnon, Robert King, William Kreml, William and Carolyn Matalene, Harry Miller, James Myers, Cameron and Donna Northouse, Annie-Paule Quinsac, Peter Sederberg, Charles Tucker, and Philip Zeltner. To all my friends who have helped me so I can only say that I hope this book justifies their confidence.

February, 1978
Columbia, S. C.

INTRODUCTION

Often enough it is easier to grasp a book and what it is up to and what is going on in it if the reader has some notion of how and why it came to be written and what the issues were which impelled the author to write it. For such a book as this the appropriate perspective is not the personal life of the author but what might be called his cultural life. The very fact of the writing of the book is odd, particularly since the academic and intellectual world is today organized into separate disciplines, each of which has accumulated a daunting body of information and theory. This book does not fall neatly into any of the accepted and professional intellectual and scientific disciplines. It is concerned with philosophical issues, but it is not a work of philosophy. It is deeply involved with the problems of language, but it is not linguistics. It struggles with the problems of psychology and sociology, but it is neither. Nor is it a work of political science, though it directs its attention to some of the problems of that discipline. It is not cultural history; yet it concludes by turning its attention to a crucial problem of cultural history.

And that last concern of the book is reasonable enough, for that is the concern with which the enterprise began that culminated with this work. It is undeniably odd, and probably suspicious, that someone whose formal training was in English literary history and whose principal interest for several decades was the literature of Victorian England should attempt a general theory of human behavior, one, moreover, based upon a single concept, that of the sign. How this undertaking came about will, I believe, illuminate the oddity of the book and its peculiar organization, an organization in which the first chapter—a chapter which should, by all traditions of expository writing, be the most accessible—is the most difficult.

Thirty years ago, fresh out of graduate school, I soon realized that I could not hope to comprehend my principal interest and my academic specialty, Victorian literature, without a satisfactory theory and explanation of a phenomenon which seemed more extraordinary the more I studied it—the cultural phenomenon of Romanticism. Certainly there was an enormous body of scholarship on the subject, but the more I studied it and attempted to use the current conceptions of Romanticism in order to understand the Romantic texts—literature, philosophy, painting, and music—the more baffled I felt. I began asking myself such questions as, What is history? What is culture? What is philosophy? What is literature? One thing seemed clear enough: literature is a mode of language. So my question became, What is language. And indeed all my questions seemed more and more to reduce themselves to or be subsumed by that one overarching question: What is language?

At that time, I soon learned, philosophy itself was intensely involved with that very question and even was beginning to think that that was not only the proper question for philosophy but even, perhaps, philosophy's sole question. One's intellectual life does not proceed neatly and logically. It proceeds by accident. And it was a matter of luck that I addressed my question about language to a colleague at the University of Pennsylvania, Professor Elizabeth Flower, who did not answer my question but said something that was to prove far more valuable than any answer then available could have been. Charles Peirce, she told me, had said that we cannot have a theory of language until we have a general theory of signs. And since there was no such theory, there could be, from that point of view, no theory of language. Another bit of luck was that one of the great works of Victorian literature is Thomas Carlyle's *Sartor Resartus*. According to Ernest Cassirer, that work is the first work which proposes anything like a useful theory of symbolism. But since no word is so confusing as "symbol," I soon found that it was far more useful to think about the book in terms of signs or, technically, semiosis, for Charles Morris's *Signs, Language, and Behavior* fell into my hands. Though his theory of signs turns out, I came to believe, to be unmanageable, far too complex to be useful, and without adequate theoretical grounding, nevertheless after I read it, I felt that I knew and could understand what Carlyle had been attempting to do. For the first time *Sartor Resartus* was clear to me.

Nevertheless, the way before me was by no means yet open. To solve the problem of Romanticism I needed, it seemed to me, an

epistemology which would bear my weight; a theory of art and literature which would make sense; and a theory of cultural history. But the
pursuit of such matters within the disciplines in which such questions
are actively tossed about, though not perhaps really studied, became
increasingly fruitless. It became evident that not only would it be
impossible to solve the problem of Romanticism within the discipline
in which I had been trained but also that neighboring humanistic disciplines would be of very little help.

I turned, then, to subjects that appeared to me to subsume these
disciplines: psychology, sociology, and above all anthropology. Yet I
soon discovered that in spite of the richness anthropology could offer
me, theoretically it was very weak. But the study of these subjects led
me into two quite different paths of inquiry: the history of art and the
philosophy of science. Though I had made little progress in any grasp
of the nature of semiosis and of understanding the concept of the sign,
that concept provided a connection from one discipline to another. At
the same time, my reading in the philosophy of science led me, no
matter how many paths I explored, to the one overwhelming question:
What is meaning? What are we talking about when we use that word?
And another problem arose, inseparable from it. When we explain the
meaning of a word or a sign, what are we doing? What is explanation?
What is an explanation of a meaning? What is the meaning of an
explanation?

The result of this struggle was the conclusion that current theories of
meaning which were to be found within the discipline of philosophy
were in fact quite useless. Nor could linguistics help me, since linguists had as yet scarcely done more than to recognize that sooner or
later they would have to come to grips with the problem. Some fifteen
years ago I found myself backed into, as it were, the fundamental
proposition of this book: *The meaning of any utterance or any sign is
the response to that utterance or sign.* I did not then know, nor know
for more than a decade, that George Herbert Mead, the American
Pragmatist, had arrived at precisely that formulation in 1900. Yet he
did little with it. Now it is also worth notice that Charles Morris, with
whom I began in my effort to understand the word "sign," was in the
tradition of Mead and Dewey, that is, of American Pragmatism. With
the arrival at my basic proposition I felt for the first time that I was
beginning to be free of the endless entanglements of philosophy. Yet if
this book is in a philosophical tradition, it is in the tradition of the

American Pragmatists. But they all started out as Hegelians. And having become familiar with the major works of Hegel, I realized increasingly as I wrote this book that it is hardly too much to say that it is a behavioral interpretation or rewriting of Hegel. But by "behavioral" I do not mean "behavioristic." As the first chapter makes clear enough, I have little respect for academic behaviorism, for behaviorists are not nearly behavioral enough.

At this point in my inquiry I had written my first book, a study of nineteenth-century cultural history, and my second, an attempt to create a behavioral theory of art built upon the theory of biological adaptation. (Some years before, I had edited Darwin's great work.) And in my proposal about art I made my first effort to construct a general theory of signs. Since I still was too dependent upon Morris and had not yet clearly extracted from my thinking my basic proposition about meaning, that theory turned out to be a failure. Still, my approach was on the right track, I felt—sign production and sign meaning as modes of behavior. A few years later having, to my intense surprise, undertaken a study of pornography, I tried again. This attempt was a vast improvement, for I could put to use my theory of the nonimmanency of meaning. Furthermore, the inadequacy of any theory of sexual behavior, necessary to explain pornography, led me into constructing a theory of explanation and, most importantly, to the place of explanation in human behavior. But that led, though I had to be told it did, to an explanation, or theory, of human behavior itself. In short, I had found I could not explain Romanticism until I had a semiotic explanation of human behavior, and it was not until much of this book was written that I proposed a theory of Romanticism which satisfied me. Indeed, considering that this book is in the tradition of Hegel and Pragmatism, it is itself in the Romantic tradition.

I have, furthermore, another great nineteenth-century predecessor. Auguste Comte provided in his *Positive Philosophy* a justification for what I have attempted. Eventually, he said, all of the sciences would be subsumed by and incorporated within what he called "sociology," that is, the study of human behavior. And I suppose that from the Comtean point of view, the leading idea of this book is the notion of behavior that it presents: behavior controls behavior. Yet I go beyond Comte in eliminating from my theory the notion of "mind." Likewise I go beyond the Pragmatists in asserting not merely that the proper way of conceiving the human organism's relation to the world is as a relational transaction but that that transaction is a semiotic transaction.

Nevertheless, it was not reasonable to begin the book at that point. One must, I felt, begin with the limiting condition of any discourse, that is, that even when one is purporting to talk about verbal behavior, that talk itself is verbal behavior. To get some understanding of what the consequences are, it is necessary to remove long-standing obstacles to comprehending meaning and explanation. That is the task, the difficult task, of the first chapter. The lions in the way are words about which philosophy and psychology continuously revolve without, so far as I can see, having done much but stir up a great deal of dust. And the first of these words is the maddening and perplexing "cause" itself. Once that has been disposed of, "meaning" can be engaged with, and the word psychologists have treated so badly, "response," and its related words. Those, in turn, are followed by an engagement with another sacred word, "logic," and then "mind" itself and its companion, "intention." With these words out of the way and with a comprehension of meaning as response, it becomes possible to understand explanation and the structure of explanation. That, in turn, leads to the conclusion of Chapter I—all verbal utterance is both normative and fictive. Put differently, the proposal is that the notion of language as communication is a sentimentality; language is behavioral control and the primary mode of such control. Or put in another way, when we affirm that a statement is true, we are only asserting that it *ought* to control our behavior.

Chapter II then asks whether what is the case for verbal signs is also the case for nonverbal signs, and it is concluded that they too are normative and fictive, whether man-made or natural. In this the primary problem is how verbal signs differ from nonverbal signs, and a theory is suggested as to what made it possible in human evolution for man to create verbal signs from the condition of nonverbal semiosis, already found among animals. And this investigation gives us a richer notion of behavior: response is now understood as semiotic transformation of the world, which, for humans, consists of signs. But that transformation, on closer examination, involves interpretation. What interpretation involves and its identity with explanation is next explored. Finally, science is explained as the norm of man's transaction with the world.

Chapter III takes up a problem for which we are now ready. If meaning is not immanent, if meaning is response, how are that meaning and response stabilized? They must be stabilized, ultimately and fundamentally, for the sake of reasonably smooth interaction in economic activity. If behavior is not controlled, it becomes random. The control of response is essential to the human enterprise. But ultimately response can be controlled only by force. Culture is defined as instructions for performance; or, culture turns behavior into performance. Meaning, it is proposed, is sustained by redundancies, the constant reiteration of cultural directions in various semiotic modes. Without that redundant reiteration, behavior disintegrates. Meanings, or culturally validated responses (the lowest level of behavior), are maintained by redundancies; redundancies are maintained by culture; culture is maintained by institutions; and institutions are maintained by force. The suggestion is that what we call culture has emerged because if force is unsuccessful in stabilizing behavior, there is no alternative. So culture is a human strategy for circumventing and postponing the use of force. The most important mode of that strategy is the institution. And an institution is identified with explanation itself, thus placing almost all of human behavior under verbal control. These kinds of explanatory controls are seen as five kinds of institutions, which, I believe, exhaust the varieties of human institutions.

Chapter IV takes up the question of questions—the individual. Theories of human behavior, derived from the dualism of Descartes and maintained by Kant, almost invariably begin with the "mind" or the individual organism as the building block of a theory of human behavior. This book, of course, proposes the sign response as that basic building block and defines the individual as a mere cultural precipitate, a randomly assembled package of behavioral patterns, held together by a "mental construct," that is, a persistent semiotic transformation. But for that very reason the individual is always and necessarily at odds with and incoherent with institutions and explanations. All human institutions work, but because they are manned by individuals, none of them works very well or can work very well.

It is for this reason that all notions of a decent society, or of a redemptive paradise, or of a utopia, or of a socialism that solves economic and moral problems, are illusory and damaging to what chance for success the human enterprise may have; and perhaps that chance is not very great. At any rate, semiosis in the rich human mode of explanation is what man is; it makes humanity possible. But it is man's cross that the constructive power of explanation is equaled by its destructive force. Man's opportunity may be his nemesis.

When I had finished this book, I felt that it was so gloomy and discouraging that perhaps it would be better not to publish it. But then it occurred to me that gloomy prophets have very little effect and that perhaps one possible moral might be—it is faintly possible—salutary, at least for a few people. And that moral is that we cannot transcend our semiotically imposed limitations, that the hope of creating a redeemed society is vain, illusory, and destructive. The effort to create a social order free of control which is sustained by force only increases the uncontrolled exercise of naked power.

EXPLANATION

An inquiry into any area of interest yields, if one judges the effort to be successful, an explanation. But the difficulty of explaining human behavior lies in this: an explanation of human behavior is itself a mode of human behavior. No matter how carefully we may observe nonverbal behavior, no matter what safeguards for that observation we may set up, no matter how exacting the controls, we still must state our conclusions, our explanations of that nonverbal behavior, in verbal behavior. We must use the language of verbal behavior to talk about explanation, but then we must use the language of explanation to talk about verbal behavior or any kind of human behavior. To discuss either, we must have a verbally constructed theory of the other, or we must "understand" it; that is, we must have an explanation of it. To explain behavior, we must have an explanation of explanation; but to have an explanation of explanation, we must first have an explanation of behavior. From one point of view a theory of explanation logically subsumes a theory of behavior, but from another and equally valid point of view a theory of behavior logically subsumes a theory of explanation. But a theory of behavior is an explanation, although, to be sure, a theory of explanation is a mode of verbal behavior. Where to begin: with behavior or with explanation?

Puzzling as this seems, the obvious answer is before us. I have already engaged in verbal behavior, and that behavior is an example of explanation, even though as yet nothing much has been explained. If one raises the question about which is logically prior, behavior or explanation, it is evident that one is explaining that there is a problem. One is already engaged in explanation. The logical priority is of no significance. But the behavioral priority is clear; it is explanation.

To define behavior, then, one must first define explanation, for that is where one begins. It is not a matter open to choice. By writing, I have already made the decision. But this means, unfortunately, that behavior must remain undefined for the time being. After explanation is clarified, behavior can be clarified; and then explanation can be further clarified, and its place in behavior can be comprehended.

Explanation is ubiquitous in human behavior, so omnipresent that to understand it, even incompletely, is to develop an insight that no other insight can match. Explanation is found constantly, at all levels of culture, in every kind of social organization, in every human situation. In what are called the higher studies—philosophy, the sciences, the study of the humanities—men devote their lives merely to explanation and do little else, certainly nothing else that makes them different from the rest of mankind. And even in this activity they are merely specializing in and concentrating on a mode of behavior that everyone engages in. Politics, for example, is the art of persuading the public and other politicians that action is properly taken on the basis of the explanation of what are perceived as problems amenable to political manipulation. Politics is engaged in social management, but so is business, and so indeed are a husband and wife, or two friends, or two children in rivalry over which will play in how much of the sandbox and with what toys. We cannot manage others without explanation, nor can we manage ourselves. We justify our actions and our plans by explaining their importance—their value—both to ourselves and to others. Social interaction without explanation is inconceivable; it may be the very condition of human existence. Yet in these simple statements lurks a number of traps, snake pits which are ordinarily leapt over, or skirted, or covered up, or bridged, but which nevertheless are there. What is more, these traps and snake pits are concealed and ignored by two disciplines which claim that they are doing just the reverse—the disciplines of philosophy and psychology. What lies in the path of understanding explanation, and thus of behavior, are certain words. These two disciplines have taken possession of these words, have asserted themselves to be their proper custodians, and fiercely resent and resist the efforts of anyone else to use them in ways they disapprove of or with an understanding they have not validated. They claim to have cleared up much in how these words are used, but they have cleared up very little, if anything. So eager have been the practitioners of philosophy and psychology to define these words and to control how they are used that they have scarcely observed their own behavior. What are philosophers and psychologists *doing*? What is the character of *their* behavior? Why are they so eager to control our behavior when we use these words, words so essential to any kind of what we call thinking?

I am talking about *causality, meaning, rhetoric, logic, mind,* and *intention;* and *stimulus, response, conditioning;* and—most perplexing of all the sacred words of psychology—*reinforcement.* We need to wonder if philosophy and psychology can properly be called "intellectual disciplines." Ever since philosophy gave birth to psychology—a most painful parturition—the two have been snarling and snapping and biting at each other—a continuous dogfight. Chemistry and physics do not attack each other in this manner, nor do poetry and painting. Yet philosophy and psychology have long been quarreling over the sacred words I have just listed. Philosophy should have enabled us to understand that special aspect of verbal behavior I have called explanation, and psychology should have enabled us to understand behavior and the place in it of explanatory behavior. But these two verbal enterprises, or rhetorics, have done neither. These sacred words, then, must be attacked head on, for they are central to all modern efforts to understand both explanation and behavior. It is necessary to spring the traps these words conceal, to drain of poison the snake pits they bridge. And in the effort to do so, much can be learned about that strange and central mode of human behavior I have called explanation.

CAUSALITY

Let us begin at the very edge of explanation, at the frontier at which perceptual observation is transformed, magically metamorphosed, transcendentally apotheosized into language. What are we doing when we make our observations? Observation and transformation are also forms of behavior. How do we select *this* rather than *that* aspect of nonverbal behavior to observe? What precisely are we talking about when we say we set up safeguards or controls? That is, what kind of behavior are we talking about? And, more treacherously, what happens when we convert our observations into words? This too is a form of behavior. How do we move from the nonverbal to the verbal? And, more confusing still, when we observe that behavior b follows behavior a, in one instance or in thousands, and when we state that observation in words, as I have here, and when we follow that by uttering some such statement as "a causes b" or, more circumspectly, "a entails b," where do "cause" or "entail" come from? How do they get into this discourse? Or if we say, with still greater caution, "*b* follows *a* in a sufficient number of sampled instances to be statistically significant," where do these new words—"sufficient number," "sampled," "statistically significant"—come from? The introduction of such words into the discourse resulting from our observations certainly cannot be justified by saying that there is something in what we observed of which these words are a direct and unmediated consequence. On the contrary, they appear to be the consequence of saying "*b* follows *a*." So the introduction of such words is itself a mode of behavior, but, since they follow verbal behavior and not the observation of nonverbal behavior, the behavior that produces them seems to be of a different order or kind than the verbal behavior that results from an observation.

Moreover, a further puzzlement appears when we state that "*b* follows *a* because of *x*." The introduction of *x* is the emergence of an entirely new bit of verbal behavior, quite different from either the original observation or from the initial verbal consequences of that observation. Once again, where does *x* come from? What is the justification for bringing it in? Moreover, we have now got into a reflexive tangle, for this new statement exports from verbal behavior a new factor into that nonverbal behavior which we began by observing. Thus "*b* follows *a* because of *x*" is transformed into "*x* caused *b* to follow *a*," and this is now taken as a sound implication that in the observed situation there was also a "cause" as well as the observed events. Thus we have at once moved farther away from the events and deeper into layers of verbal behavior, and at the same time we have returned to our original event and added something to it. If we now take a further step in this kind of discourse and say, "Since *x* caused *b* to follow *a*, *b* is the result of *x*," or "*b* is the effect of *x*," or say, more circumspectly, that "*b* is the effect of *a*," we have introduced one or two new words, depending on whether we consider "effect" and "result" as interchangeable. And, again, where do these words come from? Confusion is now further increased if we return from the nonverbal to the verbal and say, "*x* exists, or we are justified in saying so, because for every effect there is a cause and for every cause there is an effect." We have thus arrived at the famous and indeed notorious cause-effect relationship or cause-effect nexus, and we have done so by the exceedingly dubious means common to both philosophy and psychology. This dubiousness can be made a little clearer.

Consider as our observed event [(a)=(Jones hit Smith) and (b)=(Smith hit Jones)]. Our second verbalization of this was "(a) (Jones hit Smith) causes (b) (Smith hit Jones)." We have one "cause" here, but, as we have seen, further verbal behavior resulted in quite a different place for "cause" in the formulation: thus, "(b) (Smith hit Jones) follows (a) (Jones hit Smith) because of x," or "x caused (b) (Smith hit Jones) to follow (a) (Jones hit Smith)." Disregarding that the "to" in this sentence introduces a new and confusing word, the dubious status of x can be shown simply enough. Suppose that (Jones hit Smith, but Smith did not hit Jones). Thus, we are in the position of saying, "Smith did not hit Jones because of x" instead of "Smith hit Jones because of x." Now x, it will be remembered, was the factor exported into the observed event from the verbal behavior that followed the observation of that verbal event. Clearly, if x can cause Smith to hit Jones and can also cause Smith not to hit Jones, x can stand for any number of statements, such as, "Some men retaliate at once to provocation, and some men do not," or "Just as Smith was about to hit Jones, there was an earthquake," or "At the time of Smith's birth, Mars was in conjunction with Venus; therefore, he hit (or did not hit) Jones," or "The last time Smith hit someone who had hit him, he was clobbered and spent a week in the hospital." For x it is possible to substitute if not an infinite at least an indefinably large number of statements. We can scarcely say that x was observable in this incident, and if we cannot say that, we can scarcely say that b was the necessary consequence of a. Jones hit Smith, but after that, Smith could have done anything at all.

Even if we turn back to the first and simplest utterance, "Smith hitting Jones followed Jones hitting Smith," that statement was not a necessary consequence of the observation. Other statements could be made: "Jones was wearing a red necktie, but Smith wasn't wearing a necktie at all," or "The bartender did nothing," or "It looked as if Smith's pants were falling down," or "Jones looked angry but, oddly enough, Smith didn't seem to be at all angry." And if we go on to the next sentence, it is just as unnecessary to say, "Jones's hitting Smith caused Smith to hit Jones." Not only is "cause" imported here from somewhere other than the observed event, other utterances would be possible: "Jones's blow resulted in Smith's return blow." This statement leaves quite open the question of "cause," of which it affirms nothing. Or "The two blows were linked." If we continue to produce sentences following each of the tracks indicated, we could arrive at three quite different sentences at deeper layers of verbal behavior. The "cause" sentence could lead, obviously, to a very general cause-effect sentence. The "result" sentence could lead to a questioning of cause-effect, such as, "A result is produced by an event that happened prior to it, but that event cannot be determined." And the "link" sentence could lead to some such statement as "An event that follows a previous event is linked somehow or other to that event, but *how* can scarcely be known," or, somewhat more strongly, "The link is not the sort of thing that we can yet know," or "The determination of the character of that link is the task of science," or "That linking can be talked about only in statistical language."

That each of these verbal tracks is the one that ought to be followed with the proper termination at sentences like those I have given has been argued passionately in philosophy and continues to be argued. For that reason, if no other, the kind of discourse I have presented can easily be mistaken for philosophical discourse, and I expect some readers will take it in that way. Some of these readers, I have no doubt, will say that it is bad philosophy; some might even say that it is good philosophy, though among them, I suspect, will not be professional philosophers. Some philosophers might say that, to be sure, it is not particularly bad philosophy; it is merely unsophisticated, naive, and primitive. But in any case, and no matter what it may look like, I do not intend it to be philosophy. Philosophy, I believe, is concerned with laying down rules about how we *ought* to move from sentence to sentence; that is, philosophy is *normative*, to use its own terminology. It is concerned with prescribing what ought to go into sentences that ought to be called true sentences and with prescribing what kind of sentence ought to follow a true sentence in order to preserve the truth value of the first sentence. Since philosophy maintains that it is not a prescriptive enterprise but a descriptive one, any philosopher—or at least any philosopher that I have run across, in print or in flesh—will tell me that I am wrong.

On the other hand, I would not claim that the discourse in question is not prescriptive. If it is descriptive, it is prescriptive, for a description proposes to its auditor that he look for *this* rather than for *that*. Thus I am saying that in observing the verbal movements from an observed event to a statement about cause and effect, the phenomenon that ought to be observed is that no verbal step in this movement is necessary, that each step introduces new words not derivable from the previous step, and that each step is but one of an indefinably large number of alternative steps that could be made at that point. The analysis that I have offered is thus an *exemplification* of the more general proposition that the movement from an observed event to a statement about the cause-effect nexus of that event is done by exceedingly dubious means.

That the notion of causality is a puzzling notion is scarcely a novel proposition. Philosophers—and others—puzzled over it long before Hume threw philosophy into extreme perplexity about the problem, and philosophers argue about it and discuss it daily. One recent commentator has this to say on the subject:

> From the foregoing considerations it is apparent that some of the main philosophical problems of causation do not yield to any easy solution. The ideas of a necessary connection between cause and effect may be, as Hume thought, an esoteric and metaphysical one, but it is doubtful whether anyone can render an adequate analysis of the causal relation without it. The idea of a causal power or efficacy is perhaps more esoteric still, and yet there is no obvious way of eliminating it from the concept of causation. . . . If, however, one professes to find no difference between the relation of cause to its effect, on the one hand, and of an effect to its cause, on the other, he appears to contradict the common sense of mankind, for the difference appears perfectly apparent to most men. . . . Here as in so many areas of philosophy, our advances over our predecessors appear more illusory than real. (Richard Taylor, "Causation," in *The Encyclopedia of Philosophy*, ed. Paul Edwards, The Free Press, 1967, II, 66.)

Really, however, the notion of causality is puzzling only if one puzzles over it. If one reads the entire essay of which this passage is the conclusion, an obvious point emerges, one to which Taylor draws attention but does not make the most of. That point is that *as science developed, the notion of causality changed*. More precisely, as science made discoveries which the current concept of causality could not adequately account for, philosophy responded by reexamining the notion of causality, refining it, redefining it, questioning it, innovating alternative notions, and so on. This is why no "advances over our predecessors" have been made. Philosophy, in response to changes in science, has changed its rules for determining whether a causal statement is legitimate or not. Thus such a statement as "God is the final cause of all events," though once regarded in philosophy as a legitimate statement, is no longer so regarded. On the other hand Taylor seems to assert that causality is a necessary but unanalyzable notion. Possibly he thinks of it as a philosophical primitive, a proposition beyond or beneath which it is impossible to go. In any case his position seems properly interpreted as the notion that when we use the term "cause," we do not know what we are talking about, but all the same it is necessary to talk about it. And this in turn appears to be a recommendation to continue to use the word without worrying about whether we are talking about anything or not. He seems to be saying that causal statements are legitimate because we cannot do without them. And this, in turn, if it is an interpretation he would accept, seems to legitimate the philosophical enterprise of discussing the notion of causality. That a philosopher should be interested in legitimating philosophy need not surprise us.

Thus I think that the real point of his essay in fact escapes him. His final statement that philosophers have made no advances over their predecessors surely is regretful in tone. Philosophers, it seems to be implied, ought to make advances over their predecessors and, in some areas, do, though not in causality. But perhaps the notion that philosophical advances should be made is *itself* illusory. If we consider the twenty-five hundred-year history of causality, all that is obvious is that the notion of causality is readjusted as the cultural conditions change in the context of which philosophical discourse about causality takes place. What appears to have happened can be understood if we turn back to an observation already made. Before "cause" is anything else, before it is a notion, or an idea, or a concept, "cause" is a word. That word appears in verbal behavior after an observation of the nonverbal has been made or even while it is being made; *when* it appears makes no difference. Furthermore, as the various successive steps in the subsequent verbal process are made, "cause" can take on different functions, though that function always exports from the verbal into the nonverbal a factor which is not observable.

If I tell someone to go find Jones and a policeman, and if I then have the latter arrest the former for disturbing the peace, or if I tell someone to go find Jones and buy him a beer for having given that obnoxious Smith a bloody nose, the chances are that that someone can find someone whom others, and maybe even Jones himself, will identify as the man who hit Smith. But if I tell someone to find the cause for which Jones hit Smith, he cannot, *in the same way,* find the cause. But *in another way* he can find the cause. He can reflect thoughtfully and consider carefully and then say, "Well, the gossip is that Smith has been making passes at Jones's wife, and successful passes at that." That what has been found is a sentence is so obvious that that fact may easily elude us. Of course, that sentence is "found" only if we take literally the metaphor that the person who utters the sentence had previously "searched his mind." In short, "cause" belongs to verbal behavior, not to nonverbal events, even nonverbal behavioral events; and an instruction to determine a cause for a nonverbal event is an instruction to engage in verbal behavior, not in nonverbal behavior.

Comparing two similar but not identical sentences will make this clearer. "My finger hits the typewriter key and causes a letter to appear on the paper," and "My finger hits the typewriter key and a letter appears on the paper." What does "cause" in the first sentence add to the second sentence? Certainly the addition of this word together with "to" gives me the feeling that I have said something of significance, but have I? Surely I know nothing more about the operation of the typewriter than I did before, but on the other hand—and this is the explanation for the sense of significance—an opportunity has been opened to me to learn something more. Suppose that I now say to myself, "If I hit the key with my finger a letter will appear on the paper." And suppose that I do that and a letter does not appear, the introduction of the word "cause" enables me to make further tests. I discover then that I did not hit the key hard enough, as a few tests show me. Now suppose that I say, "If I hit the key with my finger a letter always appears on the paper." But this is an IBM Selectric typewriter, and sometimes instead of a letter appearing on the paper (a letter that corresponds to the letter on the key), a hyphen appears. At this point I am at a loss. So I ask my IBM serviceman about the matter, and he tells me that this model does sometimes make that particular mistake. He also starts to tell me why but gives up. I *think* the hyphen appears when I hit two keys in too close succession. At least when I do get a hyphen instead of the letter I want, it seems to me that that is what has happened. On the other hand I have yet to *make* it happen, though once or twice I think I have succeeded in doing so.

Thus, the previous statement that the word "cause" is an instruction to engage in verbal behavior, not in nonverbal behavior, needs to be qualified. If the causal statement is recast in an "If . . . then . . . " form which consists of instructions for nonverbal behavior, then the behavior initiated by the word "cause" can eventuate in nonverbal search behavior. At this point, however, it is advisable to introduce a caution. If I "search" for both verbal and nonverbal behavior, I tend to *subsume* (a word to be given a detailed analysis later) both kinds in such a way that a similarity between the two appears to be asserted. Clearly, when I talk about verbal search behavior, I am using "search" metaphorically. On the other hand, when I talk about nonverbal search behavior as initiated by the term "cause," I am initiating not only search behavior but also "test behavior."

This is obvious from my testing of my typewriter behavior, but a further example will make the point clearer. "The water in the mill race by striking the water wheel paddles causes the wheel to revolve." To test this I can restate it in an "if . . . then . . . " form, or I can proceed without further behavior to diverting the water from the mill race. If the water wheel continues to revolve, I can be at a loss, *unless* I am in possession of the general notion, "An effect is produced by a cause." With this as a very general instruction, I search for another cause for the water wheel revolving; and I discover, let us say, that an electric motor inside the mill is causing the water wheel to revolve, for this particular water wheel is in a commercial amusement park. Again, armed with the general notion "cause," I can ask myself why this ingenious mechanism is necessary, and further searching and testing then disclose the fact that the mill race does not contain a sufficient flow of water to turn the wheel. Why not? What is the cause for this situation? I ask the park engineer and am informed that studies and tests had shown that it is less expensive to run the water wheel by electricity than to provide enough water to run it by water alone.

Thus, the word "cause" does not add information, as philosophers such as Taylor have believed (or at least hoped) or have denied, as in the Humean tradition. Its appearance can eventuate in both verbal and nonverbal behavior, though, it is to be remembered, it need not eventuate in any behavior. When philosophers, or anyone else behaving in the philosophical mode, asks what the word "cause" means, all they can do is to provide simple and elaborate verbal substitutes for it, concluding, if they are like Taylor, that it certainly means something, though they cannot say what.

MEANING

Once again we are faced with the kind of puzzlement we have encountered before. What do such words as "information" and "meaning" mean? The meaning of "meaning" is an ancient problem, worked over time and time again but on the whole with as little result as the endless discussions of causality. Until very recently it was assumed that a word has a determinate meaning and that careful analysis would reveal that meaning. However, when such attempts are made, all that happens is the substitution of other words for the word in question. It appears reasonably clear that what is in fact happening is not that the determinate meaning is uncovered but rather that *someone determines* the meaning; such discourse concludes with a prescription of what meaning *ought* to be found in the word, or it concludes, less frequently, with a statement that the meaning of the word is obvious and that we cannot get along without it, even though the meaning cannot be uttered. More recently, baffled by the traditional way of struggling with the question, some philosophers, led by Wittgenstein, have proposed that an unequivocal meaning can be discovered from the use of a word. This proposal seems promising until it is realized that an investigation into use involves an examination of all the factors, verbal and nonverbal, present in the situation in which the use takes place and involves further an unlimited examination of similar situations. Similarity is, and must be, *determined* by neglecting those factors in two situations which are judged not to be found in both. As the range of situations determining usage is extended, more factors found in the beginning situation will have to be abandoned. Eventually the only factor left will be the word itself.

An interesting example of this process can be found in William S. Newman's splendid series of three volumes on the keyboard sonata from late in the seventeenth-century to the present time. He began by assuming that "sonata" has a determinable meaning, or "essence." The successive situations he examined were identifiable enough, each consisting of a piece of music with "sonata" at the beginning. He expected to discover in the musical pieces certain constant factors, and these having been discovered, he would then have a definition of "sonata." But as his historical investigations continued, carried out in the chronological order of the writing and publication of the sonatas—hundreds and hundreds of them—in European and American music, he discovered something that surprised him a good deal. Under

the rubric of the word "sonata" the actual pieces, examined in historical succession, dropped some factors and added others, so that eventually none of the factors common among the first sonatas were left in the
later ones. A "sonata" thus turned out to be a piece of music with the
word "sonata" in its title. At best the word could mean a piece of
music to be played rather than sung and one which the composer hoped
would receive serious attention. But such factors apply equally well to
any number of musical pieces with titles other than "sonata." In short,
Newman began with the usual assumption that the word he was studying had a determinate meaning, but he discovered eventually that he
himself was not even in a position to determine its meaning. The
notion that a determinate meaning can be discovered by its usage was
Taylor's effort in his historical study of "causation," even though
he does not say so and may have been quite unaware that that was what
he was doing. His conclusion that the word has a meaning but that the
meaning is unanalyzable even though we cannot get along without the
word is an example of the attempt to discover an "essential" meaning
by examining its usage. His conclusion was simply that the word has a
valuable use but that its meaning cannot be determined since its determinate meaning—even though he is sure it has one—cannot be discovered.

Newman's radical conclusion, however, is much more significant:
the word "sonata" has no meaning; it is merely a label attachable to
music pieces which have no musical factor in common.

If it occurred either to Taylor or to Newman that what they concluded about their two words is common to a great many words, and
perhaps to all words, they do not say so. Yet this may well be the status
of words. This implication can be grasped if we permit ourselves to be
puzzled by the italicized words in the following phrases: "the meaning
of the word," "the word *has* a meaning," "the meaning of the word *is*
such-and-such," "*what* is the meaning of this?" All these italicized
words imply that the meaning is *in* the word or, to put it differently,
that a word determines how we shall define it. This would apply to
polysemy as well, the notion that many words *have* a variety of
meanings, sometimes related and sometimes not. "Polysemy" merely
says that a word can have various ways of defining it. But as
Humpty-Dumpty said of words, "The question is, Who is to be mas-
ter?" The word or the man uttering it? If the meaning is *in* the word, or
if words *have* meaning, or if we can say what the meaning of a word

really is, then a word does dictate our definition of it, or, if we say that a word cannot be defined, then it does dictate the way we use it.

But it is evident that this is not the case. Different people *find* different meanings in the same word, and the same people find different meanings in that same word at different times. Thus words do not dictate our definitions of them. And this for a simple enough reason. The utterance of a word by a human being is a behavioral event. All that is observable is the utterance of that word and the word itself, in either spoken or visual (written or printed) form. The meaning of that word, no matter how "meaning" is defined, cannot be observed. It is not an "observable." If we return to the observable nonverbal event at the beginning of this chapter and the subsequent sequence of sentences to the termination of that sequence in a cause-effect statement, it is obvious that all that is observable is a series of sentences, that is, a series consisting of an (imagined) nonverbal behavioral event followed by a sequence of verbal behavioral events. And this is the case whether we consider the entire sequence of sentences or select from it only those sentences within quotation marks. The latter were proposed as abstractions of one kind of sentences that succeed one another in discourse purporting to be an acceptable track of uttering sentences after an observed event. The former consisted of sentences that I wrote, each sentence emerging from the writing situation that included the previous sentences. On the other hand, I could not possibly say that each sentence *necessarily* followed the preceding sentence. To say that would be to affirm that no matter who wrote any of these sentences, he would have had to write the ensuing sentence that I wrote, obviously an absurd affirmation. An indefinably large number of reasons may be generated to explain why I wrote the sentences that I did, but the only observable is that I wrote the sentences that I wrote.

Moreover, it is reasonably certain that at any point in that sequence of sentences another person would write not the sentence that I wrote but quite a different one; and it is almost equally certain that that sequential step would be justified by asserting that the step I made was an illogical one. It is quite possible that someone would even say that each step in that sequence was a violation of logical discourse. If one reads at all widely in the field of polemical philosophy, it is quite apparent that it is relatively easy to demonstrate that two sequential sentences of an opponent are illogically related, that the step from the first to the second is not a logical step and is a violation of logical rules or, more pretentiously, logical truth. It is true that I have yet to find a philosopher who asserts this in print; but in conversation, philosophers have admitted to me that the tools of modern logic are so powerful that any position can be dissolved.

But this is not true merely of modern logic. Logic, like causation, has a history. There is a number of logics, or there are varieties of logic, if one prefers. All have emerged in Western European culture in the past twenty-five hundred years, and most of them survive either intact or in fragments and are still in use. Just as various ideas of causation have emerged, these various logics have emerged as a consequence of the changing circumstances in which logicians engage in the logic mode of behavior. Moreover, an examination of the history of the use of logic indicates that it is constantly used to dissolve positions, metaphysical, religious, scientific, philosophical, which, because of those changing circumstances, are no longer judged to be pertinent, or useful, or "true." The enterprise of logic, it has always been asserted, is to determine "truth," but logic appears to go about its enterprise by determining that certain sentences or sequences which have had the status of "truth," that is, have been judged for some reason to be acceptable statements, are not in fact "true," are not to be judged acceptable. It certainly appears to be the case that the unacceptability is determined before the logical tools are applied. One of the most common ways of doing this is particularly pertinent here. A word or a sentence is determined to have a meaning other than the meaning which the author of that sentence is judged to have asserted it has. As I have proposed, and as I shall discuss in greater detail later in this book, philosophical discourse is prescriptive; it tells us what we ought to say and do. Logic, then, is a mode of prescriptive verbal behavior which philosophers use to demonstrate the invalidity of an existent prescription. Logic is a prescriptive mode of verbal behavior which is used to control philosophical verbal behavior in ordinary, alogical language. If a word or sentence or any discourse *had* a determinate meaning, this control would be impossible. It would be possible to demonstrate logically that a step from one sentence to the next is logical or illogical, but counterdemonstrations would not be possible. Yet such counterdemonstrations are not only possible but constant, and counter-counterdemonstrations as well. Polemical philosophy is full of them.

In short, if meaning were immanent, logic would not only *not* be prescriptive; it would not even be necessary.

Yet this excursus into that strange form of verbal behavior we call logic makes it clearer that though meaning is not determinate, meanings are determined. The determination of meaning is a mode of human behavior. If I give a definition of a word, if I follow a sentence with another sentence, if I follow a sentence with nonverbal behavior, such as causal searching and testing, I have determined the meaning of that word or sentence. It does not follow, to be sure, that my determination of meaning is final or complete. Since the verbal or nonverbal determination is itself a bit of behavior which can give rise to a determination of its meaning, and since any determination is one of an indefinably large number of determinations, no determination can be complete, except for the individual who *repeats* that determination. But since even *that* repetition can give rise to further behavioral determination, this exception is itself only a hiatus in the chain of determination of meanings. A determination can be regarded as final or complete only for an individual who does nothing, who ignores it.

Moreover, something very disturbing follows from this. Any attempt to discover the determinate meaning of a word or any utterance is an attempt to cut into a chain of determinations that extends backwards to the very beginnings of language, to the emergence of man as linguistic animal. It is an attempt not merely to ignore but to deny the existence of that inconceivably intricate web of determinations of meanings, determinations both verbal and nonverbal, which is the total history of verbal behavior. It is an attempt to say, ''The world begins at this point and did not previously exist.'' But since such an attempt to discover a purely illusory determinate meaning is itself a mode of verbal behavior inextricably woven into that vast tapestry of previous determinations, it is impossible to make a new beginning. Attempts of philosophers, such as Descartes, or scientists or theologians or literary artists, to rethink the world from scratch, from a single position, are hardly more than farcical. Whatever they are doing, they are not doing what they say they are doing.

RESPONSE

At this point it is possible to introduce the first general proposition of this inquiry. Since the meaning of an utterance is the behavioral determination of the meaning of that utterance, it is possible to define the meaning of an utterance as the response to that utterance. *The meaning of a verbal event is the response to that verbal event. Further, the meaning of a verbal event is any response to that event.*

A proper place to begin is with the word "response" itself. In the formulations of the preceding paragraph "stimulus" can be substituted for "verbal event," "word," and "utterance." Evidently what that formulation depends upon is the stimulus-response theory of traditional experimental psychology. That theory, however, is anything but satisfactory. It assumes, in the first place, that the link between stimulus (S) and response (R) is causal, thus S→R. This formulation, used as a verbal direction, has led to and justified the typical experimental procedure. A stimulus configuration is detached from a nonexperimental setting—an existential setting it might be called—and exhibited or otherwise introduced into the experimental setting. A subject, or responder, is then exposed to the configuration and his response is recorded. Either a subject is repeatedly tested, or a series of subjects is tested, or a series of subjects is repeatedly tested. The response of the experimenter, however, remains the same. He records what he judges to be the responses, and of the greatest number of what he judges to be the identical response he asserts that this response is the response to that stimulus. To be sure, he puts this in much more circumspect terms. What he really seems to be asserting is that that response will occur on exposure to that stimulus with such frequency that the other responses, or perhaps most of them, may be safely ignored. Indeed, at such times the ignoring is fairly drastic. It is reported by one whom I take to be a responsible psychologist that in reinforcing experiments on laboratory rats the behavior of which does not indicate that reinforcing is occurring, such rats are frequently discarded from the experiment as being rats unsuitable for experimentation. The question asked is, "What response does that stimulus elicit?" and the answer is, "The response that occurs with the greatest frequency or with a frequency of statistical significance."

Obviously, there is much in all this that is puzzling and disturbing. Why do not all responses occur with equal frequency? This would appear to the inquisitive observer, the experimenter, as it were, whose subject is experimentation, to be the interesting question. Innumerable experiments have indubitably shown that in the laboratory situation—in virtually any experiment—there will be more of one response, or one kind of response, than of others. This is the case with both animal and human subjects. Why should this be so? A similar question is, Why is there a limited number of responses? Is this simply because there is a limited number of responders? If, instead of a few dozen, or some hundreds, or even several thousand subjects (though such a large number of subjects is quite rare), several millions of experimental subjects were exposed to the same isolated stimulus in the same experimental situation, what would be the result? Are there finite limits to the number of responses?

Further, experimental psychology is a recent mode of behavior, occupying only a tiny fraction of the total length of time man has existed as a species. Would there be the same limitations on the number of responses, and would there be even the same responses if millions of Paleolithic men were the subjects, or millions of ancient Greeks, or millions of eighteenth-century Frenchmen? These are idle questions if one judges that questions that cannot be answered are indeed idle questions. But unanswerable questions are not idle questions if they put the questions that can be answered in a puzzling light and if they suggest that the answerable questions are being asked in circumstances that are neither analyzed nor explained, that possibly the wrong questions are being answered, and that trivial answers are being arrived at. In short, it seems not unreasonable to suggest that the discovery in an experimental situation of a high frequency of one response and a low frequency of other responses is not what the experiment discovers but is rather the condition that makes the experiment possible.

One objection often made to psychological experimentation is that such experiments are not "real," that they do not reproduce an existential situation and therefore the results cannot be applied to such situations. The difficulty, it is maintained in this kind of objection, is that experimental situations are not isomorphic with existential situations. There is something of significance in this objection, but at this point it is important to deny the validity of the "unreal" allegation, for the experimental laboratory *is* part of the real world. What happens to an animal or human subject in an experiment really happens. It *is* an existential situation.

This existentiality can be grasped if the analogy between the psychological laboratory and the theater is proposed and explored. A scrupulous and detailed examination of the analogy between the two will expose the dubiousness of the results arrived at in the psychological laboratory. We will, it may be, gain some understanding of why the immense effort, time, and money expended in psychological experimentation has been so very nearly fruitless; and we will be in a position to question sharply some of psychology's sacred words.

Both theater and laboratory present configurations selected from existential situations, and in both there is a selected audience. A theater audience is not randomly selected. It is made up of people who for some reason want to go to the theater. This does not necessarily mean that they are interested in the theater. They may be interested in making a socially desirable appearance or in keeping their wives from nagging them; or they may go because they have nothing else to do. A variety of interests is present in the audience, yet it is not a random variety of interests, but a selected variety. In the same way animals are selected by laboratory breeding. And human subjects are selected because they are offered money, or because they are interested in psychology, or whatever. But these human subjects are rarely selected at random from the population. They are usually selected from a body of students. The assumption is that what is being tested is so basic to human behavior that it is free from cultural contamination or that statistical manipulation of material collected from questionnaires administered to the subjects can eliminate the factor of cultural background or reduce its relative unimportance.

The weakness of this position has already been suggested. The condition of experimentation is that a high frequency of one response can be discovered, and this suggests that the elimination of the factor of cultural background is impossible. That is, it may be that if you put any group of individuals in the same situation, either simultaneously or separately, the tendency is that one response will be dominant over other responses. In that case, the laboratory situation is but a special case of a more general behavioral "law,"—or, more precisely, is an instance of a general explanatory statement. To put matters even more grimly, at least grimly for the psychologist, it may be that even the most random selection of humans is a culturally biased selection, simply because they are humans.

Further, in both theater and laboratory there is an individual or a group of individuals who manipulate the presentation of the selected configurations. In the theater there are the playwright, the scene designer, the director, the stage manager, the lighting man, the prompter, and so on. In the psychological laboratory all of these functions are performed either by a single individual or a group of individuals. The experimenter as playwright designs the experiment; as director he controls the presentation of the experimental configuration. In some experiments there is a lighting man, while the presentation of the configuration involves the tasks of the stage designer, even if the configuration is presented against an absolutely neutral background. After all, some plays are presented on neutral stages. The task of the director, moreover, bears further analysis. In directing the play he is a stand-in for the audience; he is engaged in predicting how enough of the audience will respond to the play to make the play a success—however success may be defined—yet another instance of his and the experimenter's relying upon the tendency for a group of people in the identical situation to produce a dominant response. Further, the various manipulators of the presented configurations, particularly the playwright and the director, mingle with the audience during intermissions in order to eavesdrop on discussions of the play. They will hear, of course, a variety of responses, but if they hear a combination of the favorable responses and interpretations of the play which they wish the audience to arrive at, and if they hear these in sufficient quantity, they will judge their activities a success. If there is no *dominant* response, they will feel they have *failed*, just as the experimenter whose efforts result in no dominant response will feel that the experiment has been badly designed.

But one further examination of what the directors and experimenters do alike is instructive. Both are making an experiment upon audience-subject response to selected configurations. If the director is seen as a surrogate audience whose responses have a feedback effect upon the performance, then the director is observing his own responses. To him the theatrical situation is performance-plus-audience. The audience is, to him, engaged in a performance. And indeed, it is often asserted on a night when a successful play is coldly received that the audience was not in a receptive mood. It is a well-worn truth of the theater that audiences vary in their capacity to respond to the same play. This is judged to be a factor different from the factor of performance quality. The audience is to the director a collection of actors whose behavior is controlled by the theater situation and by the performance itself. Just as his directing modifies the behavior of the actors, so a cold, unresponsive audience can chill the actors, defeating the customary effectiveness of the performance. Such audiences are, therefore, discounted in deciding whether or not the performance should be restudied or revised in various details. The experimenter is in an analogous relation to his subjects. He is judging their performance, and, as we have seen, if the performance is not what he predicted, even if he predicted only a dominance of a single response without predicting what this response will be, he may revise the experiment, or he may simply eliminate from his experimental data certain subjects, as well as eliminate as unimportant those subjects whose responses have the sort of low frequency which is not only not dominant, but relatively rare.

One recent series of well-known psychological experiments brings out the performance quality of the subject and emphasizes the usefulness of the theater-experiment analogy. In these experiments the subjects were also the configurations to be studied, for these were the subjects of the Masters-Johnson experimental studies of sexual behavior. One of the most interesting results of those experiments, a result that made it possible to turn the experimental laboratory into a clinic, was the effect of the experiments on individuals who offered themselves as subjects because they were having sexual difficulties in marriage. In case after case their sexual difficulties were alleviated and at times entirely removed. In the setting of the experiment they were either observed through a one-way mirror or, more often, observed through television cameras or recorded on teletape. Moreover, they knew it. That is, they were giving a performance for an audience. It is not surprising that their performance improved. (In this case the director was absent from the performance itself, but—and this was the source of the development of the laboratory into the clinic—they were given directorial criticism afterwards.) Once again, the improvement, or, more properly, the judgment that an improvement had occurred, is not the significant factor but rather the tendency of the responses in this situation to pile up, to manifest a high frequency of one kind of response. The subjects themselves, moreover, were at once actors and audience. The deprivatization meant the removal of the assumption that sexual behavior ought to be impassionedly spontaneous. They thus became audience to themselves and, one may hazard the guess, to cooperative directors.

Another factor common to this notable situation and to the ordinary experiment, as well as to the theater situation, is that the subjects *know* they are to be subjects in an experiment. Members of a theater audience certainly have this awareness. They anticipate being exposed to preselected configurations and that their responses will be examined. Once again, eavesdropping during intermissions shows that this examination and overt response to response is a common phenomenon, and consideration of one's own behavior can show as well that covert verbal response also occurs. That there is no significant difference between examination of one's response by oneself and by another is an important point that must be postponed until later for detailed analysis. Here it is sufficient to point out that by examining their responses, audience members are, first, doing the same thing that the director and playwright do when they hover in the lobby and eavesdrop and also the same thing that the director does when he provides feedback to the actors. That is, the audience is *giving feedback to itself* on its own performance. That this behavior has an effect on response to the next act of the play cannot be doubted. (One is thus inclined to raise curious questions about the college student who repeatedly participates as subject in a great variety of experiments.)

Efforts have, of course, been made to overcome this effect by an experiment which involves the deception of the subject. In such an experiment the subject knows that he is an experimental subject but is told that he is to engage in one kind of experiment when in fact he is to engage in quite a different kind. One such experiment on sensory deprivation had curious results. Previous experiments had shown that subjects deprived of sensory stimulation exhibited various kinds of disorientation—hallucinations, sensations of weightlessness, and so on. In this experiment the subjects were placed in the sensory deprivation experimental situation but had been previously informed that they were to be subjects for quite a different experiment, totally unrelated to sensory deprivation. The result was surprising. They exhibited none of the responses of the previous subjects. Once again, however, their responses showed the piling up or high frequency of one kind of response, albeit of a negative sort.

Experiments in sensory deprivation, furthermore, bring out another attribute common to experiment and theater. In both there is a certain amount of sensory deprivation, effected in two ways. In the laboratory the selected configuration is ordinarily presented against a neutral background, and the history of the theater shows that audience response becomes more predictable if the same principle is followed. Until the mid-seventeenth-century theater stages were neutral. (To be sure, in the Elizabethan theater, for example, there was an architectural setting, even if it was but the inn-yard background to boards laid across trestles. But that setting was unchanged; it was permanently used for all plays even though there is reason to think that there was considerable use of props. If there was an inner stage—a matter on which there is some doubt—curtains on occasion may have been drawn back to reveal a bed or some other prop necessary for the action. Otherwise, if the place of the action was important, a description of that place was presented in the script, verbally.) In the course of the seventeenth-century the closed theater became standard, the proscenium arch was introduced, and elaborate stage spectacles were developed for opera and ballet. However, for ordinary plays the settings were relatively undifferentiated. The Bibbienas designed innumerable stage settings of magnificent baroque architecture, possibly the most magnificent of all baroque designs. However, these settings were quite interchangeable, useful for virtually any play and rarely designed with relation to the action taking place in the play itself. By the end of the eighteenth-century, however, stage settings were increasingly differentiated, changes of scenery within a play became more frequent, and "realism" was heightened. (By "realism" is meant here the inclusion of configurations that might be found in the nonstage world in a place in which the kind of action presented on the stage might conceivably occur.) This realism steadily increased, reaching its American apogee in the early twentieth century in the productions of David Belasco.

Since then, the history of stage production has exhibited a steady reduction of "realistic" configurations, a reduction pioneered by Adolphe Appia and Gordon Craig in the late nineteenth and early twentieth centuries. Today there is an increasing frequency of productions presented on bare platforms, the constructions of which are not even concealed. Frequently they resemble the scaffolding around a building under construction, and often enough the settings are in fact made of standard, mass-produced scaffolding materials. Virtually all that remains of the realistic stage is the lighting, particularly of the backdrop or cyclorama, and even that is usually expressionistic rather than realistic. Even historical dramas, such as those of Shakespeare, long presented with the most magnificent and detailed settings possible, as in the productions of Edward Irving, are now presented in this manner. As a further indication of what has happened, the famous Bayreuth Wagner productions of Wieland Wagner, beginning in the early 1950s, stripped away the realistic trappings of the traditional Wagner production, which Wagner himself authorized though he was never satisfied with them, and revivified the Wagner music dramas.

In the twenty-five hundred years of European theater, the realistic stage has been a brief experiment lasting only about three hundred years. (That the realistic stage survives on Broadway and its imitators is a consequence both of the cultural level and the intellectual triviality of the plays so presented.)

It is said, of course, that the aim of the realistic stage was to provide theatrical illusion, but even if the creators of the realistic stage thought so, they were mistaken. It seems improbable that anyone has ever taken a stage for the real thing. There is such a phenomenon as that responded to by the phrase "theatrical illusion," but that phrase is merely a response that does little or nothing to explain what in fact is happening in the response to the stage spectacle. And it is also said that the bare, or abstract, or neutral stage is more effective because it allows freer play to the imagination. Aside from the obvious fact that the term "imagination" is a real puzzler, the contrary effect seems rather to be the case. That is, the realistic stage presents an enormous amount of information which is relevant only to establishing the kind of place in which the action *might* take place. Once it has served that function, it has no other. It is quite irrelevant to the action of the play. Nevertheless, it is always present. That is, it is always capable of eliciting a random response. Anyone can notice that the lamp is just like the one Aunt Gracie has in her living room, or that in a realistic setting of a library the books on the wall facing the audience are solid, but those on the side walls are only painted, or that the portrait over the fireplace is not a real portrait but only a crude daub. Thus, the realistic stage reduces the probability of a high frequency of a dominating response. An example of an absurd and possibly idiosyncratic response (yet the kind of response that is exceedingly common) is that even in the nonrealistic production of *Die Walküre* in the current Metropolitan production (1975) in the last act it looked to me as if the Valkyries on their mountain peak were trudging through half-melted snow, or slush. It is equally pertinent that in the hey-day of the realistic stage, the nineteenth century, there was an even lower production than usual of scripts to which high literary merit is ascribed, and this in a period in which the other arts were exhibiting exactly the opposite kind of pro-ductivity, one of high quality. Likewise, the greatest scripts of theatrical history come for the most part from periods in which they were acted against a neutral or quasi-neutral stage setting.

The history of the cinema, short as it is, presents a similar set of data. The cinema began when the realistic stage setting was at its height, and it maintains that tradition. It has been little affected by the revolution in stage settings, a revolution, of course, that has merely returned to what the stage always was before the developments of the seventeenth century. The one film which I can remember as having been affected in significant ways by that revolution is Carl Dreyer's *The Passion of Joan of Arc*. Not only was it the first film in which the actors wore no makeup, thus breaking with theatrical tradition, but the settings were equally reduced in the degree of irrelevant information serving only to establish a place. For interior or exterior scenes the walls were white and free of all specification except the minimum needed to establish Gothic architecture. The flooring was either cobblestones for exterior scenes or stone flags for interiors. The furniture was only that necessary for the action. A good many shots used only the sky as background, the equivalent of the theatrical cyclorama. The effect was a concentration or piling up of response. Everyone I have talked to who has seen the film and every cinema critic I have read attests to its extraordinary emotional power. I saw it as a boy and felt like weeping at the execution of Joan. I endeavored to suppress my tears, as the manly thing to do, until I noticed that the tears were pouring down the cheeks of a big, strong man sitting next to me. Then I learned that to weep openly in the theater is permissible, even for adult men. The performance of the audience permits weeping, another indication of the high frequency of the single response in the theater-laboratory situation as well as of audience as performer.

Just the opposite device was used by Robert Flaherty, particularly in what may have been his greatest film, *Man of Aran*. The genius of Flaherty was to solve the problem of the realistic film by using the setting not to establish the place for the action but as the action itself. The film was about the setting. The setting was the film's subject. The actors, natives of the region, were made part of, and perhaps equivalent to, the physical setting. The camera explored with equal interest the people and the place. The technique was to select and dwell upon all the configurations of the place, from the majestic headlands jutting into the Atlantic to seaweed carefully placed in rock crevices as potato beds. The weather-worn faces of the characters were as lovingly explored as the weather-worn faces of the cliffs, and with the same caressing and revealing leisureliness of contemplation. And again the extraordinary emotional power and impact of the film has been attested to by critics and audience members.

Griffith, however, was the first to develop the cinema method of eliminating the realistic setting. That device has become standard in cinema—the close-up. The irrelevant is thus eliminated. But as soon as the camera moves back again to include all or a large part of the actor, the setting reappears, the irrelevant once more is visible, and the probability of increasing randomness of response is multiplied.

These examples from theater and cinema serve to show the effect in the psychological laboratory of that kind of partial sensory deprivation accomplished by selecting a configuration and isolating it against a neutral background. Randomness of response is reduced by depriving the subject of alternative sources of stimulation and, thus, alternative modes of response. To be sure, the aim of the theater is to produce a specified response, to make the audience laugh or weep, or, as in the rare case of Bernard Shaw, to make it think, to reverse its accustomed value behavior. Given the long tradition of the theater, compared with which the tradition of the experimental laboratory is miniscule, the stimulus is produced with a capacity to predict what stimulus will produce what response; and likewise the audience, as is indicated by my learning how to weep in the theater, also is able to predict and thus produce the appropriate response, depending for the individual, of course, on his experience with the theater. A further dissimilarity is that the laboratory isolates but a single configuration, while the theater isolates a great many and mingles them in complex ways. On the other hand, much of the stimulation in the theater is redundant. The tear-producing stimulus is presented again and again, or the emotion-producing stimulus is presented with extreme redundance, thus producing in time an explosion of laughter or tears, but, it is to be noted, in individuals who are there for the sake of the emotional response and explosion. Like the subject, they know that they are supposed to produce a response. Yet the aim of the laboratory is to discover the response to that particular configuration as stimulus. But what is discovered is the high frequency of a dominant response.

The conditions which make this possible become clearer if another attribute common to audience and subject is examined, another form of partial sensory deprivation. This is the attribute of psychic insulation.

Both audience member and experimental subject are protected from another kind of irrelevant stimulation. The drama or performance aspect of the theater audience involves going to a special kind of building for a special purpose, entering, ordinarily, through a lobby decorated, according to the economic strata to which that theater is appealing, with as much glamorous pretension as possible, a way of saying, "You are now going to have a special experience, an experience at a considerably higher level than ordinary. You are entering a magic realm." The interior of the theater, often even more richly decorated, heightens the excitability of the audience, its ability to experience stimulation. It is then protected from the rest of the world by darkness and the filtering out of as much external noise and other sounds as possible. There is even a psychic insulation of touch, for, depending on the cost of the seats, comfortable chairs are provided, but not so comfortable that excitability is too greatly reduced.

There is a strikingly similar drama in the entrance to psychological laboratories. Bare and unattractive as they usually are, they have nevertheless the same sense of unfamiliarity, of a strangeness in the very elimination of all decor, and the message is the same: "You are going to have an unusual experience, quite different from your ordinary experiences." Dentists have discovered that if they decorate their operating rooms like comfortable living rooms and conceal the laboratory character of the dentist's chair, their patients are considerably less likely to experience pain. They are instructed by the setting that their performance does not require heightened excitability or capacity to produce strong responses. Thus the most modern dentists' rooms are profoundly different from the psychological laboratory. Like the theater, it is a stimulus configuration that encourages response excitation. And this is facilitated by filtering out random stimuli which can interfere with the piling up of a dominant response, a point which is further illustrated by observing how frequently audience members complain if they do not in fact experience a dominant response. (Sometimes they blame this on the play, or on the performance, or on the setting, or the direction, and sometimes they blame it on themselves: one is in a bad mood, for he has quarreled with a lover; another is lamenting the fact that wealthy Aunt Mary did not remember her in her will; another is wondering if she remembered to turn the gas off.) In both theater and laboratory the decor and the psychic insulation serve to elicit heightened responsiveness.

Further, it is not only that the audience and the subject enter their respective situations with the expectation that their responsiveness is to be heightened and that the situation will aid in that heightening; the tendency of some members of an audience to complain of their failure to experience heightened response indicates that one goes to the theater with the awareness that one's capacity to experience heightened responsiveness is to be tested. It is no accident that "test" and "testing" are words so commonly employed in psychological experimentation, nor that subjects who display insufficient responsiveness are eliminated from the experiment. Thus the whole laboratory situation can be seen as a stimulus configuration designed to heighten the responsiveness to a selected configuration.

This extended analogy between laboratory and theater can lead reasonably to several conclusions. The dubiousness of psychological experimentation of the standard sort is not that it is not isomorphic with existential situations. It is itself an existential situation. What happens is that a configuration asserted to be a stimulus is selected from the situation in which it is believed to be normally found and placed in a quite different situation; and this situation, like the original situations from which the experimental configuration has been extracted, is itself a complex stimulus configuration. Further, the laboratory situation is so like the theatrical situation that it is barely a metaphor to call the former a theater for experiment. It is probably more accurate and certainly more satisfying to categorize theater and experimental laboratory together and judge them to be two instances of a category of behavior that includes, it may well be, a great number of behavioral situations—the classroom, or a royal audience chamber, or a great many, if not all, art-perceiving situations. All of these call for heightened excitation, even though, as in the experimental laboratory, it is not always forthcoming. All of them present a stimulus configuration extracted from its normal stimulus environment, and all of them likewise ordinarily result in the dominance of a single response or a small group of responses. At the same time, in each there is a spread of less dominant responses, some of them very infrequent.

Thus it seems reasonable to conclude that the piling-up effect on response in the experimental laboratory is not a unique factor in the situation of exposing a selected and extracted configuration in what is asserted to be a neutral situation (but in fact is not). Rather, the piling-up is a factor in the kind of situation of which the experimental laboratory is but one instance.

Yet it has been already suggested that the claim that the laboratory experiment is not isomorphic with existential situations has something to be said for it. What that something is has also been suggested. When a stimulus is selected from situations in which it is normally found and is transplanted into the experimental laboratory, the result is a situation that is not isomorphic with existential situations—if the existential situation is defined as the situation in which that stimulus is normally found, that is, found when it is not found in the experimental laboratory. But this observation immediately raises the question, "What is the stimulus?" If response varies as the perceptual environment of the stimulus varies, then it is to be wondered if any stimulus can be selected from its normal perceptual environment and continue to be the same stimulus.

STIMULUS AND RESPONSE

The argument that the experimental situation results in dominant response, and thus belongs to the behavioral category to which theater belongs, can be countered by the argument that, after all, the stimulus does elicit a particular dominant response. To this the counterargument is that if the stimulus configuration is truly isolated and if there is a causal relation between stimulus and response, then there should be no range of response. But there always is. This difficulty with S→R theory has long been felt, and it was long ago proposed to meet the difficulty with the utterance "intervening variable." This recognizes that the S→R formula is unsatisfactory and that something must account for the range of response in the experimental situation. Various candidates have been proposed for the position of intervening variable—brain physiology, past experience of the subject, cultural background of the subject, emotional and physiological condition of the subject, and so on. But the trouble, as was recognized when the theory was proposed, is that all of these are speculative and none is accessible. That is, at best they are accessible only through questioning the subject, either directly, or by means of a questionnaire, or through some other means of studying the previous history of the subject. Such inquiries, however, contradict the behaviorist principle of not depending upon verbalizations by the subject, which are regarded as suspect, with reason, as we have seen in considering the movement from observation to verbal response. Furthermore, it is not known and cannot be known if any list of intervening variables is exhaustive. The theory of the intervening variable has led to the difficulty for the S→R behaviorist that the intervening variables can be discovered only by experimentation, but that experimentation cannot proceed without taking account of the as yet undetermined intervening variables. It may seem surprising that traditional behaviorist S→R theory should continue, but it does continue, and indeed it is surprising.

Yet the survival of classical behaviorism is not surprising if it is remembered that the assumption of behaviorism is that there is a causal link between stimulus and response and that stimulus as well as response are observables or, more precisely, that the stimulus can be located, can be determined. It is that assumption that in fact led to the theory of the intervening variable. However, without denying the validity of that theory, the assumption of that theory—that stimulus can be determined—is, as I have already suggested, questionable. One may approach the problem by asking why experimental theory is founded upon the selection and extraction of a stimulus from existential situations. And of course, the answer is obvious. It cannot be experimented with in its existential situation because the response would not be pure; it would be contaminated by the other stimuli in that situation. The obvious answer was to remove it to a pure and neutral situation. However, that pure and neutral situation is nothing of the sort; it is a quasi theater for experiment, a rich and complex stimulus situation. The stimulus has not been selected from a stimulus field and placed in a neutral field; it has merely been placed in a different stimulus field. It is no different from removing a cow from a pasture and placing it in a barn. It is true that farmers tend to behave differently towards cows in barns than they do in fields, but it could not possibly be said that the cow has been selected from the pasture stimulus field and placed in a neutral or pure stimulus field. The stimulus in the laboratory is merely a cow in a barn. Clearly, the selection of the stimulus must be done not by the experimenter but by the subject. Unfortunately, faced with a stimulus field, the subject is in no better position to decide what in fact he is responding to than the experimenter. Experimentation in terms of S→R theory, or even S→IV→R theory, cannot be undertaken unless it can be demonstrated that in nonlaboratory existential situations the stimulus to which the subjects to be tested in the laboratory are responding can be determined before the laboratory experimentation can be undertaken. The problem to be considered in human behavior, then, is not what stimulus yields what response, but, rather, Why it is that in existential situations—such as the laboratory—there is a tendency for a particular response or class of responses to be elicited when everything in the stimulus field has been varied except the stimulus configuration in question (that is, when all possible stimulus configurations but one have been removed and different stimulus configurations substituted for those removed). Thus, all that S→R experiments have demonstrated is that when a selected stimulus is presented to subjects in the psychological laboratory, the theater for experiment, a particular population of subjects shows both a range of responses and a tendency towards a dominant response or class of responses. It scarcely takes elaborate experimentation, however, to demonstrate that. Simple observation of behavior can discover it, and long since has. It is an old wives' tale. Of greater significance is the kind of existential non-laboratory experimentation in which the stimulus properties of a complex stimulus configuration are varied. Thus, the change in size or color of a box of detergent can increase or decrease sales of a detergent in supermarkets, but it has also been observed that a red box, for example, can increase sales as well as a gold box. In marketing, on the other hand, it has equally been observed that any change of design of packing for a well-known product can increase sales. So even here the case remains dubious. It cannot be said that a particular color can increase sales permanently, only that design innovation can at least temporarily win some customers from a rival product. Once again the stimulus cannot be isolated from its stimulus field.

The result of S→R theory is what might have been expected. The assumption that a stimulus can be identified and that its response can be determined in the neutral laboratory has simply led to an immense proliferation of experiments on what is apparently going to be an endless series of configurations. Little that is not trivial has been discovered, and little of significance has been done with the nontrivial discoveries. But even this distinction is evaluative. S→R behaviorism has discovered little more than that people do respond—to something or other.

CONDITIONING

Before returning to the problem of meaning, it is desirable to examine briefly another kind of conditioning theory, one that has aroused great attention in recent years and has been put into effect in modifying behavior and has been offered as the way to achieve a society of harmony, order, and peace. This is known as operant conditioning and its therapeutic application as behavior modification.

A basic form of operant conditioning involves placing a rat in a soundless, lightless box, devoid of everything but a bar which, when depressed, delivers food or water, whether the bar is hit with nose, paw, or tail. In this tiny theater most rats will tend to increase the frequency with which they press the bar. One obvious lesson appears to be that if you reduce the sources of stimulus for any animal to a near minimum, it will respond to what is available. But this triviality is overwhelmed by the greater triviality that rat behavior is, in this situation, under the control of human behavior. What controls the human behavior is the object of our inquiry. At any rate, from such experiments, so obviously theatrical, has been developed a therapy for humans—behavior modification. Two examples must suffice.

It has been discovered that the infliction of pain can modify behavior. Some unfortunate creature whose behavior is defined as undesirable is placed in a chair wired to produce an electric shock and is shown pictures of what he is not supposed to find attractive. A homosexual, for example, is shown pictures of attractive and naked young men and at the same time is given electric shocks. This is known as aversive therapy. It has been claimed that a certain number of homosexuals given this treatment have ceased their homosexual activity. One suspects that these are either rather stupid homosexuals or homosexuals who were looking for some reason, any reason, to terminate homosexual behavior. Others, the smarter ones perhaps, soon return to their sinful pleasures.

Now the discovery that behavior can be modified by the infliction of pain is scarcely novel. It used to be known as torture. The Spanish Inquisition discovered that if you tortured Protestants, they would abjure their vicious heresy and embrace the One True Church and that even some of those who left the territories controlled by the Inquisition maintained their new faith. The effect of the torture seems to have made it possible for them to entertain seriously an alternative religious possibility. It is also known that *any* therapy practiced on a population of homosexuals will have the result that some of them abjure their sexual heresy and enter the True Church of Correct Sexual Conduct.

In another form of operant conditioning, and one used in schools, particularly schools for retarded, difficult, or otherwise deviant children, the child is given a token if he behaves as the teacher wants him to. These tokens may be exchanged for various goodies or otherwise put to attractive uses. The child undoubtedly learns something about money, but what else does he learn? Well, he learns about bribery. In Russia under the bureaucracy established by Peter the Great, it was virtually impossible for the ordinary citizen to get any satisfactory response from a bureaucratic official without bribing him. In fact, the bribery was so open that bribery was certainly part of the bureaucratic system and not in any but a moral sense a deviation from it. The behavior of the bureaucrat was modified by giving him a token which he could exchange for goodies or could otherwise put to uses attractive to him, such as (so badly was he paid) sufficient food. In short, the system was that the bureaucrat was supported in part by the government through money collected by taxation and partly by direct payment by the public. The only difference in token therapy is that the tokens and the goodies are both supplied through taxation. In the one case the public paid directly and indirectly; in the other the public pays indirectly. But in both cases the pattern is precisely the same. Undesirable behavior—for the official, refusing the service, for the child, refusing to do what the teacher wants him to do—is modified in the direction of behavior considered desirable by the modifier.

It is exasperating that bribery and torture should be rediscovered and presented as profound and innovative revelations of the foundations of human behavior. Once again the true point has been missed: torture and bribery are pervasive factors in human behavior or are, it may be, special cases of pervasive factors. To this possibility the present inquiry will return, for the question is not whether torture and bribery are pervasive and effective, but why. One thing we can now be sure of, however, is that the torture and the bribery are not stimuli that necessarily elicit behavior modification, that is, a particular kind of response. Rather, they are part of existential situations filled with innumerable, complex, and undeterminable stimuli. That sophistication of S→R theory known as reinforcement has in fact added nothing to our knowledge of human behavior and has contributed nothing to a theory of human behavior. All it says is that people respond to what is happening to them and that there is a tendency for a population of respondents to respond in more or less the same way to the same kind of happening, although there is also a tendency for a good many members of that respondent population to respond in different ways. This is not to say much, nor is it to say anything that everyone is not perfectly aware of, that is, that human behavior is up to a point predictable but that what that point is in any particular situation cannot be predicted.

A theory of human behavior cannot, then, be built upon S→R theory, for it is scarcely a theory at all; or rather, it is hardly more than a formulation of what everybody has always observed. If a configuration with which an individual is familiar is encountered against a novel background, he will tend to behave just as he behaved in previous encounters. This point seems obvious enough but is far from satisfactory. The fact is that if an individual encounters a familiar configuration against a novel background of a sort quite different from the sort of background against which he is accustomed to encountering that configuration, his behavior will not only not be the same, but the chances are that he will be unable to respond at all. One always knows what one is supposed to do when one encounters a stop sign at an intersection, yet it is not predictable that everyone will behave as he is supposed to. But what if mischievous boys have placed the sign beside an open stretch of country highway with no intersection in sight? In that case one is not sure whether one should stop or not. An even more puzzling case arises when one encounters a stop sign, a perfectly ordinary commercially produced stop sign, hung on the walls of an art exhibition. If one has had no experience with Pop Art, one is even more at a loss. It is not simply a question of choosing between alternative modes of response, in this case regarding it as art or nonart, though some would take that way out, but rather of knowing how to respond to it on the assumption that one ought to have an artistic response. Clearly its position on the walls of an art gallery is an instruction that it is to be taken as a work of art, but how is one to do so?

From this point of view S→R theory appears to concentrate on only one aspect of response, its predictability, and indeed behaviorist psychologists rest the validity of their position on the fact that they can make predictions not only in the laboratory but also outside of it. However, it appears to be obvious that a theory of human behavior cannot rest on predictability alone but, rather, must account as well for a deviation from the predicted response and from the failure to respond, for inability to respond is, in fact, a common human behavioral phenomenon. This emphasis upon predictability in psychological theory, moreover, indicates what the behaviorist psychologist is really up to. When asked for a justification for his activities, his usual response is that if we understand human behavior, we can live better lives. He wants us to live better lives, and that is very good of him, but this attitude in conjunction with his activities suggests very strongly that we can live better lives if our behavior is entirely predictable. What many people have always suspected about behaviorism has been confirmed in their minds by B. F. Skinner's *Beyond Human Freedom and Dignity*. The aim of behaviorist psychology is to make behavior more predictable and less free. As I have proposed, the experimental laboratory is a theater for increasing predictability of behavior.

Thus, the psychologist is like the philosopher. Though he imagines he is engaged in descriptive behavior, he is in fact engaged in prescriptive behavior. But he is not to be condemned for this. The "humanist" who objects to the prescriptive character of behaviorism assumes also that nonprescriptive behavior is within the realm of possibility, but, as this inquiry will in its course attempt to show, that is not the case. *Like the philosopher and like everybody else in the world, the behavioral psychologist has no choice but to engage in prescriptive behavior*. The failure of behaviorism lies in its using an unanalyzed common-sense notion—that people tend to behave in the same way when they encounter the same configuration in similar circumstances—and in assuming that the S→R formulation can explain exceptions to that formulation (i.e., the negation of that formula). (Even the intervening variable theory assumes that were it not for those variables, S→R would always obtain, and that by discounting those variables, one can arrive at the true S→R link.) A more adequate explanation, then, must include S→R and S→IV→R, and the terminology of such an explanation must be other than that currently used in S→R theory. An inquiry into why that should be so leads to the problem of explanation, with which we began, and thus back to the point at which this excursus into behaviorism left that discussion, the problem of meaning.

MEANING AND RESPONSE

The long excursus above has been necessary to make it clear that the formulation "The meaning of an utterance is the response to that utterance" is not an example of classical S→R theory. That is, the utterance to which the response is made cannot be considered the stimulus to that response, for, as we have seen, a stimulus cannot be discovered. One can begin by saying that it is possible to observe that the verbal response (to exclude, for the time being, the consideration of nonverbal responses to utterances) is a response to the entire stimulus field, but even that is not sufficient and indeed says very little. It is a constant in behavior that two individuals responding to the same utterance in the same stimulus field can and usually do generate different verbal responses. And the factors so tentatively and vaguely included by the theory of the intervening variable must also be taken into consideration. Even if we assume that it is theoretically possible to isolate each of the stimulus configurations in a stimulus field—to separate, for example, the tone in which an utterance is spoken, or what is metaphorically called the tone of written discourse, from the words themselves or the color red from the configuration of an apple—it would be impossible to calculate and determine the ways these configurations are combined by the responder in such a way as to predict invariably the verbal response to the verbal utterance. The intervening variables, of course, have to be accounted for as well, including all of the factors in the stimulus-field response history of the responder. Since these belong to the past, they cannot be determined. Even if on metaphysical grounds we find it pleasing to say that behavior is determined, we cannot say how it is determined; we cannot determine all the factors responsible for the response to the utterance in question, the response that is the determination of the meaning of the utterance. The reason is that a statement that behavior is determined is itself a verbal response to observed stimulus fields, and how we get from the observation to the verbal response is the heart of the mystery. The most that can be said is that the stimulus field is the occasion for the response, but even this weak statement cannot be put into a negative form: were it not for that stimulus field, the response would not be made. Some individuals, whom we call the severely insane, make the same verbal response no matter what the stimulus field, and any inquiry into human behavior can hardly discount the response of the insane, for insane behavior is just as much human behavior as what we judge to be the sanest behavior in the world. In fact another kind of behavior we also call insane is also instructive. The response appears totally unpredictable, instead of totally predictable. The responses in this form of insanity appear to be equally unrelated to the stimulus occasion, but it seems that any response at all serves the purpose, whatever that might mean, of that particular kind of insanity. To be sure, it is often maintained that certain threads of continuity or patterns of meaning are to be found in such responses, but all the examples I have seen do so by neglecting much of the verbal data recorded. Thus, there is one extremity in the range of response which is characterized by unalterable singleness of response and at the other extremity by an equally unalterable randomness of response. Normal verbal response behavior, then, lies between these two extremities.

This can be explained by deriving two corollaries from the proposition that the meaning of an utterance is the response to that utterance. *Every utterance is capable of eliciting all possible verbal responses, and all utterances are capable of eliciting but a single verbal response.* But certainly these are not the normal modes of verbal response, which are not independent of the verbal situation in which the response is being made. By "not independent," however, I do not propose to introduce some notion of a necessary causal link between verbal stimulus occasion and response, nor to suggest that meaning is, after all, immanent in normal verbal response. Rather, "not independent" is to be interpreted as meaning that in the judgment of an observer, either the one who originated the utterance to which the response is being made, or a third party, the response is not an inappropriate one. Someone *judges* it to be a relevant response, but this is very different from saying that it *is* relevant. The latter implies all kinds of ontological propositions or at least traditionally has led to all kinds of ontological propositions about the nature of being. The former merely asserts that someone other than the speaker, overtly or covertly, judges the response to be relevant, not independent of the verbal occasion.

Further, the very biological individual who made the response can judge and does judge whether or not the response is relevant. Every writer knows this. He writes sentence *a* and responds to it with sentence *x*. He then judges *x* to be irrelevant, crosses it out, and writes sentence *y*. Furthermore, this kind of extemporized editing is a common phenomenon in ordinary verbal behavior. A person says something, then says, "Oh, I didn't mean that," and offers another verbal response instead. It is useful to take a term from the publication world and call this process "editing," since no other term seems to be available. The explanation for this is that the person who utters the response and the person who withdraws it and utters another in its place, having judged the first response not relevant, are not the same person, although they are the same biological individual and, as persons, may have much in common. That is, if the theory of the intervening variable has anything to it at all, it means that response is not merely a function of the stimulus occasion but also a function of stimulus-occasion history. The person who enjoys the Franck Symphony today is not the same person who does not enjoy it tomorrow, although the biological individuality of the two persons is continuous. The utterance to which the response is made and the withdrawn response are now part of the history of the person who proposes the alternative response, but that second response was not part of the history of the person who uttered the withdrawn response. It may be objected that a good many individuals seem entirely unaffected by their own or anybody else's editing. They do not "learn"; that is, there appears to be no modification of behavior after they have been judged to have made an irrelevant response. They are therefore the same person. But this is not the case. The probability is increased that in a similar verbal occasion they will not make the same response as the one not judged relevant. Their history has modified them; they are not the same person.

The person, then, is a factor in the response, and this is implied, of course, in the notion that meaning is not immanent but is actively determined, that a meaning is a behavioral determination. Indeed, "the person" is not much more than a restatement of "behavioral determination." To this are to be added the verbal occasion and the judgmental behavior to make what might be called "the behavioral triad of meaning," each member of which, since meaning is not immanent, can vary independently of the other. That is why arguments about the true meaning of a term are not futile, since they often result in behavioral modification, but are not what they seem to be. Modern analytical philosophy—and indeed such philosophy is no more than abstraction of or concentration upon what has always been true of philosophical discourse—is full of statements about what the meanings of words really are. These statements often take the form of saying that a certain word refers to, or *properly* refers to, such-and-such. But "refers" here is obviously metaphorical. A word does not refer. Persons refer. A reference to something is an instruction to respond to that something, with the proviso that so long as the behavior confines itself to verbal behavior, a reference to something is not to something non-verbal but in fact to a word or some sequence of words. This implication that words refer—ignoring the fact that persons are involved in referring—conceals the true character of such philosophical discourse. It is to ignore the judgmental aspect of the behavioral triad of meaning and to ignore the fact that the writer of such discourse is in

fact doing the judging. When, then, it is said that a word means
so-and-so or that a word refers to such-and-such, what is going on can
be described by saying that what ought to be said is that the writer is
judging that the word *ought* to mean so-and-so or, more fully, that the
responder to the utterance ought to respond in a particular way. For
"real meaning" we may properly substitute "appropriate response."
Once again what is asserted to be a description of meaning turns out,
under behavioral analysis, to be a prescription. For "real meaning,"
then, can be substituted "appropriate response," for the term "appropriate" in its ordinary usage generally includes the notion of judgment.
Nor is "judgment" used here in any mentalistic sense. Judgmental
behavior is something that can be observed. For the time being this
discussion of such behavior will be limited to verbal behavior, but this
is not to be taken to mean that judgmental behavior is limited to verbal
behavior, though that question must be postponed. An example of
observable judgmental behavior is the utterance "He truly understands
that sentence." Translated into the language of the behavioral triad of
meaning, this sentence is transformed into "I judge that he has responded appropriately to that sentence."

All this can be clarified and extended by considering a couple of
examples. Soldiers are instructed that when they are captured, they
must answer questions only by giving name, rank, and serial number.
The captors, however, always want to know considerably more than
that, especially information about the military unit to which the captive
belongs, since this will give them more detailed information about the
forces opposing them and, sometimes, quite new information. To any
questions, the soldier responds as instructed. To all verbal utterances
of his captors he offers but a single response: name, rank, and serial
number. In his judgment that response is appropriate. To his captors,
however, that response is inappropriate. The questioning proceeds then
in such a way as to trick him into a response which in their judgment
will be appropriate but in his judgment will be inappropriate. Another
example of the same sort comes from Poe's "Raven." Whatever the
speaker asks the bird, it always replies, "Nevermore." The drama of
the poem lies in the shift of the speaker from judging that response
inappropriate to judging it appropriate. Since there are occasions in
which a single response is judged by someone, either the speaker or
someone else, to be appropriate, it cannot be said that a single response
is necessarily a symptom of psychosis. Since the most frequent kind of

response does not evince this singleness, and since such "normal" response is the determination of meaning, the soldier's and the raven's responses may be called overdetermined, that is, more frequently repeated than at first seems to be appropriate.

Other examples show exactly the opposite tendency. An extreme case is glossolalia, or speaking in tongues. This consists of an apparently random utterance of sounds found in the language of the speaker but so combined as to make determination of meaning impossible. Somewhat less extreme is the speech disorder known as logorrhea. The meaning of short sequences of sounds can be determined, but each determinable meaning sequence is followed by what is judged to be an inappropriate determinable meaning sequence. Thus the meaning of the total logorrhea discourse is indeterminable. Less striking is the kind of discourse most people have experienced in which the initial response is judged to be relevant or appropriate, but the speaker's response to that response, though relevant to the preceding response, is not relevant to the initiatory verbal occasion, and the relevance decreases as the discourse proceeds. Each of these three examples can be regarded as moving away from normal or most frequent response behavior in the direction of randomness. Again, since such normal response is the determination of meaning, these three examples may be called in various degrees, "underdetermined."

Verbal behavior oscillates between the overdetermined and the under determined, and this oscillation is accompanied by a continuous effort to bring it back to the center. But what the center is is a matter of judgment, not an abstract sort of judgment, but of judgmental behavior, which takes the form of asserting that the central, or correct, or true behavior is the right behavior in view of the verbal occasion. Actually, however, it is a normative judgment. Since the verbal occasion does not determine the verbal response, the center cannot be objectively determined by language. Claims that overdetermined or underdetermined responses are appropriate and therefore central responses are as frequent, as impassioned, and as normative as claims that response is neither over- nor underdetermined.

As our various examples suggest, the claim that a response is not central is one that shifts judgmental behavior from the verbal occasion to the person making the response. The deviance from what is judged to be appropriate is accounted for or explained by the attributes of that person which are alleged to be responsible for the deviant response.

Moreover, since the judgmental behavior is itself verbal response, the counterclaim is that a judgment of inappropriateness is itself inappropriate, and once again that inappropriateness is accounted for by the attributes of the person making the judgment. Thus, the interaction of response and judgment of response is the oscillation between what is judged to be overdetermined or underdetermined. Obviously smooth verbal interaction depends upon judgmental behavior that the response to which one is responding is itself an appropriate response to the verbal occasion. Or rather, smooth response, response which does not question the appropriateness of the response to which the response is being made, is a judgment that the response is appropriate to the verbal occasion. But, in addition, it is to be observed how often a response to a response is initiated by utterances like, "Yes, you're right," "I agree with you," "Uh-huh," "You've hit the nail on the head," and so on. Thus, even smooth response is permeated with verbal judgmental behavior. When an individual's responses are judged to be excessively full of such remarks, a judgment is made about that individual. "He agrees too readily," or "What's wrong with him that he has to say he agrees with you before he answers?" or "He says he agrees so much that I wonder if he really does agree," and so on. The verbal behavior is judged to be overdetermined, and judgment is shifted from the verbal occasion to the person of the respondent, or, more precisely, as a succession of persons with an overdetermination of statements of agreement common to many of them, or, perhaps, in extreme cases, even all. However, the difference between what is considered normal statements of agreement and excessive or overdetermined statements of agreement is a quantitative one and, moreover, is a judgment made by an observing judge. Hence, the punctuation of smooth interaction by occasional statements of agreement is itself overdetermined. Those statements are instructions to the respondent that his responses are appropriate.

On the other hand, smooth verbal interaction does not necessarily mean agreement. Peppering responses to response with such utterances as, "No," "I don't agree with you," or "You're wrong," does not necessarily mean that the response is being judged to be inappropriate. What follows immediately after, in the judger's subsequent responses, is significant. Only if the responses shift to the person whose responses are being judged is the judgment one of inappropriateness. The distinction comes out in such utterances as "You're going about it the right way but you're getting the wrong answers." The judgment is that an error has been made in the response, not that the error is a consequence of some oddity in the history of the person making the response. Such errors are reprehended by referring to the convention of logic or to a neglect of significant data. These conventions are formally and sophisticatedly organized into what is called "methodology," the conventions that control scientific behavior and increasingly, amusingly enough, the humanities, with philosophy seen as (and seeing itself as) overarching and determining the behavior in both. Ordinary verbal interaction, however, shows exactly the same verbal behavior in unsophisticated form. "I can't understand why the wheels are dragging." "Idiot! You forgot to take the emergency brake off"; or "I believe you have made a mistake in my bill; you entered the sales tax twice." Thus, appropriateness of verbal response may be imagined to have two axes at right angles to each other. The horizontal axis is the personal axis, a continuum from the extreme of overdetermination to the extreme of underdetermination, and a vertical axis, a continuum from the verbal behavior of ordinary life to the most sophisticated and refined modes of mathematics and logic. This may be called the *procedural axis*, a term that emphasizes its behavioral aspect as "methodological" does not. When verbal interaction is absolutely smooth, the judgment of both participants is that each other's responses are appropriate both procedurally and personally. At such times there are no overdetermined or redundant remarks of "right" or "wrong," no judgments of procedural inappropriateness. The responses are themselves judgments that both procedural and personal appropriateness obtain.

A further aspect of verbal behavior revealed by this analysis is that procedural judgments, whether judgments of "right" or of "wrong," are overdeterminations. As instructions, they are instructions to the responder to whom the instruction is directed that he should continue the kind of behavior, judged procedurally appropriate, which he is currently performing. Their effect is the stabilization of that behavior. If the judgment is that the behavior is procedurally in error, it is an instruction to continue responding in obedience to the conventions of procedure but to respond more conventionally, to pay more careful attention to the rules of the appropriate procedure, or to learn them better. If it is observed that the movement from the extreme underdetermined to the extreme overdetermined is a movement from the completely random to the completely repetitious, and if procedural and

personal appropriateness is placed in the center of this continuum, then
these overdetermined instructions fall towards the direction of the repetitious; but since they are not verbally repetitious, they are best called
redundant. *The link thus emerges between the redundant and the
stabilization of verbal behavior.* Further, this stabilization of procedural appropriateness of behavior is also the stabilization of personal
appropriateness of behavior, for a judgment that procedural response is
appropriate is also a judgment that personal response is appropriate,
since it is a judgment that nothing in the history of the person responding is distorting his procedural behavior.

RHETORIC AND REDUNDANCY
For this stabilization of procedural and personal verbal appropriateness
there is an ancient term which requires only slight modification to be
useful for the present purposes. That term is "rhetoric." Rhetoric is
traditionally defined as the art of persuasion, and that is an excellent
definition. An examination of the ancient treatises on rhetoric, from
Aristotle to Quintilian, and of the great examples of ancient
rhetoric—written within this tradition and some of these very books as
controlling directions—such as the orations of Cicero, reveals clearly
enough what the practical instructions amounted to, as distinguished
from the theoretical justifications and explanations. Rhetoric was considered to have as its object persuading the listener to a particular
course of action, but that might very well be and frequently was a
verbal course of action, a particular verbal behavior, such as persuading a jury to utter the judgment of innocent or guilty or persuading an
assembly of the citizens to vote or support by verbal behavior a decision proposed by the speaker. Its object was to reduce the randomness
of response to a given situation, to reduce it, if possible, to a single
response. It was, then, the attempt to move the verbal responses to a
situation from unpredictable randomness to predictable identity of response or repetition of the same response by all members of the group
addressed. Its aim was the overdetermination of behavior and its
stabilization, if only temporarily.

The "figures" of rhetoric are phrases and words and verbal formulas to be employed with frequency in a discourse. Rhetorical discourse was peppered with the "rhetorical figures," a phrase more
comprehensible today if for it is substituted "verbal configuration,"
and the character of "figures" is further brought out by the phrase

"patterns of verbal configuration." The examples given above of expressions of agreement or disagreement with procedural appropriateness are thus rhetorical figures; though they may not be repeated in a series of responses, they constitute the repetition of a pattern. This notion of pattern, then, brings out the redundancy in the actual use of rhetorical figures. Further, although we do not and cannot know how the figures were arrived at, it is reasonably certain that the first rhetorical treatises that have been preserved have a tradition of earlier treatises behind them and that these in turn were preceded by oral instruction, particularly by the Sophists, whose boast was that they could teach anyone how to persuade.

The question remaining is whether the figures were discovered or were invented, that is, whether they were observed as occurring in verbal behavior or whether they were imposed upon it. Perhaps the answer cannot be certain, but it is of significance that the first Europeans who encountered American Indians and learned their language were impressed by the stately mode of speech of the chiefs and other tribal leaders. They observed a language of ceremony, marked by what in the European tradition was called rhetoric (that is, rhetorical figures). The observation of figures in ordinary verbal behavior, such as those given, suggests with this nonliterate occurrence of figures in Indian rhetoric that formal Greek rhetoric was originally based upon observation of verbal behavior, especially in situations in which the overdetermination of response was the obvious purpose, such as civic assemblies or courts of law or religious ceremonies. In the latter extreme overdetermination of response is the characteristic, and the verbal behavior in all religions is marked by a rhetoric which goes beyond the patterned redundancy of ordinary rhetoric to exact repetition of verbal formulas. Thus, the principle of rhetorical overdetermination is linked to what has been already pointed out about the kind of situation of which the theater and psychological laboratory are instances. In the theater, for example, personality is established by presenting the character as responding in the same way to a variety of situations. Randomness of response is reduced in the theater situation by selection and isolation of configurations, while in other types of situations it is reduced by redundancy. The two types of situation emerge when both types of overdetermination are combined, as in religious or political situations in which the physical setting is of the theater type, as in churches or throne rooms, and the verbal behavior is redundant to the point of being formulaic. The overwhelming power of such overdetermination can be experienced in such a work as Wagner's *Parsifal*; during the Grail scenes religious verbal formulas are presented in the theater.

The preceding example about the establishment of character and personality in the theater suggests what is probably the most important device of rhetoric, *the repetition of nouns and pronouns*. This can be observed in any sequence of verbal behavior involving two or more people, but it also can be observed in discourse sustained by an individual. This chapter began with the puzzle of how we get from one sentence to the next. To the responder of the response to a sentence the problem is how to know that the ensuing sentence is related to the preceding sentence except by contiguity. However, the question that "know" here involves is rather, "What in the ensuing sentence controls this person's behavior in such a way that it can be called a judgment that what he is responding to was in itself an appropriate response?" And this in turn involves the question of how that judgment is indicated to the respondent to his utterance. Let us take an example used before. "Jones hit Smith." "Yes, and he hit him." The question arises here as to the antecedence of "he" and "him." However, if the stress is indicated, the problem is resolved. "Yes, and *he* hit *him*" is linked quite differently to the first sentence from "Yes, and he *hit* him." In the former the antecedent of "he" is "Smith," but in the latter the antecedent of "he" is "Jones."

If discourse sustained by an individual is presented in an unspoken or written manner, the problem becomes particularly acute because stress cannot be indicated. It becomes even more acute because the behavior of the respondent to the discourse cannot be overdetermined by responses to the writer's verbal and nonverbal behavior, such as facial expressions, gestures, and so on. Consequently, the redundancy must be increased over that in spoken verbal behavior, especially behavior in which fairly rapid alternation between two or more individuals is going on. In the preceding sentences, for example, the following are redundant: "In discourse sustained by an individual . . . it . . . problem . . . stress. . . .It . . . of the respondent to the discourse . . . overdetermined . . . " and so on. They are repetitions of words previously presented or pronoun substitutions for such words.

In addition, there are two words that also are examples of rhetoric: "because" and "consequently." They clearly belong to the same category of rhetorical devices as those first mentioned, expressions of agreement or disagreement. They are instructions to the reader that his procedural response is to be continued, the writer judging in hope that it has so far been appropriate, in the judgment of both. What is being aimed at is the stabilization of reader response. A judgment that a writer writes "smoothly" is an indication that the rhetoric of redundancy is effective. This does not, as we have seen, necessarily mean that it is convincing, that agreement is the accompaniment of the reading behavior, though if agreement is absent, the term used is "slickly" or the like.

In the event that the reader refuses the "because" or "cause" or "consequently" or denies its validity—as he may do by a shake of the head, a restless motion of the body, or by a covert verbal response (a verbal response uttered subvocally, not audibly, or, with some readers, an overt or vocal verbal response, or a marginal note)—he is denying, of course, that the writer's procedural response to his own discourse is appropriate. He may then proceed (probably covertly) to generate an explanation for his disagreement; and "proceed" is the proper word here, for that explanation will be procedural, an explanation of the failure of the writer's procedure or methodology. This explanation is frequently preceded by the verbal judgment that the writer's procedure is illogical—"logic," in its fullest sense, being the term for what is judged to be appropriate verbal procedure.

On the other hand, his disagreement may take a personal form, an assertion that an event in the history of the writer is responsible for the failure of appropriateness. That failure is ascribed to a bias, to a prejudice, to a lack of information which, in the judgment of the responder, he ought to have known about. This ascription is an explanation. Both kinds of explanation, then, personal and procedural, are "causal" explanations in answer to the question, "Why is the writer's (or speaker's) response inappropriate, personally or procedurally?" as the case may be judged. (It must also be remembered that the writer or the reader may say either of these of himself.)

It is equally important to remember that since the stimulus situation does not dictate the response, nor the utterance the response to that utterance, there is nothing immanent in any utterance which dictates that the response be either of disagreement, that is, procedural, or one of over- or underdetermination, that is, personal. For example, consider the sentence, "The Japanese started a war against the United

States and bombed Pearl Harbor because Roosevelt maneuvered them
into doing so.'' A judgment of procedural inappropriateness would be
that there is no necessary connection between starting the war and
bombing Pearl Harbor and that even if Roosevelt was responsible for
the Japanese starting the war, it does not follow that the Japanese had
no choice but to begin it by bombing Pearl Harbor. Or it could take the
following form: ''That Roosevelt maneuvered the Japanese into starting the war is an interesting interpretation, but no one has yet produced
evidence that such was his intention.'' Both of these disagreements are
logical objections; as the word *logos* indicates, they are objections to
the verbal procedure. Actually, if one were to take this example seriously, it would be perfectly feasible to argue that for the Japanese
there was no other way to start the war than by bombing Pearl Harbor.
The second objection is different. The logic of it is that the case cannot
be decided unless evidence is produced and that until then it must be
presumed that it is improbable that a president of the United States
would deliberately maneuver his own country into a war. But the
difference is only superficial; although there is an appeal to something
outside of the verbal behavior in which the utterances are occurring,
nevertheless the decision about inappropriateness would still be verbal
and would be an extension or continuation of that verbal behavior. (But
further consideration of the problem of ''outside'' must be postponed
until we take up nonverbal behavior in Chapter II.)

A judgment of the personal inappropriateness of the sentence about
the Japanese and Pearl Harbor would be quite different. It might take
the form of ''The man who says that sort of thing can think so only
because he is an extreme Roosevelt-hating reactionary,'' or '' . . . because he is an extreme Roosevelt-hating radical.'' Or it might take a
form something like this: ''The man who said this was severely
wounded in the war, but because of bureaucratic stupidity he has never
received adequate compensation, the kind every other veteran received. He is naturally bitter and unjust.'' Or ''The man is extremely
sensible on most subjects, but on the subject of the Navy his good
sense always seems to leave him.'' Or ''The author is well-known and
has been for half a century as one who adores everything Japanese.
Indeed, he has come to hate every aspect of European culture, although
he is a Frenchman by birth and was educated at the Sorbonne. The fact
is that when he was young he fell in love with the daughter of the
Japanese ambassador. Although that attachment came to nothing, and

indeed didn't last long, as a result he became enamored of Japanese culture.'' These last examples, particularly the last one, indicate that explanations of personal inappropriateness move very easily in the direction of randomness. They are underdetermined responses. (Yet, on the other hand, explanations of personal inappropriateness may just as easily move in the direction of overdetermination. It is this that has made so many people suspicious of Freudian explanations. The judgment of the Freudian judgment is that the individual who makes such judgments makes them to excess; it often seems the only judgment of personal inappropriateness he can make. And, of course, the same objection has been made of judgments made according to the Christian principle of original sin.)

These examples, moreover, suggest that the binding element in a community is an overdetermination of judgments of personal inappropriateness and that this overdetermination is maintained by rhetorical redundancy. Thus in Victor Hugo's *Les Miserables* Jean Valjean's action, smashing a shop window and stealing a loaf of bread because his family is starving, is judged inappropriate, and the explanation is personal; the judgment is that his person is that of a thief. Valjean himself accepts this judgment and behaves accordingly. He steals, both from a boy and a bishop. The word controls his behavior. The rhetorical overdetermination of the courts overdetermines his responses. This overdetermination, however, is reversed by the rhetoric of the saintly bishop. Jean Valjean, accepting the bishop's judgment that he need not stabilize the judgment that he is a thief, now overdetermines his behavior so that he becomes a transcendentally honest man. Victor Hugo's judgment is that Valjean stole not because he was a thief but because his family was starving, because he was ignorant of how to get help, because indeed there was probably no one to help him, because of the social conditions of France which ground the poor into terrible and helpless poverty, and so on. What bound France into a community is that the sentence ''A man has stolen'' is the overdetermined judgment that the inappropriateness was personal; the man stole because he was a thief. Hugo's judgment is that ''A man has stolen'' is a personal inappropriateness to be explained by the utterance that he stole because of the failure of society to provide adequately for all its members. From one point of view this is a random judgment, moving itself in the direction of inappropriateness, or underdetermination. From the point of view of Hugo's community membership when he wrote the book, it is an overdetermined judgment, for at the time he was living in Guernsey, an emigré from Napoleon III's France, and living in the company of other emigrés. His was the explanation of a community of liberal-radical socialists and quasi-socialists. In both a legal system and in such a community the overdetermined judgment is maintained by redundancy, in the one through the course of legal proceedings, and in the other on the occasions of meetings and conversations.

LOGIC AS BEHAVIOR

The distinction between procedural and personal inappropriateness has long been recognized, though in a somewhat odd way. It is a common assertion that an *argumentum ad hominem* is an improper argument, at least under certain conditions. But these conditions are, of course, those in which a convention of the conditions is that an *argumentum ad hominem* is not to be used. Webster defines it as an appeal to prejudice and feelings rather than to intellect and reason, but it would be unfair to Webster to ask it to tell us how to respond to "intellect" and "reason." It is the traditional assertion that the laws of reason are expressed in the rules of logic; these laws and rules, and reason and logic, are then isomorphic with each other. But in that case it hardly seems necessary to have both terms. The reason is not observable, but the rules of logic are. At least they are often uttered, though the assertion that an utterance is not logical or reasonable or rational is more frequent than the actual utterances of rules of logic. Still, in European culture there is an enormous body of discourse on logic, and logic is studied in colleges and universities. Yet there continues to be great disagreement not only on what the rules of logic really are but, indeed, on what logic itself really is. And, furthermore, logic seems to be curiously ineffective. We have certainly long passed the position at which we can say that scientific discovery, for example, is the result of logical operations. And, in purely verbal behavior, it seems not unfair to cite an example already given, Taylor's conclusions on causation. As a professional philosopher he is presumably trained in logic, yet he admittedly ended his discussion of causation in a perfect tangle, unable at all to tell us what causation really is, except that it must be something because we talk about it. Well, "cause" indeed is something; it is a word, as we have seen, a word giving instructions for a performance, but only, let us remember, instructions to someone who has learned how to respond to it. This interpretation of "cause" can be fruitfully applied to logic itself and to logical rules. They are instructions for performance—in particular, verbal performance. Indeed, it is a common modern position that logic is tautological. Behaviorally, that means that the only appropriate way to respond to the utterances of logic is to produce more utterances of logic. This, in turn, means that a logical utterance cannot determine how nonlogical utterances are generated and how two such utterances are joined (how one gets from one utterance to the next).

Logic and rhetoric emerged pretty much at the same time and at the same place; that there is a difference seems to have been recognized very soon, if not immediately, but it was not at all easy to say what the difference is. The confusion between the two lies in the fact that both are modes of overdetermination of verbal behavior. Both are efforts to control response, but logic in particular is the effort to control verbal response. Furthermore, rhetoric is the effort to control response by redundancy of directions which take into account the history of the person to whom the directions are uttered, but logic is the effort to control response by redundant directions which ignore that history.

The consequence is the separation of logic from behavior and, since logic is an effort to control by *verbal* redundancy, the separation of *language* from behavior. Since only behavior is observable, language and logic are therefore said to be an expression of something nonobservable, "the mind," and the "secretion" of mind, "thought." In the nineteenth century the physiological metaphor "secretion" was not uncommon for indicating the relation of thought to mind. The significance of all this is indicated by a not uncommon modern philosophical position, that logic is the model for how natural language ought to be used, though, to be sure, natural language cannot conform to that model, that it can only approximate it. The fact that logic consists of directions for putting utterances together and for generating utterances, the two aspects of verbal behavior, is thus clarified, and the normative role of logic emerges, as well as the objection to the *argumentum ad hominem*. Logic consists of directions for controlling verbal behavior responded to as divorced from all other behavior. Its effect is to select verbal behavior from the stimulus field in which it is occurring and to isolate it; the effect of that is to facilitate control over it by creating a situation in which the randomness of response is reduced and, ideally, eliminated. It thus falls into the category of that kind of behavior we have already glanced at, the category that includes the theater and the psychological laboratory.

What logic is actually about, that is, what it directs responsiveness to and gives directions for response to, is words, words such as "yet," "nevertheless," "but," "not," "however," "on the other hand," and so on. Some logicians have reduced these possible relations to only four, but Richard von Mises (and no doubt others) reduces those four to merely "and" and maintains that this copulative is the fundamental logical relation. Very likely many, possibly most, logicians would disagree with him, but from the behavioral point of view disagreements among logicians are, in regard to the respective disagreements, of no great interest; the fact of disagreement is what counts. And to this position von Mises's conclusion is a valuable enlightenment, for it confesses, as it were, that logic is concerned only with contiguity of utterances, the fact that one utterance follows another—and that the other logical relationships are an imposition upon that "and," not derived from it; i.e., other logical relationships are means of modifying and controlling contiguity. This is another way of saying that elaborate systems of formal logic are tautological, that is, have no immanent relation to ordinary verbal behavior.

This can be further grasped by considering such a phrase as "intuitive logic." "Intuition" is a word used when we have arrived at a conclusion, that is, have added a sentence to the preceding sentence and regarded the added sentence as appropriate and satisfactory but cannot say how we did so. Intuition is a nonobservable; it is a word. It subsumes a particular kind of behavior and thus explains it and justifies it. It is not derived from an observation of the intuitive process itself, which can scarcely be observed, but merely places an instance of that process in a category which ascribes dignity or value to it. "Intuitive logic" further dignifies the intuitive process (intuitive behavior) by ascribing to it the value that is considered to inhere in arriving at a conclusion by a logical process, that is, one in which all the connecting and articulating words are presented. Equally revealing is the term also often met with in the writings of the less severe logicians or of philosophers who use logic and respect it but are not primarily logicians. This term is "logical intuition," an assertion, in effect, that logical relations, even the most formal, are in fact governed by an intuitive process, one that can only be categorized by a word which admits that one cannot state what it is.

It is an old saw that women are more intuitive than men, but this means merely that their utterances are less characterized by the appearance of the logical connectives and less controlled by stated rules for the use of those connectives. But it is doubtful that any innate or physiological factor accounts for this difference. It is more likely that the history of women is marked by a less frequent exposure to the verbal redundancy of logical connectives and to formal rules for their use than is the history of men. The social situations of the masculine world, political, commercial, intellectual, and proletarian, are marked by high redundancy of these terms; this can be seen in recreational situations for men, such as bars, at any cultural level. Bar arguments show a high incidence of redundancy of logical terms and also of arguments about what is or is not logical.

The two expressions discussed, "intuitive logic" and "logical intuition," suggest that "logic" and "intuition" are coordinate, or parallel, terms, the first asserting that correct verbal conclusions are arrived at by statable rules, the other that the process is unstatable but nevertheless correct. Further, both terms are at once explained and validated by the statement that they are both mental operations. It has already been suggested that if logical laws are isomorphic with mental laws, then "mind" is an unnecessary term. Claude Lévi-Strauss, for example, maintains that mythology and music are "about" nothing outside of themselves, that they are, as it were, elaborate games or amusements, the point of which is that they permit the free expression, unconcerned with "empirical reference," of mental structure. Thus the structure of mythology and music is isomorphic with the structure of the mind. Though, as will appear subsequently, I do not believe the alleged nonreferential character of mythology and music to be tenable, it seems clear enough that if one accepts the notion that mythology and music are engaged in for the sake of a gamelike behavior, or play, to say that the structure of that play is isomorphic with the structure of mind is to add no information about that behavior. "Mind" thus has the same relation to "logic" as the latter has to the connective words the use of and response to which logic struggles to control. "Mind" merely subsumes "intuition" and "logic" and places them in the same category as a number of other kinds of behavior. It is, as it were,

imposed on "intuition" and "logic" and not derived from the behavioral processes categorized by those two words. This is made even
more obvious if one considers the history of the philosophy of logic, or
of formal logic, and if one considers as well the occasions in which one
has heard the word. It is apparent that, considered in isolation—apart,
that is, from the possibility that the word and the behavior it purpor-
tedly describes is under the control of quite different words—the history of philosophical logic shows a remarkable degree of randomness.
And if one observes the use of the term in spoken rather than written
situations, the same randomness is easily remarked on. This randomness, moreover, is readily understandable if the use of the word is
observed in the particular situation, that is, observed not as a word that
has an immanent meaning which may be arrived at but as a means of
moving verbal behavior and the nonverbal consequences of that verbal
behavior (at least in those instances in which there are nonverbal consequences) towards what the user of the word judges to be appropriate
procedural response.

MIND

This discussion of logic has introduced the subject of explanation, the
proper subject of this opening chapter and the subject to which all that
has gone on so far has been preliminary. But "explanation" has been
presented in conjunction with the word "mind" and not inappropriately, for explanation is usually asserted to be a mental activity, a
secretion of the mind. Before tackling "explanation," it is useful to
clear the ground—and also the air—of this troublesome word "mind,"
about which even more has been written than about logic. In spite of all
this effort, however, to quote the always exemplarily useful Taylor,
"our advances over our predecessors appear more illusory than real."
Worse, they scarcely seem even illusory. Indeed, as with the word
"logic," taken by itself, without reference to personal appropriateness, the responses to the word "mind" evince a striking amount of
randomness.

We may begin, however, with a distinction which is common to
most appearances of the word: the mental is not the physical or, more
precisely, is not the physiological. This has led to the mind-body
problem, on which no progress has been made whatever. To be sure, it
has been said to be a pseudoproblem, but on grounds such that all
intellectual problems may be said to be pseudoproblems, and indeed

they may be, but not to us. In fact, even if one does say that it is a pseudoproblem, one continues to use the words "mind" and "body," anyway. Clearly, both words serve a useful purpose. That is, both direct attention to different observables, and each controls behavior in different ways. The question is not whether or not the mind-body problem is a pseudoproblem but, rather, what the useful purposes may be which the two words serve.

The mental is not the physiological, then; the mind is not the body. Yet we may speak of physical or physiological response and also of mental response. The place to begin is with the word "response," which has been used so far very heavily, and I fear is headed for continued heavy use in what is to follow. One often hears such sentences as these: "A response is accompanied by a physiological effect," or "The consequence of a response is a physiological effect." In this inquiry into human behavior my aim is to use a behavioral language. "Behavior" I wish to use in the simplest sense: somebody does something. That something can be anything at all, from writing a book to having stomach cramps. It takes a certain fraction of a second for a stimulus received at a nerve ending to travel to the brain, but in the sense used here, that activity of the nervous system is also behavior, behavior of the organism as organism, if you wish, but behavior nevertheless. Thus, the previous sentences can be recast as "A response is accompanied by behavior" or "The consequence of a response is behavior." Such formulations, however, create a spurious distinction between response and behavior and imply that a response causes behavior. There is perhaps some justification for this in the sense that response is often used in the sense of *observable* response, but the application of electrodes to various parts of the physiology brings internal responses within the area of observation. Thus, it seems reasonable to identify "response" and "behavior": response is behavior. Putting it this way serves to bring out the usefulness of having two terms. "Behavior" is a term that subsumes "response." Responses are instances of the more general term "behavior." Further, "behavior" can subsume not merely what are asserted to be individual responses but also categories of response. Indeed, this is the way the term "response" is ordinarily used. When a particular response of a particular organism is the subject of an utterance, its particularity is designated, hence the distinction mentioned above between "physical response" and "physiological response." The former seems normally to imply behavior which can be merely visually observed; the latter to imply behavior which can be observed only by interfering with the body in some way, a way that involves both tools and measurements, such as a stethoscope or implanted electrodes. "Physiological" is equivalent to "what happens inside of the surface of the skin." And this ordinary distinction I shall use. Both terms, however, are subsumed by the term "body."

The first question is whether or not there can be mental behavior without bodily behavior, either readily observable or instrumentally observable, either physical or physiological. As an example, consider the behavior process I am currently engaged in, writing a book. Sometimes the process goes smoothly. Since I have an unusually rapid electric typewriter, and since I learned touch typing in high school and have been using that method of typing for over forty years, sometimes I type as rapidly as I can "think." What that involves I shall return to, but I wish here to point out what happens when the writing process does not go smoothly. The situation is this. I produce a sentence. That sentence is now part of the phenomenal world to which I am responding. At times it is necessary, as with almost all writers, to reread what I have already written in order to go on. That is, the writing process is interrupted. Such interruptions occur when I am incapable of responding to what I have already written. I must stop, think, reconsider, plan what is to come, occasionally all the way to the end of the book, or at least what I think at the moment is going to be the end of the book. But these are all mentalistic words. What actually happens as well is that I pause, light a cigarette, lean back in my chair, go and make some tea or coffee, go out and rake some leaves from the lawn, play the piano a while, listen to a recording of Reger, all the while wondering why I seem incapable of following the music, daydream about my proposed trip to Italy if the damned book ever gets itself written, check my library to see if I have a play of Hebbel's I propose to lecture about next term, telephone a friend, in desperation go to bed, where I am foolish enough to read history, which keeps me awake, instead of a novel, which can put me to sleep in short order, or set off to do a suddenly remembered errand of the *utmost* importance, and so on, and on. (It is of interest that a recent study of professional writers who have given up smoking reveals that without smoking they cannot write. To continue their writing careers they must smoke. Without that physical activity their "minds" simply will not produce.)

The effort of psychosomatic medicine to solve the mind-body problem is not, of course, as impressive as it claims to be. Nevertheless, it has indubitably shown that a great many internal lesions are found in individuals with a history of "mental" stress or trauma. Indeed, as research into cancer proceeds, one is almost beginning to suspect that there is no substance which some human being cannot use as a carcinogenic agent if he has made up his mind to develop a cancer. Furthermore, more daring researchers have speculated that what really kills us is stress. Profound discovery. Response cannot occur without physiological stress. So long as we are alive, we are continually engaged in response. What kills us, it follows, is being alive. This is unquestionably so, but it is hardly helpful, at least if one wants to stay alive indefinitely. But it is helpful in considering the mind-body problem.

Before drawing the conclusion, let us return to the problem of what happens when writing behavior *is* proceeding smoothly. In the smoothest process I type the words as rapidly as they come to me, and in this sentence the important phrase is "come to me." In writing, one is engaged in covert verbal behavior. Words, phrases, often complete sentences appear. One says them to oneself, and, in my own case, as I say them covertly, I type them. In a somewhat less smooth process I say them covertly before I type them, frequently recasting them before typing. In ordinary verbal behavior the words are uttered covertly, but sometimes they are received, or generated covertly and recast, before vocal behavior is entered upon. That process is no different from what happens when I type a sentence with the utmost smoothness and then discover that it is necessary to change it or delete it. Responding to the sentence on the page in relation to the sentences that preceded it, I may judge that it is inappropriate, either procedurally or personally. It is not what *I* want to say. This recasting and deleting process is best defined, again, as editing, for whether the author edits his writing or an editor edits, what happens is the same process in both cases. The significant matter here is not that mental process is accompanied by physical process—for writing a book is surely one of the behaviors covered by the term "mental," a product of secretion of the mind—but rather that one use for the term "mental" is to talk about, or respond to, a physical process.

The question is this: When the word "mind" is used, what am I being directed to look for? What is the appropriate way to respond to it? The usual way of asking the question is to ask whether or not there is such an entity as the mind. "Entity" is defined by *Webster's Third* as something that has "a self-contained existence." The puzzles in the word and this phrase of definition are endless, and endless are the books and articles that have been written about them. It is possible to skirt them by asking whether or not the body is an entity. From one point of view it is. To give a crude example, certain stimuli processed by the brain produce an ulcer. The ulcer is now a stimulus to which the brain responds. Or to give another example, when I get stuck in writing, when I cannot respond at all, let alone in a way I consider appropriate, I squirm in my chair or I pick up a lighted cigarette and take a pull at it. These are observable phenomena to me, and I respond to them. On the other hand, the brain could not produce bodily phenomena to which it responds if stimuli from outside the body had not initiated the process. From this point of view the body is not a self-contained entity separable from what is outside of it but part of a continuum in which both itself and what is outside of it are segments. From this platitude it is but a step to the platitude that the entire observable world is a continuum. That, however, is only a verbal conclusion, for we do not respond to the world as if it were an unbroken continuum. We respond to segments of it. The very act of perception is a selective, segmenting act, just as logic selects from the verbal continuum certain words which it calls logical connectives and proceeds to build its structure from that act of initial perceptual selection. Thus, the appropriate way to respond to "entity" is not to engage in verbal behavior which struggles to define whether something is an entity or not—for that cannot possibly be determined—but to act *as if* it were separable from the continuum. When such a phrase as "notional entity" is used, what happens is that a word, a phrase, or a sentence, or a series of sentences, is selected out of and separated from the verbal continuum in which it has been encountered, and then subjected to analysis, that is, to complex verbal response or behavior, according to certain stated and unstated procedural rules.

We cannot say whether anything is an entity or not, because it is just as sensible to say that there are no entities. In either case it is merely something that we say. Yet when we respond to the word entity, we engage in selective behavior, whether it is verbal selection or perceptual selection, or both. For twenty-five hundred years the struggle has been going on to decide whether or not the mind is an entity. No conclusion has been reached, or, rather, innumerable conclusions have been reached, but they are not culturally validated. Someone always comes along and shows the procedural failure of the argument. This is not difficult, for the reason that we have seen. One has only to respond to a word with a slightly different definition from that in the discourse in question in order to dissolve any argument. The study of logic has at least reached the point of realizing that any argument can be dissolved, and this can be done because no procedural rules are immanent in language.

The question has rarely been asked, however—indeed, I have never heard it asked—as to what the word "mind" directs one to respond to.

Consider the distinction made above between words coming to me and my responding to them covertly. To which category does the "mind" direct me to respond? To which should I be ascribing the word "thought?" Let us say that a man, in response to a question about his opinion, responds by saying, "I think," then pauses for thirty seconds and then says, "I think that such-and-such is the case." During the pause either of two events takes place; one is that his mind goes blank, and words do not come to him; the other is that words do come to him covertly. Is that covert behavior mental activity? Or is wherever the words come from the mind? Let us suppose also that words come to him but that he edits them before renewing his overt verbal response to the question put to him. In editing, he has responded to his covert utterance with a modification of that utterance; that is, other words or even the same words in a different sequence have come to him. Is that and only that process to be called a mental process? Further, if the mind is where the words come from, and if the coming of those words is behavior, then can a distinction be made between words coming and nonverbal behavior coming, such as striking at a tennis ball? I know of at least one philosopher who maintains that no distinction can be made. He puts it in an odd way, however. We think, he avers, with our muscles.

To these various questions various responses have been made. It seems to be the case that the distinction is commonly made by using the terms "conscious" and "unconscious" minds. In that event "conscious mind" merely instructs me to observe the fact that I observe words and images coming to me covertly. I am, we say, *aware* of that, and thus by a common English method of making nouns out of verbs, consciousness is sometimes defined as self-awareness, but this term appears to do nothing more than to direct me to observe my own covert verbal and imagistic behavior. It is difficult, then, to grasp any difference between my observing my covert verbal behavior and my observing my leaning back in my chair and my observing the camellias in a vase on my typing table. And it is equally difficult to grasp any difference between my responding to my covert verbal behavior by typing a sentence and my responding to the camellias by the covert verbal behavior "I need to get some fresh ones." The definition of mind, then, as the organ which secretes thought seems to do no more than to tell me to observe the fact that covert verbal and imagistic behavior, including aural, olfactory, gustatory, and other sensory images, do come to me covertly and that I can observe them as they arrive, as, indeed, I can observe any behavior as it arrives.

But where do these words and images come from? It is commonly believed that they come from the brain. At least, if the physiology of the brain is instrumentally interfered with, behavior is modified in predictable ways. We even know the geography of the brain, or at least something about it, that is, what areas of the brain can be instrumentally interfered with to produce a particular category of behavioral modification. Frontal lobotomy, for example, can produce a considerable reduction of unpredicted behavior. That is, the patient is more likely to do what you tell him to do. But that is all we know. We have yet to trace a neural path from stimulus to response, and I believe that this is so for the reason already given: it is impossible to know what the stimulus was that was responsible for a particular response in a particular individual. The use of "mind" in this situation is merely an instruction to observe that between stimulus and response something happens, though we do not know that. "Mind" thus merely means "the abyss of ignorance that lies between stimulus and response."

So far, then, it appears that "mind" does no more than subsume various categories of observations. The assertion that it is an entity seems clearly to be a mere case of hypostatization or reification. To hypostatize is to assume that because there is a word, particularly that kind of word grammarians call a noun, there must be something not that word which that word names or otherwise refers to. After all, we are taught from childhood that a noun is a name of something. There must, then, be a something for the noun to be a name of. The theory of hypostatization is that there are a good many words, of which "mind" appears to be an excellent example, for which there is no something. It is an illusion that there is a something. The something that the word allegedly names does not exist. The only thing to do, then, is to stop using the word. But this creates difficulties and involved circumlocutions. Behaviorist psychologists, for example, having decided that there is no such something as "mind," eschew the word. However, if they recognized that "mind" merely gives instructions to perform certain observations or to look for certain observables, they would find it very handy. The theory of hypostatization, in short, is unsatisfactory because it does not recognize the kind of instructions a great many words give, that is, the way they are observably responded to.

Presented differently, the usefulness of hypostatizations can be recognized. A word instructs those who know how to respond to it to respond to an instance of a class of configurations. Among such classes are words themselves, for a word, whether presented visually or orally, is never presented in precisely the same way twice, and in addition it is selected from a situation simultaneously verbal and nonverbal, as a member of a class. A word can be, then, an instruction to respond to instances of that class of words of which the word itself is an instance. Thus, the appropriate behavior for responding to a stop sign at an intersection is to bring the automobile one is driving to a halt. For other words, however, the appropriate response is to respond with other words. "Mind" is such a word, and it must be admitted that philosophers and psychologists and hordes of other individuals under their influence have been responding verbally to "mind" for a long time and with untold billions of words. To explain the character of such responses is clearly of greater use than to engage in the necessarily inconclusive and even hopeless task of attempting to determine what the word "mind" really means or what mind really is.

This can be entered upon more readily by examining another use of "mind," seen in expressions like, "He has a powerful mind," "He has a very strange mind," "He has an interesting mind." In these three examples the adjectives are differential or contrastive. They direct that this particular mind be distinguished from other minds or some other minds, that is, that this particular mind is not to be placed in the same category as the minds with which it is contrasted or from which it is differentiated. In the "If . . . then . . . " form such sentences predict that "If you will observe the way this mind works [an expression which can only mean the verbal and nonverbal behavior of the individual who is alleged to have this mind], then you will observe that the ways in which its workings differ have a certain attribute in common"—interesting, powerful, strange, repulsive, trenchant, perceptive, intuitive, logical, and so on . . . and on. Such sentences in more general form amount to the assertion that if you put two individuals in the same situation, their observable responses will be different, at least sometimes, though at other times they will be the same. A similar assertion is that if you put the same individual twice into what you judge to be two situations sufficiently alike to be placed in the same category, then his behavior will be different on each occasion, or it might be the same; that is, the two behaviors will be sufficiently similar to be judged as appropriately placed in the same category or so dissimilar as not to be so placed. What this boils down to is the proposition that human behavior is both predictable and unpredictable. I do not think that such a notion will surprise anyone, but what has been made of it is quite astonishing, for one of the most important uses of the word "mind" is simply to explain this predictability and this unpredictability by subsuming both under that word.

"Mind" thus has an explanatory relation to the predictability and unpredictability of human behavior. As is usual with such explanatory words, it is then hypostatized into an entity that can be investigated and talked about, or so it is supposed. Since it is easily observable, given the triad of reality-behavior-mind, that behavior varies unpredictably, it is concluded that mind, which explains behavior, causes that unpredictability or is responsible for it in some way. That is, if reality is held steady, or, more precisely, if a situation is held steady, and if behavior varies, then mind must be the source of that variation. Moreover, since reality or situation is held steady, behavior does not necessarily vary; then surely it must be the case that the mind has a direct relationship to reality. In such instances, mind is said to know reality, but when behavior, given this triad, does vary, then mind is said not to know reality. Thus arises the question, How is it that mind sometimes knows reality and sometimes does not? Attempts to resolve this quite insoluble conundrum have taken the various philosophical modes of idealism, realism (in its medieval sense and in its modern sense), empiricism, and phenomenalism, each of which is based on a solution to what is called the epistemological problem, the problem of the relation of the mind to reality. No universally accepted solution to the epistemological problem has yet been arrived at, nor, so long as the discussion is continued in the traditional way and with the traditional terms, is it at all likely that it ever will be arrived at. It is one of those philosophical questions on which no progress has been made, except for the fact that a few people have come to the conclusion that the wrong question is being asked. To ask how the mind gets to the world, or how the world gets to the mind, is to ask how a word gets to the world, or how the world gets to a word. Since both "world" and "word" are words, this is to ask how a word gets to a word, and the answer obviously is that a word does not do anything.

Thus, the problem is not how the mind gets to the world but, rather, how language gets to the world. But, again, since language does nothing, the question properly is how human beings get from language to the world and from the world to language. Further discussion of this must be postponed until we have moved from the verbal to the nonverbal, and for the time being it is sufficient to note that the terrible and puzzling epistemological problem begins with and can be reduced to the observation, not that *behavior* is both appropriate and inappropriate, but that human beings are constantly engaged in *judging* that a response is either appropriate or inappropriate.

INTENTION

Another use of the word "mind" occurs in such expressions as "I have a mind to go to the movies," and "He has evidently changed his mind about what he only started to do." This use occurs at a lower cultural level than the type of use considered in the preceding section. At the higher cultural levels its equivalent is "I intend to," or "My purpose is to," or "His intention has evidently changed." But at all cultural levels it is the same kind of expression as "I am going to." All of these are said to refer to an activity of the mind, an activity at one time judged to be a subcategory of mind, a mental faculty—that is, intention, or purpose, a pair of words involved with such terms as "goal," "aim," "direction," and so on. Looking again for the kind of behavior which such words direct us to observe, one does not find it difficult to locate. To the question, "What are you going to do this evening?" the answer might be "I have a mind to go to the movies," or "I intend to go to the movies," or "Go to the movies," or, simply, "Movies." Granted that the response to each of these might be different, the behavior to look for is the "mental" factor in producing the utterance. Each of these might be preceded by either covert verbal behavior or a covert image, such as an image of the advertisement for a particular film. On the other hand it might not be so preceded. In the latter case the production of the utterance and the production of the covert utterance or image is the same kind of immediate response. So would be a leap for somebody's throat in a hostile atmosphere in which the challenge is flung out, "What are ya gonna do about it?" Consider also the following interchange: "What should I do tonight?" and the immediate response, "You ought to go to the movies." In this kind of case, the immediate response, "You ought to go to the movies," is of the same sort not only as the preceding immediate response but also the covert response which preceded an utterance. That is, in the interchange the responder gives the questioner instructions for behavior, while in the covert response the individual gives himself instructions for behavior before producing the utterance. I shall call the latter a mediated response if it is followed by an overt response. To take another example from my own behavior in writing this book, the normal or appropriate response to typing a sentence is to type another, ordinarily preceded by a covert verbal response. But when I am unable to produce an appropriate verbal response and its ensuing typing response, I tend to have covert images of some other response, such as an image of sticking a fork in the corned beef to see how it is coming along, although in fact I tested it only ten minutes before; or to glance at the coffee cup, and on the observation that it is empty, to produce a covert image of myself going to the kitchen with the cup and pouring a fresh cup. On the other hand, let us suppose that in the hostile situation the attack eventuates in the death of the individual attacked, and the attacker states, "I didn't intend to kill him or even to attack him. I just reacted to what he said." In such a situation the claim, whether true or false, is that the attack was not preceded by covertly given self-directions to attack, let alone kill. "Intention" as a "mental" activity, then, categorizes mediating covert responses if covert verbal or imagistic behavior is categorized as mental behavior.

Yet if it is used to categorize an unobservable activity within that inaccessible area of behavior bracketed by stimulus and response, is "intention" anything more than a metaphorical extension into the unknown? Is there a kind of behavior other than immediate response which the word gives us directions to look for and observe? It seems probable that this indeed is the case, for what on first glance appears to be another kind of intentional behavior is sustained intentional behavior. Some years ago in Bologna, Italy, wanting to get a haircut and a beard trim, I asked the concierge at my hotel for directions to a barber shop. I followed them—they were not very intricate—but found no barber shop. I went beyond the point where it was supposed to be, fruitlessly; I returned to the hotel and started all over again, with the same result. Feeling stupid and sheepish, I returned to the concierge and told him of my failure. He looked blank and then said, "Oh, it's Monday. I forgot. On Monday the barber shops are closed. But the one at the railroad station is open." I at least knew where that was, went there, found the shop, found it open, and got what I wanted. Here is an instance of sustained intention, and it appears to justify the view that the notion of intention which I suggested above might be a metaphorical extension of the term. However, if one could examine my covert behavior—and I remember it quite distinctly—one would have observed that I sustained my intention by covert images of a barber shop and covert repetitions of the concierge's directions. Nor was that the only factor. Consider such common expressions as, "Watch what you're doing" or "Look out where you're going." These occur when someone judges that, considering covert directions already given, or judging that covert directions have been given, or observing the inappropriateness of the behavior, the behavior of the individual to whom the utterance is directed is evincing randomness. But often enough we say to ourselves when we get lost or just miss another automobile when we are driving, "I ought to watch where I'm going." Such utterances are to be taken most seriously, for they reveal how behavior is sustained. Not only do we sustain behavior by reiterating directions, but we also sustain behavior by responding to our own behavior. Thus both verbal and nonverbal behavior are directions for response, or further behavior, whether that direction-giving behavior is our own or another's.

Two other kinds of sustained "intentional" behavior, historical and unconscious intention, are worth noting. In the case of the murderous attack, the statement might be "If he has a history of such murderous attacks, then either he is not to be believed in his assertion that he did not intend to kill and has sustained his murderous behavior by redundant self-directions, or he has an unconscious intention to kill." But it also might be said, "Although he is to be believed in his assertion that he has never intended to kill, in spite of the fact that he has done so more than once in the past, this repeated murderous behavior indicates an unconscious intention to kill." Statements about historical intentions do no more than categorize what is asserted to be the past repetition of a particular kind of behavior. If such an intention is said to be conscious, this amounts to a statement that one attribute of that historically sustained intention was redundant self-direction. If it is said to be unconscious, either this amounts to an assertion that it is known that no self-directions have been given, or it merely asserts that the various incidents of murderous attacks are instances of murderous attack; that is, it is tautological, or, more complexly, it categorizes murderous attacks with other violent and destructive acts. In the last case, the word "unconscious" is a direction to observe or to remember a pattern of behavior, commonly called a syndrome. When we use "intention," then, we are doing no more than categorizing a bit of behavior or a series of behaviors in a way that results in generating a response which we judge to be appropriate.

One final example of the use of the word "mind" shows with particular clarity the purely explanatory use of the word in the subsumption of what are often called occult behavioral phenomena. Two examples will suffice. The first comes from the Rhine experiments on extrasensory perception. In carefully screened or blind experiments it has been demonstrated to the satisfaction of various highly skeptical psychologists—though by no means to all of them—that at least some subjects can guess which card an experimenter is looking at and that these guesses are of such frequency that they cannot be accounted for by statistical probability. One skeptical psychologist has come to the conclusion that the Rhine experiments have uncovered something, though the experimenters cannot say what. To be sure, what they may indicate is that statistics is less sophisticated than statisticians imagine, but let us assume that this is not the case and that an inexplicable phenomenon has indeed been discovered. (That it is inexplicable need not surprise us. Psychology is a young science; its theory is primitive, scarcely developed; its experimental procedures are unanalyzed and dubious, at best. Perhaps there can be no such science.)

The second example is even more perplexing, the modification of objects just by looking at them or at the very most by holding them but without exerting muscular pressure. Let us again assume that this sort of thing does happen, though certainly the number of people who can manage it is in itself so small as to arouse suspicions, and let us assume also that skepticism is not justified, that such phenomena, even such phenomena as teleportation, do indeed take place and are indeed inexplicable. Nevertheless, for some responders to such phenomena, they are not inexplicable at all. They are phenomena produced by the mind, and since no physical intervention has occurred, and since in ESP telepathy no known perceptual physiology appears to be responsible, such responders assert that therefore the mind is an existent separable from the brain. Others go further and aver that such phenomena are under the control of inhabitants of Unidentified Flying Objects, who are indeed the gods of ancient mythology. Mythology thus turns out to have been accurate in its observations, though possibly a little weak in its interpretations. A further leap produces the assertion that the phenomena in question evince the existence of true gods, not merely wanderers from other planets, or of God Himself. What has happened in the production of such explanations is easy enough to see. Here are inexplicable phenomena. They must be caused and caused, moreover, by unobservable (not, note, unobserved) forces. The unobservable force-producing entity for which a word exists is the mind. Therefore, if the responder judges himself to be culturally modern, he asserts that such phenomena are mentally produced. If he is willing to be judged to be more old-fashioned, if he prides himself on being more than archaic, he uses another word which is said to refer to an unobservable force-producing entity, God. The case is, however, that, granted that such phenomena do occur and granted that they are inexplicable, what the statement of inexplicability amounts to is that such phenomena are not explicable by the currently available explanatory modes and the currently available procedural rules for manipulating explanatory modes of verbal behavior. The assertion that such phenomena are not mentally produced observables amounts to an assertion that the attributes of such observables are not sufficiently identical with the observable phenomena of behavior subsumed under the word "mind" to justify the inclusion of these inexplicable observables in the set of linguistic and nonlinguistic observables categorized by "mind." Wallace Stevens's famous line, "It is never satisfied, the mind—never," may be an excellent general cultural directive, but if explanation is one way the mind operates, then it is clear that the mind is in fact very easily satisfied. Inexplicability is satisfied by an explanation, and everybody is satisfied by any explanation some of the time.

The mind-body problem is not a problem; nor is it a pseudoproblem in the sense that it refers to a distinction which does not exist. "Body" subsumes "physical" and "physiological," as I have been using those words. "Mind" subsumes in its full explanatory development various faculties, functions, processes, operations, activities, and so on, such as the "memory." To be sure we do engage in the behavior we call "remembering," but it does not follow that there is such an entity as the "memory" or, in more fashionable terms, taking the metaphor from computer technology, a "memory bank." "Memory" merely subsumes all instances of remembering. Thus, the various faculties subsume various categories of acting, or behaving, or performing, all of which, after all, are done by the body. The observational response to "mind" is to look for certain kinds of behavior in the continuum of bodily activity. It is not that the body produces mentation. Rather, the body produces observable behaviors which we categorize as the productions of the mind, particularly when those behaviors are observable only by the observer and no one else. "Mind" is a word which has an explanatory relation to such responses. To explore that relation is the next task, which—with "mind" out of the way—can now be undertaken.

EXPLANATORY REGRESS

To begin once again at the beginning, the meaning of a word is the response to that word. (Such responses may be either verbal or nonverbal, but since explanation is verbal behavior, in what follows, verbal behavior will be examined.) Put differently, the response to a word is the determination of its meaning. However, this can also be put thus: the meaning of a word is the determination of a response. This third way of putting it places the emphasis on the activity of determining, and also the use of the indefinite article "a" before "response" indicates that the word does not determine the response; or, to repeat what has been offered above, though in different form, the response to a word is indeterminate. Thus, any response can be determined for a word. The problem now appears of how that determination takes place. What is the behavior that determines meaning?

To get at this behavior it is first advisable to scrutinize the word "meaning" more closely than has yet been done. Once we free ourselves of the notion that meaning is immanent in a word or that a word determines the response to it, it becomes evident that "meaning," like "mind" or any of the faculties of mind, such as memory, is an example of hypostatization. It is a matter of the occasions in which questions about meaning arise, occasions in which sentences such as these are uttered: "What is the meaning of this word?" "I do not know the meaning," "Where shall I find the meaning?" "This word has several meanings; which is the right one here?" and so on. These questions appear to be themselves responses to the word and, as responses, appear to be themselves meanings of that word. This seems strange until we consider such sentence responses as, "That word doesn't mean anything here." This is a clear assertion that the speaker is unable to respond. Thus, all of these sentences about meaning are not so much responses to the word itself, but rather responses to the inability to respond appropriately, in the judgment of the speaker. They are the same kind of response as exemplified above in my own inability to respond to a sentence I have just written. If my personal history is removed from consideration, the various behaviors I engage in in such circumstances would, to an observer, look like random behavior. However, I have observed from many years of writing that such responses are not random but, rather, are quite patterned. On the other hand, the longer I am engaged on a particular job of writing, a book instead of an essay, the more patterned become those responses and the more limited the range of response. I respond to failures to respond to my own writing in an increasingly smaller number of ways, and each of those ways is increasingly patterned. My failures to respond to meaning are increasingly determined. I am engaged in determining the meaning of my failure to respond to my self-produced written utterances. Since there is always response, however, this kind of sentence, as a response to a failure to respond, is actually better understood as a response to what is judged to be an inappropriate response. Failure to respond verbally to an utterance, then, is an inappropriate response. However, in the case of the sentence "That word doesn't mean anything here," quite the contrary appears to have taken place, for the inappropriate response is asserted to be, after all, an appropriate response.

What is going on here can be grasped if such a situation is presented in full verbal form. A question is asked. The individual to whom the question is addressed does not respond. He is asked why he does not, and his answer is, "Under the circumstances, the question is meaningless." This amounts to an assertion that no response was made because the original question was an inappropriate utterance, and therefore no response can be appropriate. The failure to respond is thus both explained and justified and is asserted to have been appropriate. The question is placed in the category of inappropriate response, while the lack of response is placed in the category of appropriate response. However, such terms as "category," "subsumption," and "judgment," which I have been using without behavioral analysis, are obviously mentalistic terms, and before further scrutiny of explanatory behavior can be continued, they require such analysis.

In *A Study of Thinking* Jerome Bruner has presented and discussed ingenious psychological tests to investigate categories, but categories can be studied even more simply by ordinary direct observation. To leave the verbal once more, if you watch someone running rapidly through a thick wood, you will observe him dodging trees. Each tree is, of course, a different perceptual configuration, tall, thick, thin, short, trunks with branches high above the ground, trunks with branches close to the ground, and so on. Yet the person responds to each tree with the same pattern of behavior. His "intention" we would say, simply by observing his behavior, is to avoid running into any tree. Consider a somewhat different case: a football player carrying the ball and, as he should, heading for the opposing team's goal line. Members of that team are running at him, throwing themselves at him, grabbing for his legs. Yet he successfully dodges each one. No matter the speed, direction, or gesture of each opponent, he responds with the same pattern of behavior. These are configurations succeeding each other rapidly. Intermittent succession, even if occasions are far apart in time, provide the opportunity for the same kind of observation. Whenever I see a dog in someone's home, or even a cat, my response is to whistle at it or make some other enticing noise and attempt to pat it. When I go for a walk, however, I merely talk to barking dogs and make no effort at more intimate interaction. I respond differently according to the situation in which I encounter these configurations. The meaning of a dog at home is different for me from the meaning of a dog on its own property.

But it must also be noticed that in watching the man running through the trees, or the football player running down the field, or in observing myself reacting to dogs and cats, each selected configuration of the individual I am observing is a different configuration. Thus in both the observed and the observer the same kind of behavior is apparent. Each separate configuration is responded to as if it were the same configuration. If we turn back to verbal behavior, an example makes this even more easily grasped. Let us assume a well-trained youth to whom his mother says, "Please go get some firewood," or "Firewood, dear," or "We need some firewood," or "The wood box is empty." To each of these utterances our admirable young man responds by fetching firewood and putting it in the wood box. He responds to each utterance as if it were the same utterance. To be sure, he may do so immediately, or after he finishes what he is doing, or after a delay; he may go out the front door or the back door; he may leave the door open and have to be reminded to close it; he may close it; his mother may be waiting for him and open and close it for him. That is, there may be any number of differences in the behavior, but the pattern, as in the preceding instance, can be judged by an observer to be the same in each instance, though with variations.

"Category" is a word like "meaning." To hypostatize it is to place it in the realm of the fictitious "mental," but to regard it as a direction-giving utterance is to make a slippery notion into a very simple and obvious one. One needs only convert it from a noun into a verb. Thus, individuals do respond to members of a set of configurations *as if* those members were identical, that is, interchangeable. And the word *category* or, in its more active form, *categorization*, directs us to observe such sets of responses. What can be observed, then, is sets of responses which we judge to be sufficiently identical to be called, that is, verbally responded to, *as if* they were identical or interchangeable responses. To understand what is involved here, let us assume that the admirable young wood-fetcher, Robert, has a twin brother, John. When Robert fetches wood at his mother's request, he smiles before he does his task, but John frowns. One observer may say, "They are both obedient young men," but another may remark, "True, but one is willingly obedient, and the other is not." The first observer ignores the differentia of the facial responses and places both behaviors in the same category, that is, responds to them verbally in the same way. The other observer, however, places the behaviors in different categories and responds by asserting that the two young men ought to be responded to in different ways. The appropriate verbal response to this categorial response is that the second observer has judged that there is a difference between the behaviors of the two boys, at least as far as wood-fetching is concerned. To judge, then, is to determine what category a configuration ought to be assigned to, to determine whether the differentia among the members of a categorial set ought or ought not to be responded to. To judge is to determine on these grounds the appropriateness of a response.

In this account the most important words are "as if" and "ought." The relation between the two is that a categorizing response is also a judging response. Thus the observer of the runner through the woods or the runner with the football can say of either of them that their behavior shows that they are judging well, or badly, as the case might be. The observer is judging judgments, and he does it the same way the observed actor does it, by categorizing. The observer's verbal response is a determination of whether the observed runners are, or are not, behaving appropriately, that is, judging appropriately. Thus, if he is informed beforehand that the woods-runner has instructed himself or has received instructions to run through the woods in as straight a line as possible, and if he observes that in fact the course of the runner is leading him back to his starting point, as so frequently happens in going through woods, then he will judge that the runner is judging inappropriately. He might say that the runner is responding to the trees in his way as if his modes of response would lead him straight through the woods. But he also could very well use the same expression if he observed that the runner's course is leading him straight through. Both appropriate and inappropriate responses are "as if" responses, for both depend upon categorial selection from the stimulus field and on non-response to differentia as well as to nonselected configurations. But it must be remembered that there are no responses appropriate or inappropriate in themselves, that there is no "immanence of appropriateness," but that responses are appropriate or inappropriate only in the judgment of someone, whose judgment is a categorial judgment involving a selection from the stimulus field. *"As if" indicates, then, the fictive character of categorization, while the "ought" indicates its normative character.*

"Fictive" is defined by Webster as "of, relating to, or capable of imaginative creation" and as a second meaning as the equivalent of "imaginary" or "feigned." My use of "fictive" is not an example of philosophical idealism, nor is it here to be judged synonymous with "fictitious," the totally made up. My emphasis is rather on "imaginative," in the sense that we pretend or feign that we are responding to the entire stimulus field, when we are responding to an indeterminable selection of the available configurations, and on "creative" in the sense that we segment the perceptual continuum, or the world. We are all like the psychological experimenter, who imagines that he can select a configuration and determine it as a stimulus for a particular response, and our behavior is as fictive as his; or, his behavior is an unanalyzed instance of ordinary response. Verbal behavior, consisting as it does of fictive responses, thus creates a linguistic fiction or, put differently, is not isomorphic with the stimulus fields to which it is a complex set of responses, and this complexity develops an independence from perceptual stimulus fields because verbal response is a doubly fictive response to utterances—doubly, for utterances can be fictively selected from nonverbal stimulus fields and are themselves subject to categorial judgment. To change the metaphor used earlier, language is a vast organism that can pursue a life independent of the world, i.e., of the nonverbal, and has done so since language first appeared in human history. (The problem of how a verbal continuum of established independence can be modified and its independence compromised, must be postponed until the next chapter.)

To the question, "What is the behavior that determines meaning?" it is now possible to respond with the words "categorizing" and "judging." *Thus verbal behavior can be defined as the determination of fictive and normative meanings of verbal and nonverbal configurations.* The meaning of any utterance, then, is the determination of a fictive and normative response to that utterance. An explanation of an utterance, furthermore, is first a determination of a fictive and normative response to that utterance and, at the next step, a determination of a fictive and normative response to the first level of explanation, and so on.

Let us take an utterance from the example with which we started. (I have, incidentally, played fair. The following sentences were produced by a series of immediate responses. That is, I have set them down exactly as they occurred to me, without editing or similar modification. I am aware that the reader may very well find the analysis of these sentences rather tedious, but tedium is often the price we have to pay for clarity of understanding. I know of no better way to shatter the illusion that our explanations are marked by an inherent necessity.)

1. "Smith hit Jones."
2. "Why?"

3. ''Because there was an earthquake.''

4. ''What did that have to do with it?''

5. ''Well, Smith always is highly aggressive whenever there is an earthquake and invariably hits the handiest thing there is to hit, especially if at the moment the earthquake strikes he is irritated by what happens to be the nearest thing strikable. Unfortunately, he was arguing with Jones when the earthquake struck, and Jones was the nearest thing to hit.''

6. ''Does he act like that only when there are earthquakes?''

7. ''Well, actually, he is a pretty aggressive and highly irritable man.''

8. ''Is he more irritable when there are eathquakes?''

9. ''Come to think of it, when he is irritated with somebody and arguing with him, he is likely to start a fight when something quite unexpected happens, something that is quite irrelevant.''

10. ''Ah, now we're getting somewhere. Tell me, when he hits somebody on these occasions, whom does he usually hit.''

11. ''Oh, it's always a man.''

12. ''He never hits his wife?''

13. ''Never.''

14. ''What kind of relation did he have with his father?''

15. ''He was always quarreling with him.''

16. ''Always?''

17. ''It began after his mother was killed in an automobile accident.''

18. ''Who was driving the car?''

19. ''His father.''

20. ''How did it happen?''

21. ''His father was drunk and went off an embankment.''

22. ''Ah, I see. He holds his father responsible for his mother's death.''

23. ''Nonsense!''

24. ''It's perfectly obvious. Whenever he is quarreling with a man and is startled by something irrelevant, he unconsciously forgets that it is not his father he's quarreling with and hits him, something he has wanted to do to his father ever since his mother was killed, but his father's authority made him repress that wish.''

25. ''You mean Smith hit Jones because of an unresolved Oedipus complex?''

26. "Undoubtedly."

This parody of psychoanalytic explanation—or is it a parody? I am not quite sure—presents a perfect tangle of explanation, but with the tools we have developed, it is quite possible to disentagle it. The first thing to note is the first utterance and the final one. These bracket the explanation. The first is a statement that is a response to a unique event. Number 24 is a statement of an unconscious mental pattern that according to Freudian explanation of behavior is to be discovered in every man. Numbers 25 and 26 terminate the explanation by resolving to the satisfaction of both speakers the demand for explanation uttered in number 2. The explanation, of course, does not have to terminate here. It can perfectly well go on again to a complete exposition of the Freudian explanation of human behavior. An explanation is terminated when someone judges that further explanation is unnecessary, when no one asks, "Why is that the case?" or here, "Why do people have Oedipus complexes?" Hence, the termination of an explanation is always arbitrary. There is no inner necessity, as the early nineteenth-century German philosophers would have put it, for an explanation to terminate where it does. Of equal significance is what the termination of an explanation does to the statement which is the initial bracket. That statement now becomes an example of the terminal explanation. An example of the Oedipus complex is Smith hitting Jones. Thus, the terminal explanation determines, for anyone who accepts the explanation, the verbal response to the utterance "Smith hit Jones."

With this bracketing before us to indicate the beginning and the end of the explanatory response, it can now be more profitably examined in detail.

The first sentence within the initial bracketing sentence is simply, "Why?" This is a demand for an explanation and begins the dialogue which follows. It is tempting to say that explanation arises when there is a judgment of either personal or procedural inappropriateness or when the consequences of a behavior fail to correspond with the expectations that the verbal or other instructions have aroused, or if there is a failure to respond, or a response that the demander judges inappropriate, as here. Such failure, however, is a special case of inappropriate response. However, once the pattern of demanding an explanation is learned, it can be entered upon in the absence of any of these conditions. It has been said, and said wisely, that genius is the ability to be puzzled by the obvious, that is, to judge the established explanation for any event or category of events inadequate, incorrect, or in some other way inappropriate. Still, a great many people make nuisances of themselves by demanding explanations when, in the judgment of everyone else in the situation, it is quite unnecessary, and obviously this kind of response to the demand for explanation is not infrequently applied to the demands of genius. In some situations, furthermore, the demand for explanation is the social protocol. Education in great part consists of demands for standardized or socially validated explanations to make sure the student has learned them, and the higher the level of education, the greater amount of time is spent in learning such explanations and in responding to demands for them.

Number 3 is "Because there was an earthquake." The full form of this is "There was an earthquake and Smith hit Jones. The link between these two events was causal." As we have seen, words such as "cause" and words derived from them can give instructions for nonverbal search-and-find behavior. Such behavior, obviously, occurs after the direction-giving-causal sentence, but in this case the event does not follow the sentence but precedes it. This is a historical use of causality. It cannot be transformed into an "if . . . then . . . " form ("If there is an earthquake, then Smith will hit Jones") because the event cannot be reproduced. The reason is not that it would be rather difficult to get Smith and Jones into some kind of argument and then arrange for an earthquake or to keep them arguing until there is one, but rather that since the response "Smith hit Jones" is fictive and normative, the total attributes of the situation cannot be reproduced. We do not know, for example, the complete internal conditions of Smith, and for all we know it was not an Oedipus complex that was an important factor in his attack but too much beer. The other response to causality expressions is a verbal response, as here. "Because" is thus one of those connective words which logic struggles to control, to little ultimate purpose, as we have seen, but with constant temporary success. Causal terms link not events but sentences, sentences that purport to refer to events, that is, sentences which give directions but which cannot be followed by nonverbal search-and-find behavior. Since the "cause" of the event is a factor introduced into the event and imposed upon it, it increases the fictiveness of the explanation, a fictiveness which began with the original bracketing sentence. Moreover, it must be noted that the two events, the earthquake and the attack, are not merely linked by "cause" but are thus fictively constructed into a single event, which is then subsumed by the categorizing word derived from "because" and "cause"/"causality." To the demand "Give me an example of causality, or cause, or the causal relationship, or the causal link," it is now possible to respond with a sentence which presents the earthquake-attacks with other violent and destructive acts. In the last case, the earthquake" can henceforth be used as an example, or case, or instance of causality. Any explanation converts the initial bracketing utterance into an example of that explanation. We have here an example of a first step in explanatory regress, a regress accomplished by moving away from a nonverbal or other-than-human event by means of subsuming sentences that respond to such events under successively more inclusive categories.

Number 4 "What did that have to do with it?" is a response that amounts to a judgment that 3 was inappropriate from inadequacy. Number 5 "Well, Smith always is highly aggressive whenever there is an earthquake and invariably hits the handiest thing there is to hit" is an even clearer case of subsumption by causality. "Smith hit Jones at the time of the earthquake because at such times he is highly aggressive and hits the most proximate hittable object." Earthquake, aggressiveness, irritability, and hitting the proximate are now linked into a more general event, i.e., category of events, than 3. Number 3 exemplifies the first sentence in number 5, which explains it, and the explanatory regression from numbers 1 to 5 is indicated by the second sentence in number 4, which subsumes 1 under 4 by way of 3. It also links arguing and irritation in such a way that irritation is an attribute of the category of Smith's arguing behavior. It is always to be found whenever Smith argues.

Number 6, "Does he act like that only when there are earthquakes?" is a new kind of response. It is a question about categorization itself; it is quite clearly a procedural question. It asks, "Is there a more general linkage than the earthquake-arguing-aggressiveness-irritability-hitting linkage?" Number 7 responds by ascribing to Smith a high probability that on any occasion he is aggressive and irritable. This enormously broadens the category of number 5, of which numbers 1 and 3 are exemplifications, and turns number 5 into an exemplification of the more general proposition that there is a high probability that on any occasion Smith is aggressive and irritable. This would bracket or terminate the explanation if it were not for the next procedural question, number 8, about the degree of irritation. The connective utterance is "more," which opens up the possibility for further explanation by limiting the nearly all-inclusive category of Smith's high frequency of aggressive and irritable behavior. The response thus indicates that the explanation that Smith hit Jones because Smith is normally irritable and aggressive is a procedural inappropriateness by providing too general or inclusive an explanation, too broad a category. It also indicates with great clarity the use of "cause" as a connective that categorizes by subsumption and pushes the explanatory regress farther away from the initial bracketing utterance.

Number 9 responds to that instruction to narrow the category of number 7 by subsuming "earthquake" under "the unexpected irrelevant," of which it is now a special case or example. This broadens the category of number 5, but narrows that of number 7. The procedural appropriateness of this is affirmed by number 10, "Ah, now we're getting somewhere," but it goes on to instruct a further narrowing of the too broad category of number 7 by directing the question at what has been so far neglected—the character of the object that is hit. Number 11 obliges by subsuming "Jones" under "man." Thus, the linkage is unexpected-irrelevant-arguing-aggressiveness-irritability-hitting-man. This is far less general than number 7 but more general than number 1, the initial bracketing sentence. Numbers 12 and 13 exclude "wife" from the category; such exclusion may be called a procedural safeguard.

Number 14, "What kind of relation did he have with his father?", raises a procedural problem which is not immediately resolved. Does "man" subsume "father" or does "father" subsume "man"? It brings "father" into the linkage but in what way is not immediately resolved. Number 15 further strengthens the link of "father" to the rest of the linkage by relating "father" to "irritable, aggressive, and arguing," since "quarreling" subsumes "irritability" and "aggressiveness." Number 16 presents another procedural safeguard by questioning the procedural appropriateness of "always." Number 17 again obliges by limiting the quarreling-father link to a time after the death of Smith's mother in an automobile accident, thus also hinting at the same kind of unresolved subsumption as that presented by "father" and "man," since "mother" and "wife" are subsumed by "woman," the opposite to the already presented "man." This problem is also left unresolved.

These unresolved problems lead to a drastic procedural redirection. A series of sentences, numbers 17 to 21, presents a fresh initial bracketing utterance, which in its complete form is "Smith's father when drunk and accompanied by his wife (Smith's mother) drove off an embankment. Smith's mother was killed, though his father survived." The last sentence in number 22 asserts that this fresh initial bracketing explains why Smith hit Jones. Number 24 clarifies how this explanation is managed. In the already arrived at linkage "man" is subsumed under "Smith's father." The former thus has an exemplary relation to the latter. Number 25 likewise resolves the mother-wife relation. The Oedipus complex explanation subsumes "wife" under "mother." It is asserted that Smith makes these subsumptions and turns "wife" and "man" into "mother" and "father," but it is obvious that the respondent makes the subsumption and that it is a verbal subsumption. It is also obvious that equally verbal is the causal relationship between "Smith" and "man," which is explained now as an example of the unconscious desire of Smith to hit his father. The linkage now is (the unexpected irrelevant)-quarreling-(aggressive-irritable)-hitting-(unconscious exemplification of Father by man). Number 25 triumphantly subsumes this as a case of unconscious motivation by an unresolved Oedipus complex. Numbers 26 and 27, by confirming this explanation, bring the explanation to a close with a terminal procedural utterance.

The case is thus proved, but all that has happened is that by a series of regressive categorial subsumptions an initial bracketing utterance is eventually subsumed under, and presented as a special case of, a terminal bracketing utterance. Further, since the movement from observation to responding verbal utterance remains mysterious, it cannot be said that Smith's action has been explained but only the utterance, "Smith hit Jones." Two further aspects of explanation are usefully pointed out. That initial bracketing sentence in itself could be a subsumptive or categorial sentence. "Smith gave Jones a bloody nose" and "Smith knocked Jones's toupee off" could be exemplifications of "Smith hit Jones." It would be very odd to say "Smith hit Jones, because Smith gave Jones a bloody nose," at least in this instance. Such a sentence would have to be explained by something like, "Smith was so happy to give Jones a bloody nose that he hit him again." A second aspect is that explanation could be continued indefinitely,

though by the same process, in a further regress from the initial bracketing utterance. The Oedipus complex could be presented as a special
case or exemplification of a more general psychoanalytic law, while a
series of regressive categorizations of this sort could be terminated by
"instinct," a word which here would subsume all behavioral events.

It is further to be observed that the entire explanation is, first,
fictive, in that each regressive linkage of categories introduces a word
not derived from the previous linkage. The first of these was "causality" itself, which in this type of explanation can be considered as
present at each stage of regression, once it has been introduced. Thus,
"instinct" itself exemplifies "causality," for instinct is presented as
the cause of human behavior. Second, of equal significance is that the
entire explanatory construct is normative. Psychoanalytic explanation,
of course, is widely accepted, but it is just as widely invalidated. Thus,
there can be as many explanations as there are explanatory ingenuities
for the initial bracketing sentence, "Smith hit Jones." These could
follow a different regressive line at any point in the explanatory regress. Thus, the earthquake could be omitted from consideration, and
there could be introduced another initial utterance, "Jones insulted
Smith." Or the earthquake could be made equally important with the
insult, and the sentence explained by the conjunction of these two
factors, earthquake and insult. Again, once the level of Jones's general
irritability and aggressiveness had been arrived at, it could be made a
special case of the irritability and aggressiveness of men in Jones's
social class. The explanation could thus regress towards a sociological
termination rather than a psychoanalytic one. The explanation given,
then, is normative, because it amounts to an assertion that the initial
speaker ought to accept a psychoanalytic interpretation.

JUSTIFICATION AND VALIDATION

This normativeness can be further brought out by considering the possibility that, after the given terminal bracketing, the procedure of the
explanation could be turned in either a justificatory or a validational
direction, or both. The subsumptive and categorizational procedure,
however, remains. Thus, Smith could be justified by the assertion that
repressing his unconscious hostility to his father does Smith more harm
than Jones could possibly suffer from Smith's blow. The common way
of putting this would be "Smith was justified, because he would suffer
greater harm from not hitting Jones than Jones would by being hit."

This is a clear case of causal subsumption. The category that subsumes this is "Cases of attack are justified if lasting harm is suffered by the attacker if he does not attack, even though temporary harm is suffered by the attacked." Thus, there are two kinds of acts, those for which the actor is responsible and those for which he is not. An individual can be condemned, or negatively justified, only for acts for which he is responsible. Since Smith's act was unconscious, he was not responsible for it. He cannot be condemned; therefore he is justified. Justified acts, that is, are judged to include both acts which can be justified or condemned and acts which can only be justified. The first subcategory includes only conscious acts; the second includes unconscious acts. Since Smith's act exemplifies the second, and since the second exemplifies justified acts, Smith's act exemplifies justified acts. It would be protested, of course, that this is very bad logic, although in fact it is the kind of logic used all the time. Normative logical efforts would resolve it in various ways. One way would be to assert that conscious acts, no matter how defined, are in fact unconscious in origin. Since unconscious acts are justified, therefore all acts are justified. (Such a resolution of the alleged bad logic leads to a conflict between law and theology. In effect the law says that an act which is not condemned is justified, since the actor is not punished. This puts theology in a dilemma, which has often been quite easily resolved by asserting that all acts are motivated by God. Since God cannot be unjust, it follows that all acts are justified.)

Recently a new kind of justification—"existential morality"—has been proposed. This amounts to the assertion that acts are justified not by absolute or terminal moral sentences but by consideration of the existent circumstances of a proposed act. This permits a novel kind of fictiveness and seems particularly useful when applied to sexual acts which by existent terminal moral sentences would be judged immoral. Adultery is justified if the adulterer in his act commits himself to a meaningful choice in an absurd situation. Since all situations are by existentialist definition absurd—and certainly it takes little effort to make such a judgment—the creation of human meaning in an absurd situation is justified. Further, since all situations are absurd, no two situations can be placed in the same category. Every situation is uniquely absurd and requires a unique choice and commitment. And so on. It cannot be denied that existentialist justification is extraordinarily handy, for it can reduce any explanatory-justificatory regress to rubble.

Validational regress is quite different from justificatory regress, though to be sure "validation" and "justification" are often, perhaps commonly, used interchangeably. Milton set out to justify the ways of God to men, he said, but *Paradise Lost* is much more of a validational enterprise. The difference appears in such a sentence as this: "You are not to be condemned for what you did, but you ought not have done it. Your act can be justified but not validated." The initial bracketing sentence "Smith hit Jones" can be validated by regressing from the terminal psychoanalytic bracketing and subsuming it in a verbal category such as the following: "One ought to do acts that release unconscious repressed hostility because such repressions are psychically damaging." This is a three-stage regression: "acts that release repressed hostility" are subsumed by "acts that are psychically beneficial," and these in turn are subsumed by "acts that one ought to do." Smith, then, ought to have hit Jones because the act made him healthier. Such verbal validational regressions amount to an instruction that for the verb in the initial bracketing sentence should be substituted "ought to + the verb."

It is indeed the case that modern ethicists engaged in what is called meta-ethics assert that an "ought" sentence cannot logically be derived from an "is" sentence. But, looked at behaviorally, this merely amounts to the sentence that "ought" sentences ought not to be derived from "is" sentences. Another verbal form of much the same position is that normative sentences cannot be derived logically from nonnormative sentences. The "cannot" here is again a verbal instruction; that is, the sentence is really itself an ought sentence. It is not merely that a universal phenomenon of verbal behavior is turning "is" sentences into "ought" sentences and nonnormative sentences into normative sentences; rather, since all sentences are instructions or directions for this response rather than that, all sentences are "ought" sentences or normative sentences. These meta-ethical arguments are, like so much of the rest of modern philosophy, a demonstration—one is tempted to say an unconscious admission—that philosophy, including logic and ethics and the third of that wearisome triad, aesthetics, is made of normative efforts to establish controls over those words which connect sentences and which instruct the responder that the response to sentence *b* is to be in part controlled by the response to sentence *a*, its immediate predecessor. Philosophy is thus still engaged in its age-old effort not to direct fruitfully the observation of verbal behavior but, on the contrary, to interfere with that observation. Why this should be so will emerge subsequently.

Explanation, justification, and validation are three different modes of categorial regress from an initial bracketing sentence. When verbal behavior is performed with great care and circumspection and according to already established procedural protocol, the three modes tend to occur in that order. Such a situation may be found in the law courts. A case of abortion, let us say, is first explained. It can then be justified, though not validated. The judge says, in effect, "Go and sin no more" or, to comply with the law, may utter a trifling sentence and then suspend it. At one time abortion could not be validated under any circumstances. It is now legally possible to validate it—by dismissing the case—under certain circumstances, if the existence of those circumstances can be legally proved, that is, if certain initial bracketing sentences are accepted as appropriate and then subsumed by categorial regression. In an increasing number of states abortion can now be validated under almost any circumstances. In other states a case of abortion cannot even be brought before the courts. What has happened is that explanation has been converted into justification and justification into validation, and the validatory regress is now so widely known that to the sentence "Mary Robinson has had an abortion," no legal response is forthcoming. The sentence is immediately validated. That is, if it is judged appropriate to do so, the sentence is followed by the response "Her abortion was a socially and legally valid act." The initial bracketing sentence can thus be responded to without delay by the terminating bracketing sentence, which can be represented by such utterances as "What of it?" or "OK." or "Who cares?" or "That's her business." When a categorial regress to a class of initial bracketing sentences is widely available, i.e., has widely and for a long time been disseminated within a society, it is not often presented in its full form or, indeed, any form at all. How and why such explanations are nevertheless maintained will be considered later. It is worth noting at this point that in such cases as abortion, cases in which the categorial regress is not widely accepted, both antijustificatory and antivalidatory categorial regress as well as justificatory and validatory regresses are constantly presented in widely disseminated verbal media, as well as in mixed media, such as the cinema.

NORMATIVE REGRESS

Verbal behavior on the whole, however, does not follow the circumspect movement from explanation to justification to validation
found in courts of law and in philosophical ethics. Ordinary verbal
behavior is a thorough mixture of all three modes. Up to this point I
have used the term "explanatory regress," but it seems clear that it is
advisable to have a term to subsume the three modes. Since it is the
position of this analysis that these three modes are equally prescriptive,
equally engaged in giving directions for behavior, behavior which is
then judged appropriate or inappropriate, procedurally or personally,
since all three modes, then, are equally normative, I shall use henceforth the term "normative regress" when I wish to subsume all three
modes. This terminology also makes obvious what I am sure must have
long since been obvious to most readers; the present discourse, an
explanation of explanation, is itself an example of normative regress. I
have been engaged in giving instructions, or directions, or prescrip-
tions for how certain words ought to be responded to. This has been
disguised, of course, in descriptive language. It has been based upon,
that is, has been a response to, observations I have made, and though
my claim is that they are observations that anyone can make, they are,
after all, observations that *I* have made. Descriptive language, then, is
language that claims that the directions that it gives can be followed by
anyone, but of course that is not the case. It cannot be followed in this
case, for example, by someone who does not know English. It cannot
be followed by someone who is bored by it, or finds it too obvious or
too dull, or someone who is puzzled or confused, or someone who has
had no experience or training in responding to this kind of discourse.
Furthermore, by the self-generated rules of my own discourse, I cannot
even say that the discourse is based upon the observations that I have
made. The sentences in the discourse are verbal responses to observations I have made, and those observations themselves are responses to
verbal instructions I have produced myself or which I have taken from
others, either orally or by means of print. This is to reemphasize a
point made before, a point which it is useful never to forget, though it
is impossible not to do so. We cannot say of verbal behavior, "This is
the point at which it is possible to begin analysis," for the reason that
such an utterance is itself a response to verbal directions, to a normative regress. But before drawing the moral of this and bringing to a

conclusion this chapter, it is useful to make a further point about categorization and the normative verbal regress.

CATEGORIZATION AND REGRESS

In the discussion of categories a traditional philosophical and logical distinction is made between the range and attributes of a category, or between extension and intension. The range is said to consist of the members of a category, the objects or events subsumed by that category, and the attributes are said to consist of those features which all members of that category have in common. The extension is like the range; it is that which the category covers or subsumes. The intension consists of those attributes or features or factors which determine whether or not something is properly included under the extension. Instead of these traditional terms I have used the word ''linkage.'' In the terminology of verbal behavior, ''attribute'' is first a direction to respond to a given initial bracketing utterance with a particular word or phrase. Thus, if it is judged that a particular object is man-made and it is judged that the appropriate verbal response is ''This object is characterized by beauty,'' then it is appropriate to respond further with the more general statement ''It is a work of art.'' Moving in the opposite direction, if it is said to the categorial term ''art'' that it is judged to be appropriate that one respond with ''An attribute of art is beauty,'' then it is likewise judged to be appropriate to locate a man-made object to which it is judged to be appropriate to respond, ''This is a beautiful work of art.'' Thus the attributes of a category, or its intension, can be either directions to utter an exemplary sentence or series of sentences, or directions to respond to an observable configuration or to a sentence or series of sentences. Moving upwards in the normative regress, one says, ''Because it is beautiful it is a work of art''; moving downwards, ''Because it is a work of art it is beautiful.''

This is all very well for established categories such as ''art,'' even though it is possible to judge that that category in its ordinary use is woefully inadequate. But innovated categories do not have conventionally established attributive words with which to respond to them. Such is the category of which ''Smith hit Jones'' is an example. The normative regress presented terminated with the instruction that the appropriate response to that sentence is ''Smith hit Jones because he is suffering from an unresolved Oedipus complex.'' ''Oedipus complex'' is an established category, but in the intervening categorial levels there are no existent words with which to categorize the initial bracketing sentence. Rather it is appropriate, it is judged, to respond at one stage of the regress with the words (among others, of course, if the response is made in sentences or phrases) "the unexpected irrelevant, quarreling, aggressive, irritable, hitting, unconscious exemplification of Father by man." These words are the attributes of a category which has no name. Moving in the opposite direction, the attributes are instructions to discriminate between Smith's irritable behavior or his arguing behavior and Smith's behavior when it is judged appropriate to separate a behavior from Smith with the fictive selection of what is judged to be the appearance of the unexpected irrelevant, together with quarreling, aggressiveness, irritability, and hitting a man. The directions for response given by these words is the intension of a category.

In the construction of an innovative category, as the normative regress moves away from the initial bracketing sentence each stage is made up of a set of words, and the next stage is moved by categorial substitution for one or more of those words, as in substituting "Father" for "man," "the unexpected irrelevant" for "earthquake." Each stage may use more attributional words, or fewer, or the same number. As we have seen, one of the most common words for moving from one stage to the next is the connective word "because." In the absence of any categorizing word to which these attributional words can be attached, it is judged to be appropriate (or said to be necessary) to use all the words. The response to a lower categorial stage of the regress by uttering a group of attributional words which have not been conventionally assigned to a categorizing word is what I have called "linkage." An innovating category can be created only by such linkage. The movement from one stage of the normative regress to the next more regressive stage or the next less regressive stage is not necessary or inherent or immanent, since such movements are *meaning* responses, the selective and normative determinations of response.

Attributes of even well-established categorizing words are not stable for the same reason. In the twentieth century, for example, in discussion of art, the attributes of beauty had to be changed, and some found it necessary to abandon beauty as an attribute of art, so innovative was the advanced art of this century. And, finally, a normative regress tends to be terminated when a responder arrives at an established categorial term, such as Oedipus complex, or instinct, or God, which is judged to be an appropriate response to an attributional linkage, either by the responder himself or by someone else. Thus a category tends to become established when there is a word with which to respond to a lower-stage linkage.

Hence, there is a tendency for the range of appropriate verbal response to narrow as a normative regress moves away from the initial bracketing sentence, sometimes gradually, and sometimes very sharply. There can even be a broadening and then a narrowing, but the usual termination is a narrowing. Indeed, it is the ordinary judgment that a normative regress is not successful unless it narrows to a single verbal response. This I shall call the *top*. At the same time the range of possible responses broadens with the upward movement. The occasions on which Smith hits somebody with whom he is arguing because there is an irrelevant disturbance are less numerous, by far, than occasions in which, so it is maintained, men do something because of an unresolved Oedipus complex. It is because of this upward broadening, for example, that such a doctrine as pantheism can be developed out of theism. To say "Because it is a man-made object of beauty, it is a work of art" is the same kind of utterance in the construction of a normative regress as to say "This man-made object of beauty is a work of art." "Because" and "is" are in such circumstances interchangeable. Thus, it is very easy to convert a causal explanation-of-all-things that terminates in "God" into a statement that all things are God by way of emphasizing the subsumptive character of normative regress that begins with all things and ends with God. The Neoplatonists simply reversed the upwards movement into a downwards movement and made all things into emanations of God. It is particularly interesting that these men, of whom Plotinus was the greatest, worked out a complete theory of normative regress, though without saying so or presumably being able to say so. Nevertheless, more than any other philosophy, theirs is a series of regressive stages back from the initial bracketing sentences to God. It is illuminating that outside that regress was nothingness. The vast metaphysic in Hegel's great *Phenomenology of Mind* is put together in much the same way. To Hegel the category of being, what is called here the observable, is an empty category. It has no attributes except what the human mind ascribes to it. At the top his regress terminates in the Absolute, likewise an empty category. Like the Neoplatonists, who had considerable influence on him, and indeed like all philosophers, Hegel baffles one's possible observation that he is talking about language, not about the mind. Nevertheless, so rigorously and ingeniously did he work that no philosophy is more easily converted into the language of verbal behavior than Hegel's.

CONCLUSION

Normative regresses explain, justify, and validate initial bracketing sentences. The basic building block of such verbal constructions is simple enough—verbal categorization of subsumed verbal categories. The "deep structure" of language offered by Noam Chomsky is merely an example of a normative regress; more precisely, it is an explanatory regress, its normative character clearly indicated by the fact that the initial bracketing sentence is called the "well-formed sentence." Well-formed sentences are not at all necessary for effective verbal behavior, i.e., for giving verbal directions and for following them in what the giver of the sentence deems an appropriate response. The appeal of Chomsky's deep-structure notion—and its appeal is very wide—is merely that it presents such an extraordinarily clear and unmistakable example of normative regress. Such regresses are normally anything but clear, anything but unmistakable, anything but stable. To clarify and stabilize a regress is the way an enormous amount of human energy is released. A clear and stable example, such as Chomsky's, is bound to have an immediate appeal, an appeal very like the appeal of a one-word termination of a regress. All difficulties are resolved; the confusing and unstable categorial process which led to the termination vanishes, and a reduction of semantic tension is the affect, an affect we call knowledge or, more impressively, cognition.

What this comes down to is that the normative verbal regress is the structure of meaning, by which is meant, to repeat, the normative and fictive determination of response. As we have seen, the normative regress at once limits the verbal response, increases the normative control of response, and at the same time expands the number of sentences which can be judged to be appropriate responses. When we construct a normative regress, we climb to the top of a pyramidal mountain; but, as we climb, the view takes in more and more verbal territory, while at the same time, through linkage or attribution, makes possible increasing discriminations within that territory. Furthermore, if the normative verbal regress is the structure of meaning, it is the condition of verbal behavior. Moreover, it is a condition from which it is impossible to escape. As I have already pointed out, this explanation of explanation, the conundrum with which this chapter began, is itself an explanation and limited by the conditions of explanation. It is of no use, as has become popular in philosophy in recent decades, to prefix "meta" and talk about "meta-explanation," any more than it is of any use to talk about "meta-ethics." A meta-explanation, which supposedly lies outside of explanation, is itself an explanation; and the notion that verbal behavior can be other than explanatory is a vanity of vanities. Normative verbal regress is the condition of verbal behavior; it is the trap within which we are caught, the trap from which there is no escape. At least it is a trap from which there is no verbal escape. Is there a nonverbal escape from it? To that problem we shall now turn.

II

THE NONVERBAL

Words are instructions or directions for behavior, and they may be responded to either appropriately or inappropriately, but the appropriateness or inappropriateness depends upon the judgment of someone. The appropriateness and inappropriateness are no more immanent in the response than the meaning is immanent in the words which are responded to. But words are only one discriminable aspect of language; verbal behavior is not linguistic behavior.

This distinction is often neglected, and in philosophy it has always been neglected. What in the past few decades has been known as the "ordinary language" philosophy, or what have been known as the various linguistic philosophies, are in fact nothing of the sort. Linguistic behavior consists of other utterances as well as words. Indeed, when one speaks, one cannot do so without employing other vocal resources. Linguists have identified these other attributes as pitch, stress, and juncture and in English have, they maintain, identified four levels of each. The meaning of "pitch" is obvious. "Stress" is the attribute of the quantity of energy release, that is, volume. "Juncture" is a pause not between words, for in speaking there is nothing to correspond with the space between printed words, but a pause in the stream of utterance. The various punctuation marks in formal written language are attempts to make visual equivalents to juncture, attempts not entirely successful.

For ordinary purposes these and other observable attributes of utterance are subsumed by the term "tone," and there is a multitude of metaphorical terms for kinds of tone—growling, sweet, hasty, impressive, and so on. The question is, What does tone have to do with the words which are uttered in a kind of tone? I shall begin with a trivial example, or an apparently trivial example, for analysis shows that what is going on here is by no means unimportant.

Two men who have been hitherto strangers to each other have struck up an acquaintance in a bar and have fallen into a sustained conversation. At one point Smith says to Jones, "Why, you son-of-a-bitch!" Smith's tone is one of jocularity. The relation between the words and the tone is an ironic one; that is, the tone and the words are inappropriate to each other. The words are denigrating, but the tone is jocular; it cancels the denigration. For Smith, friendship—that is, ascription of value to Jones, not denigration—is the appropriate way to interpret the words. The tone, then, is an instruction to respond *in*appropriately to the words. If Jones responded appropriately to the words, he might throw his beer in Smith's face, or hit him, or break off the conversation and turn on his heel. And it is perfectly possible that he might do anything of the sort, including stabbing Smith to the heart. Some people are very upset at denigration, especially from a comparative stranger. The protocol of the situation is that Jones ought to respond to the tone as cancelling out the denigration of the words, but he may or may not obey the protocol. He may judge it to be appropriate *not* to respond inappropriately to the words; he may judge it to be appropriate to ignore the jocularity of the tone. Or he may judge that it is inappropriate to respond to the tone, for rightly or wrongly he may believe that Smith really meant to be denigrating and that the jocular tone was hypocritical.

The tone in which words are uttered, then, consists of instructions for responding to the words. Furthermore, as the above analysis of possibilities of response shows, there is no immanent connection between tone and words, nor, since the meaning of neither tone nor words is immanent, is there any necessary response that determines the relative importance of, in the case, a pair of instructions ironically related, one instruction asserting what the other denies.

THE SIGN

Another example will get us closer to what is going on here and how we should organize our analysis. Say that a subordinate has been called into the office of his superior and has been reproved for some failure or other. He reports on it to a fellow worker at his own hierarchical level. "His words were pleasant enough. He said that my slip wasn't very important, but that he felt he should call it to my attention. However, the tone of his voice showed that he was really very upset, and the expression on his face meant that he was really very angry. However, you know, everything in his office is arranged just so, excessively neat, everything too much in its place. Either he is terribly precise and even petty about everything, or else that amazing neatness indicates that he is not at all secure, not at all sure that he should be in the position he's in.'' This can be rewritten as follows: "His words were a sign that he didn't judge my slip very important, only that he should call it to my attention. However, the tone of his voice was a sign that he was really very upset, and the expression on his face was a sign that he was quite angry. However, you know, the striking neatness in his office is either a sign that he is terribly precise about everything, or else it is a sign that he is not at all secure in his position." This rewriting suggests the appropriateness of subsuming words, tone, facial expression, and office arrangements under the explanatory term "sign." The unfortunate subordinate now has the problem of trying to make sense out of inconsistent signs. His task is to determine which signs are to be judged as the signs he should respond to: signs of good temper, of disturbance, of anger, and of hyperneatness, the last in itself capable of quite different interpretations. We may leave him with his puzzle. It is enough to observe that his superior's behavior and office were rich in signs which had a bearing on his response and that "sign" subsumes verbal behavior, nonverbal behavior, and objects.

We use the word "sign," then, when we are indicating (or signifying, or making a sign that) there is in the perceptual field before us a configuration (a figure perceptually discernible against its ground) to which it is appropriate for us to respond. That judgment, however, does not entail any particular response, as the ambiguous signification of the hyperneatness of the boss's office shows. The proposition, then, that the meaning of a word is not immanent can thus be extended to or transferred to "sign." The meaning of signs is not immanent. To put that proposition in terms of hierarchical explanation, one attribute of words, nonimmanency of meaning, is not a unique or defining attribute of words, but rather it is an attribute of words because it is an attribute of the category "sign," which subsumes words. Nonimmanency of meaning is an attribute of all signs.

And this point can be made behaviorally in a way that will prove useful in what follows. I have asserted that it is appropriate to respond to "word" with the words "meaning is not immanent." I now assert that it is appropriate to transfer that response to "sign." This gives us an insight into what is behaviorally involved in subsumption. A subsumption is an instruction to transfer a response already learned in connection with one configuration, in this case a word, to another configuration, also a word. The only attribute common to "sign" and "word" is, if printed, letters; and if spoken, sounds (phonemes, as the linguists say). The question now arises: Are there other attributes of words which can appropriately be transferred to signs, such as normativeness and fictiveness? Are there attributes of words which cannot be appropriately transferred to signs? To answer these questions will require considerable fetching about.

Normativeness certainly seems transferable. Just as the judgment that a configuration (or set of configurations, as in the boss's office) is a sign that does not entail a particular response, in the same way any configuration in any perceptual field can be judged to be a sign—that is, a configuration which we ought to respond to by controlling our behavior in some way or other, even if that behavior involves momentarily judging the configuration to be a sign and then dropping it from consideration. From this it seems reasonable to conclude that in any perceptual field, any configuration can be judged to be a sign. What we have already seen to be the case with words—that any word can be responded to with any of all possible responses and that all words can be responded to with but one response—is also the case with nonverbal signs; and these propositions are also transferable from "word" to "sign." They are, of course, but corollaries of the proposition that meaning, whether of verbal or nonverbal signs, is not immanent. But this line of analysis can be pushed even further. Any configuration can be perceived in a perceptual field. That is, there is no limiting factor which determines what can be seen as a configuration. Thus, for example, the outlines of configurations can be perceptually assembled in quite extraordinary ways, ways which to the "normal" observer can seem utterly bizarre. There is nothing to stop an individual from perceiving the edges of a pair of trees, some bushes, a lake, a couple of clouds, and mountains on the horizon, as the face of God. The person who avers that the face of God is the configuration he sees and that that configuration is a sign which appropriately controls his behavior we may judge to be either religiously inspired or psychotic, depending upon our own mode of judgment in such matters. We may say, that is, that it is either appropriate or inappropriate to see the face of God in a landscape in the form of a configuration which no one else perceptually assembles.

Another kind of bizarre response is responding to a sign in a way others judge to be inappropriate. For example, a man may rush into his house from an evening's walk, asserting that he was about to be attacked by two muggers. Investigation may reveal that what he interpreted so threateningly was in fact two sizable bushes recently transplanted by a neighbor. Judgments, in short, that sign responses are inappropriate are indications of the normativeness of response to nonverbal signs. A consideration of three puzzling words, about which much has been written (entirely too much, perhaps), can bring out the normative character of sign response. These words are "attention," "interest," and "intention."

When a teacher tells a student to pay attention to the lesson on the blackboard, and not to the birds in the trees outside in the window, he is instructing him to respond to a particular set of signs *and no others*. He is giving instructions to the student on how he ought to control his behavior. When an officer calls a company of soldiers to attention, the very posture they assume is an instruction to themselves to respond only to the orders he is about to give *and to no other signs*. When we say that an individual is interested in, let us say, literature, we are predicting that when he distinguishes from their ground any signs, verbal or nonverbal (such as a rare edition of Byron), judged to be subsumed by that category, he will respond to those signs *to the exclusion of others*. (This can even be demonstrated physiologically, for when an individual perceives a configuration which he judges to be a member of the category of his interest, the iris of the eye expands.) How the individual maintains an interest is a problem to which it will be necessary to return; here it is sufficient merely to suggest that in being interested he simply takes the place of the teacher and instructs himself to respond to a category of signs. As for "intention," we use the word when we assert that an individual in a certain category of situation customarily responds to a particular set of signs, and this judgment can apply to the single act of an individual whose behavior is controlled by the protocols of sign response in that situation (as Smith deciding that Jones was joking, not denigrating) or to the recurrent acts of a single individual (the boss's intention being to keep a tight control over the behavior of his subordinates). That is, we are explaining the behavior by subsuming it under the norms of everyone's behavior in that kind of situation or by subsuming it under the norms of the behavior of a particular individual in a number of similar situations. All three words—"intention," "interest," and "attention"—subsume the recurrence of response to a category of signs. They point out that the individual's behavior is controlled either by the cultural norms of sign response or by the norms of sign response peculiar to the behavior of some individual. What is common to all three is the limitation of sign response by an "ought" instruction; that is, normativeness is an attribute of verbal behavior appropriately transferred to all sign behavior.

As for fictiveness, the transfer of this attribute from verbal to nonverbal signs requires that a subtler question be asked. How does a configuration become a sign? Consider a lumberman in a forest, searching for a good example of a particular kind of hardwood tree. He finds such a tree; and, after examining it, he marks it as a tree to be cut down. What has happened? First, he has responded to certain perceptual attributes of the tree—bark, shape of leaves, and so on—in such a way that he identifies the tree as the kind he is looking for. The total configuration of the tree can be perceptually broken down into attributes, that is, signs, which are in common with certain other trees the lumberman is already familiar with. He has transferred an already established response to a configuration he has never seen before. Second, other attributes, or signs, such as freedom from branches, straightness of bole, and girth, he interprets as indicators that the tree is one that is economically valuable, worth cutting down; he has transferred another established response to this particular tree. This he has done on the basis of perceptual attributes common to this tree and trees he has previously encountered. In nonverbal behavior, then, a hitherto unencountered configuration is responded to with an already learned response if certain perceptual attributes are in common to a class of configurations. Our lumberman has categorized his tree as the kind of tree he was looking for and one sufficiently excellent of its kind to be worth economic exploitation. The important matter to be observed, however, is that not all the perceptual attributes are identical. They are enough, however, for him to make two acts of subsumption; kind of tree and quality of that kind. To use the definition of subsumption used above, the lumberman has nonverbally instructed himself to transfer two kinds of response already learned in other situations. Nevertheless, he performs this act of nonverbal subsumption or categorization by neglecting or ignoring a large number of perceptual attributes. He may even make a mistake, not noticing that a recent bolt of lightning has hit the tree and that by the time it is lumbered it will already be decayed beyond the point of being worth lumbering. This gets us a step closer to justifying the transfer of fictiveness from verbal to nonverbal signs.

The lumberman, however, already has a repertoire of responses at his disposal before he encounters the tree. It is necessary now to consider the initiation of the learning process, whereby a configuration is turned into a sign. When I first occupied my present house, I was occasionally startled when almost asleep by the sound of something hitting the roof. What was it? An animal? A burglar? Initially I could not even identify the location of the noise. Eventually I realized that it must be a pinecone falling from one of the many pines which surround my house. I had, after all, observed pinecones lying all over the property and had already been busy in picking them off the lawn; and the theory was subsequently confirmed when I saw pinecones fall on the terrace at the back of the house at a time when I was sitting on the terrace myself. Initially my response when I was in bed was most akin to fear. I learned, however, that the appropriate response was to ignore the sound. The interesting point to be made here is that the unidentifiable, uncategorized, unsubsumed aural configuration elicited a response. From a state of being almost asleep I was suddenly wide awake. Unable to categorize the configuration, I immediately made attempts to do so, finally, after some time, succeeding in so categorizing it that I was no longer disturbed by that kind of unexpected sound. I do not wish to imply for a moment, however, that such an attempt at categorization was "automatic" or "instinctual." On the contrary, from infancy we are instructed to categorize the unidentifiable configuration, and such instructions are a normal part of teaching technique, maintained by themselves for the scholar and scientist throughout their lives. But in this self-instructing behavior they are, of course, like everyone else, although some people are certainly more curious than others. That is, they have learned better than others to attempt to categorize unidentified configurations. The effort to categorize a configuration, then, is the effort to search among one's available patterns for a response pattern that one *judges* to be appropriate. In this case I could eventually respond either by saying to myself, covertly, "Oh, that was another pinecone," or by producing an image of a pinecone falling from a tree and striking the roof. Eventually I learned to dismiss it from my attention, to exclude it from the signs I was currently responding to. I was no longer interested in such sounds. It had become my "intention" to ignore them. I daresay that by now I no longer even hear them, but there is, of course, no way of being sure of that. In any event I have learned to transfer my response of attentional dismissal to every sound on the roof I categorize as one made by a falling pine cone.

SEMIOTIC BEHAVIOR

Semiotic or sign behavior, then, involves the categorization of a configuration as a sign. Such categorization enables the transfer of a behavior already employed in response to members of a category of configurations to a new configuration. It is made possible by the identification of attributes of the configuration (they may be appropriately called subsigns) with attributes of configurations to which response has already been established. But this may be more narrowly and more basically defined and understood. *When a configuration, or figure, is perceptually distinguished from its ground, it is then a sign.* An interesting experiment made some years ago shows that if people are faced with a totally unfamiliar configuration, within a matter of seconds they will categorize it, will say "what it is." It is to be observed that we cannot say what anything *is*. We can only say what it is *like*. That is, we can only make an analogy between it and some other configuration, frequently on the most slender possible evidence, or attributional similarity, or, as this experiment shows, on no evidence at all. Verbal definition of a configuration, then, is ultimately based on transfer of response. When that transfer of response, however, is impossible, or when we judge it to be impossible, the result is not that the configuration ceases to be discriminable from its ground. Response can then vary from complete randomization of behavior to the fixation of attention on the unidentifiable configuration. But that fixation of attention, as well as the random behavior, is itself a response. We can then henceforth occasionally dismiss from this vocabulary of semiotic analysis the term "configuration" and content ourselves with the simple term "sign" and also be content with the almost equally simple phrases "semiotic attributes" or "subsigns," the signs into which any sign can be perceptually analyzed, as a tree can be perceptually analyzed into its individual leaves, which we can then, if we wish, count. Thus we can say that an entire perceptual field, including the perceptions of the entire sensorium, is a sign which can then be further visually analyzed into semiotic attributes—a tree, a lake, a boat, sky, clouds, and so on, as well as the pressure of the breeze and the scents of the newly mown hay. Each of these, by our act of attention, i.e., eliminating response to other signs, becomes a sign in its own right; each can then be further perceptually analyzed into semiotic attributes—and so on, so that if further analysis by sight, for example, becomes impossible, analysis into semiotic attributes can be continued by touch, taste, or hearing, or temperature testing.

This consideration makes it possible to return to the problem of transferability of the attribute of fictiveness from verbal to nonverbal signs. Any sign can be resolved into a set of semiotic attributes. Since, as we have seen, there is no immanent connection between a sign and a response to that sign, no immanent meaning to signs, it is possible to say of any two signs that there is a sufficient identity of their semiotic attributes to justify placing both signs in the same category or, on the contrary, sufficient nonidentity of their semiotic attributes to justify placing the two signs in different categories. In the former instance we act as if the signs were interchangeable; in the latter we act as if they were not. Such judgments, of course, depend on our interest, our intention, our purpose, whatever one wishes to call it. The interest of our lumberman is to find economically exploitable examples of a particular category of tree. Having located a member of the category of that tree, he has then to decide whether or not it is an exploitable example. He may or may not subsequently decide whether his judgment was the appropriate one, that is, "correct," but at the same time he acts as if the tree were or were not interchangeable for his economic purposes with other trees of the same category of hardwoods. The act of perception, then, is not only categorial, it is also judgmental. It involves a decision, or we may call it a determination. Jones, in deciding that Smith meant to denigrate him, acted as if, from the combination of denigrating statement and jocular or friendly or value-ascribing tone, the tonal signs were appropriately eliminated from attention. Smith might explain this by saying that obviously Jones has an interest in judging himself to be insulted.

The world that our various modes of perception make available to us consists of signs. On the basis of their semiotic attributes, themselves discriminable as independent signs, or signs in their own right, we can subsume those signs by perceptual categorization in ways that if not infinite are certainly indefinably many, and we can recategorize them in equally various ways. Since there is no immanent link between a sign and a response, there is no inherent or "natural" response. To be sure, if a man is hit by a roof hurled through the air by a tornado, an object he did not see coming his way, one can say that his death was natural, but on the other hand it cannot be said that he responded. The sign to which he might have responded was not in his perceptual field, for he was lying face down on the ground, clinging to a tree. To be more exact, then, it is better to say not that the world consists of signs but that perceptual fields consist of signs. *As the world comes into our perceptual field, the world turns into signs.* And once that happens, by acts of categorization and judgments of interchangeability and noninterchangeability, we construct perceptually a fictive world. This statement is not to be taken as an example of philosophical idealism in its extreme form. It does not assert that the world is not "really" there. Let philosophers argue about that, as they have been arguing for centuries with no resolution of the problem and no possibility of a resolution. Whether the world is "really" there or not, it might as well be. And whether the human observer of that world is "really" there or not, he might as well be. It appears to be the case, then, that the attribute of verbal signs which I have called "fictiveness" can be appropriately transferred to nonverbal signs.

The corollary of this proposition is one that has also been pointed out as an attribute of verbal behavior. We cannot speak of the truth or falsity of any sign response but only of its appropriateness or inappropriateness in the judgment of someone. Furthermore, just as in verbal behavior, the connection between a categorization and the signs it subsumes is not immanent. It is therefore the case that any connection made is inherently unstable, as in verbal subsumption, that is, explanatory regress. Consequently, the fictiveness of our semiotic behavior—and now, since all behavior is semiotic, we can simply speak of behavior without the qualifying adjective—the fictiveness of our behavior, then, is the basic explanation for what we judge to be error and the equally basic explanation for what we judge to be innovation. The first is a judgment of interchangeability which is judged to be unproductive of what are determined to be desirable consequences. Just the reverse is the case for innovation, the judgment of interchangeability which is judged to be productive of desirable consequences. This inherent instability of our categorizing perception of the world is how we get into trouble and also how we get out of it. Judgments of "truth" and "falsehood," "correct" and "incorrect," "right" and "wrong," then, are efforts to stabilize that which is inherently not stable. This gives us our first inkling of how and why behavior is managed.

But these are verbal judgments, and it is now possible to turn to the question asked above: "Are there attributes of words which cannot be appropriately transferred to nonverbal signs?" This is much the same as asking, "What is the connection, the link, between verbal and nonverbal behavior?" As we shall see, this is the question of questions, the epistemological question. But before moving into that problem, it is pertinent to consider here three quasi digressions, both for what has preceded this point of fresh departure and for what will follow.

THREE QUASI DIGRESSIONS

The first has to do with what has already been touched upon—learning, a subject on which much has been written, on the whole to little effect. Thus far, academic psychology has learned little or nothing about learning. Let us take an apparently simple example of what might easily be called "natural" learning: The burnt child avoids the fire. What has happened? The child extends its hand toward the fire. It feels pain. (Without falling into a simple-minded hedonism, I think we can say that humans do experience pain and that, generally speaking, they try to avoid it, though of course there are exceptions—masochists and martyrs—both of whom, however, generate very sophisticated responses.) The next time the child encounters the fire—or perhaps the third or fourth time—it will not reach toward it. On the contrary, the most likely response will be to shrink away from it. The attributes of the sign "fire" are changing, bright, parti-colored shapes, its placement in a recess in the wall, probably surrounded by a configuration different from that of the configuration of the wall, and heat. On the second encounter—though very stupid children and very curious empirically minded ones might try again—the child transfers from the first occasion the avoidance response, doing so on the basis of the identification of the semiotic attributes of the total configuration or, more simply, the attributes of the sign. Or take a child who has patted a strange dog and has been nipped. There are shrieks, tears, hugs, comforting words, antiseptics, bandages, and then from the child's mother, "That'll teach you not to pat strange dogs." Or, "The avoidance response is appropriate when one encounters the dog sign, the attributes of which are indicators (subsigns) that one has not previously encountered that dog sign.'' In short, the fundamental pattern of learning is recognized in ordinary verbal behavior. And that pattern is the judgment that two or more signs are or are not interchangeable and that transfer of response is or is not appropriate.

Closely connected with this is the second digression. It has been maintained by Thomas Carlyle, George Herbert Mead, and various others that the basic relation of the human organism to the world is the manipulation of the world, the quite literal movement about of objects, and that a sign is a substitution or displacement for the object of such manipulation. I think this is in error, for two reasons, the first theoretical and the second observable. The theoretical objection is the position which claims that it is possible to get outside of words and also outside of signs. Since fictiveness is an attribute appropriately transferable from verbal signs to nonverbal signs, what is true of verbal signs— there is no meta-verbal position possible—is also true of nonverbal signs: no meta-nonverbal position is possible. Or, to subsume both propositions under one, no meta-semiotic position is possible. Signs are opaque; we cannot understand the world without converting the world into signs. We cannot assume a meta-semiotic stance.

The observational objection can be made by examining the activity of infants. An infant moves its arms and hands about randomly and also randomly closes and uncloses its fist. Occasionally these two actions coincide with manual contact with an object which can be grasped. After a certain recurrence of such random coincidences, contact with a graspable object will elicit the grasping response, though it is to be noticed that before this response occurs, there will also be numerous occasions when it does not. As the grasping response develops, the observant parents will say—and I have heard them say it—''Look, he's learning to grasp things.'' Quite so. Certain objects have attained the attribute of graspability, just as for the burnt child a particular object has attained the attribute of nongraspability. In short, *semiotic categorization precedes manipulation.* Semiosis, not manipulation, is the basic relation of the human organism to the world.

The third digression is of quite a different sort. It can readily be observed that human constructs of paradise, and of utopia, and also such verbal constructs as metaphysical or political or philosophical systems that claim to be coherent and final, and likewise such constructs as scientific theories—that all these and similar constructs have one attribute in common. They imagine or attempt to create situations in which response is stabilized. They claim to be right, or true, or absolute, or perfect. The final throes of the Enlightenment of the eighteenth century were efforts to create systems of moral and social and economic perfectibility, such that conflict and inequality entirely disappeared. One suspects that the Marquis de Sade parodied them in his *100 Days of Sodom*. What they all have in common is the effort to defictionalize the world, to remove judgment from semiotic discrimination, or, rather, to do away with semiotic discrimination. Nothing is more obvious in the history of human behavior than the susceptibility of human beings to such constructs. They will not only believe them; they will fight and bleed and die for them. Heaven is a place where no one makes mistakes, where no one lies—or innovates. Configurational discrimination, or semiotic categorization and recategorization, involve energy loss, tension, anxiety, uncertainty, risk. What man does is to transfer the avoidance response he learned perhaps from fire to the fictiveness of semiosis itself. *And this struggle to avoid that fictiveness is precisely the fundamental source of human manipulatability*–to use the term metaphorically—*manipulatability of oneself by oneself and by others. It is the basic condition which makes social management both necessary and possible.* As the ensuing chapters will attempt to show, the consequences are immense.

SEMIOTIC RESPONSE TRANSFER: NONVERBAL AND VERBAL

What, then, differentiates verbal from nonverbal semiotic behavior or, simply, behavior? A nonverbal sign, that is, the world, gives directions for response. Indeed, to distinguish a figure from its ground is at once to turn it into a sign, and as a sign it elicits a response, even though the response is mere attention without further behavioral consequences. In socializing infants, in turning them into human beings, the first task is to get them to respond to a sign, and initially any response will do. What we judge the randomness of infant response is the raw material from which human behavior is shaped. As we have seen, sign response requires learning appropriate response, since neither the meaning nor the response is immanent in the sign. For this reason I use the terms "instruction" and "direction" rather than "dictation." That a sign ought to be responded to is the first thing we learn. And how a particular sign ought to be responded to is the second, a learning behavior that continues until the repertory of sign responses achieves an indefinably large number; and we continue to learn new appropriate sign responses as long as we live. The third step is the transference of a learned response to a sign we have never encountered before, and this is possible because we judge that the new sign includes a sufficient number of semiotic attributes to justify placing it in the same category as a previously encountered sign or series of signs, therefore justifying the response learned in those previous encounters.

This transfer of response to a new sign on the basis of shared attributes is not only something the individual human organism can do on its own, without instructions from another organism, but it is also a behavior that is prehuman. Young monkeys frequently demand attention from a mother monkey when the latter is in no mood to render it. The mother administers a blow, and the young monkey ceases its demands, most frequently moving away. The blow is struck against no specific part of the young monkey's body. It might hit the head, an arm, a side, a back, a rump. If it strikes a part of the young monkey which has never been struck before in this kind of situation, the young monkey nevertheless exhibits an avoidance response. A behavior learned in response to blows on other parts of the body is transferred to a blow on a part hitherto unstruck. One of the attributes of some attention-demanding situations is a blow; having become a sign that avoidance is appropriate, that attribute is effective in eliciting that response no matter what part of the body the blow hits.

From this point of view, what verbal behavior does is immediately apparent. Words can give instructions to transfer a response to a sign which has no perceptual (i.e., semiotic) attributes in common with previously encountered signs, except the minimum attribute of being a sign, that is, a configuration, a figure discerned against a ground. A few examples will exemplify this difference between verbal and non-verbal behavior. Our lumberman can, without verbal instructions, decide that a particular tree is suitable in kind and quality for his purpose. In doing so, his behavior is no different from the avoidance response of the young monkey hit by its mother. But without verbal instructions our lumberman cannot decide that his tree is in fact the home of a dryad and that, instead of cutting it down, the appropriate response would be to place before it an offering of milk and flowers. It is true that he may suddenly be overcome "intuitively" with a conviction that to make an offering is the appropriate response, but that intuition could not occur to him if verbal behavior had not already constructed a mythology and instructed him in it. On the other hand, his decision to make an offering might very well have been made by covert verbal behavior or an image. Another example is more basic. How do we learn to read? The answer, from this point of view, is simple enough. Reading instruction can be boiled down to "Johnny, respond to these marks on the page as you have already learned to respond to the sound 'tree.' " A dictionary definition is no different. It is instructions to base your response to a particular word on what you have already learned to be the appropriate response to the words in the definition. To be sure, as not infrequently happens, particularly to the young, definition itself can include words which one has not learned to respond to. The only hope is to look them up. Thus, and gradually, the "meaning" of the word is learned (rather, a meaning, or a *variety* of meanings). The word and the definition thus become interchangeables, just as for Johnny the printed marks and the sound have become interchangeables. However, since instability of response is the character of semiosis, the complexities of interchangeability of response in verbal behavior are obviously infinite or at least might as well be. The result is that verbal instructions can initiate patterns of behavior in an individual which he has never previously performed. It is possible to teach swimming to an individual who has never seen anybody swim, though of course it is easier to do so if he has. (The latter involves what is known as imitative behavior, and consideration of it must be postponed for the moment.)

A second difference between verbal and nonverbal signs is that though some words can elicit a response identical with some nonverbal signs—as for some people the word "snake" can elicit the same response as the covert or overt production of an image of a snake or of an actual snake—there are other words to which there are no corresponding nonverbal signs, "corresponding" in the sense of interchangeability. Such words are connectives, verbs such as "is" or "have," and articles, prepositions, conjunctions. Given a succession of nonverbal signs, whether overt and in a perceptual field (available to more than one individual) or covert (available to only one individual), it is possible to say that the successive contiguity implies the copulative "and." And indeed it is constantly so said. But such a response to a nonverbal succession assumes that the meaning of the signs is immanent and also that the meaning of the succession is immanent. That is, what "and" does is to give instructions that the appropriate response is to judge these signs as belonging to the same category. When we say that the connection between any two members of the succession is "and" or "but," it is we who say so, not the succession itself. To use the word "implies" is to assert normatively that the responder ought to make that connection. It is exported from language into the succession of nonverbal signs. It is not derived from that succession. Thus, there is no place in covert or overt nonverbal signs for anything that corresponds to the connectives or such words as "is" and "have" or the other verbal particles, as they are traditionally named, listed above. Configurations made up of words, therefore, are not structurally analogous to configurations made up of nonverbal signs.

Indeed, it is precisely these connectives which make explanation possible. And this we have seen in Chapter I, in the discussion of logic and in the example of explanation beginning "Smith hit Jones." Richard von Mises, it will be remembered, reduced all logical relationships—that is, the use of connective words—to four and reduced those four to one, the simple copulative "and." And what "and" does in the simplest situation is to place two words in the same category, as in "the horse and the cow." A little more complexly, the "and" at the beginning of the previous sentence merely proposes that there is a connection, though unspecified, between that sentence and the previous one. Had I written "furthermore" or "moreover," the connection would have been more specific. Moreover, instead of that "and" I could have written, "*But* what 'and' does in the simplest situation," etc. That would have made the connection somewhat harder to determine, though more specific. I leave it to the reader to puzzle out how to respond to that possible "but." He will find it a troublesome but useful exercise in comprehending what connectives do.

Nor are connectives the only words for which there are no corresponding signs or semiotic interchangeables in nonverbal signs. As we have seen, for such a word as "cause" there is nothing in the nonverbal that corresponds to it. For the word "explanation" itself there is no correspondent, nor for such words as "mind" or "unconscious," or any such related words, such as "nature." These are subsumptional and explanatory categories. The old distinction between "abstract" and "concrete" words was inadequately defined and expressed, but it is nevertheless a useful distinction. What it distinguishes is not two kinds of words but the two polar directions of explanatory regression. One moves from verbal to nonverbal behavior and nonverbal sign response; the other moves in the direction of terminating explanatory regression. For example, if I am asked to go find a mind and bring it back, I am at a loss. On the other hand if I am asked to point out a set of behaviors which could reasonably be subsumed by the word "mind," I am given a possible task. All I need do is to point to two people in the same situation whose observable behavior indicates that they are responding differently to the same perceptual field. If one is capable of discriminating more signs within that field than the other, we are likely to say that he has a more acute mind. In such an ordinary language statement as "*I* have a mind to go to the movies," the speaker is indicating that though you may not wish to go, he does. He is differentiating between two responses. If we say that Tom has an interesting mind, we are asserting that in any situation or at least in certain kinds of situation, Tom is likely to produce more unexpected and perceptive responses than most people. Again differentiation between two kinds of response, or noninterchangeability of response, is subsumed by "mind."

Or take such a word as "God." This is a word used so very often in the culture of Europe (and in other cultures as well) for the purpose of terminating an explanatory regress that it is not surprising that Kierkegaard almost recognized it as such, insisting that from the proposition that there is a God no other propositions can be derived. Again, if I am asked to find God and bring him back, I am at a loss, but if I am asked what signs the word "God" subsumes, I have no problem. The world is full of thousands of objects—statues, pictures, stones, trees—which in various languages are said to be gods. To be sure, in some religions—and we need not here concern ourselves with what kind of behavior religious behavior might be—it is said that these objects are merely signs of God or of a god. But the phrase "sign of" is merely an instruction as to what category of response is appropriate. Thus when a hunter says that a hoofprint is a sign of a deer, he is merely giving directions about what category of behavior from the repertory of hunting behaviors is appropriate or would be appropriate if one wanted to locate and shoot or capture a deer. Thus the statement that a statue is a sign of a god or of a lesser deity such as a saint, is an instruction to engage in the appropriate behavior of that category of verbal behavior known as prayer, if, of course, one feels so inclined. It has even been proposed that monotheism was developed out of a more primitive polytheism by explanatory subsumption or regression, and, given the character of explanation, this account seems more than likely.

These examples provide a way of comprehending the connection between verbal and nonverbal signs. Response transfer by means of identification of semiotic attributes common to two or more signs is the foundation of categorial subsumption. Verbal signs are hierarchically imposed upon nonverbal signs by categorial subsumption. The only difference is that response transfer in verbal behavior does not require commonalty of semiotic attributes. For example, to the question, "What kind of tree do you have?" one appropriate answer might be, "an elm." But equally appropriate in a different situation would be the answer, "It is entirely Anglo-Saxon." In the second of these two answers what is being talked about is the individual's family tree. This is an obvious metaphor, and it certainly seems to be the case, if philologists have been at all on the right track these past two hundred years, that metaphor is the lowest level of verbal behavior. (Level of "language" is the usual expression; but we have seen how misleading that term can be.) However that may be, certain attributes of the structure of trees—root, bole, branches—have been transferred to a verbally constructed system of family relationships, even though there is no identity of perceptual attributes, no semiotic commonalty, between trees and verbal constructs.

FROM NONVERBAL TO VERBAL

It is worth considering what factors in nonverbal behavior made possible this extraordinary leap from response transfer justified by perceptual continuity from one sign to another to response transfer not so justified. What has made possible this leap to "conceptualization," or to "thought," or to "ideas," whichever of these uninstructive words one wishes to use? The leap was extraordinary. It is the distinctively human behavior; it is what differentiates us from animals and is the only behavior that does differentiate us. In evolutionary speculation the development of the brain was an explosion (in terms of biological time), so rapid was the mutation. It is not difficult to understand why. When verbal behavior was established, one imagines, it became totally selective; that is, infants incapable of entering into the verbal community were simply allowed to die, and such infants are occasionally born today, so few generations have passed since man became man, compared with the same number of generations birds have gone through in the same amount of time. How that leap was accomplished we can scarcely recover. The factors which made it possible, however, can be identified, for they are still with us. Or rather there was one factor which took two forms: randomization.

That the human brain is capable of random response is very possibly its most interesting attribute. This is obviously contrary to the usual praise heaped upon man for his capacity to create order. But "order" from one point of view merely means "predictability." And from another viewpoint "order" merely subsumes all explanatory regresses. And from another the word only sees to it that the behavior in question conforms to socially established protocols. In the last analysis "order" is neither more nor less than the manipulability or manageability of human behavior. As we shall see, the predictability of behavior is accomplished by explanation, as has already been suggested in the identification of explanation with justification and validation. That in the course of evolution—if we choose to use that explanatory construct—randomness of response had survival value is not difficult to comprehend. As the situation for a species population changed, the best adapted members of that species—those the behavior of which was maximally determined by genetically transmitted responsive behavior—would be less likely to survive than members capable of a random response appropriate for survival in the changed situation. In the course of evolution there was a genetic accumulation of randomness of response, until the point was reached at which successful interaction within the group depended upon a counteradaptation, counter, that is, to randomness. That counteradaptation was semiosis, for only the response-transfer capacity of semiosis can be the material for culture, or learned behavior.

But this speculation of mine, designed only to introduce into the argument what anthropologists have neglected, the human capacity for randomness of response, is not essential to the argument. (It is merely an exemplification of the theory of historical evolution.) *It need only be observed that semiotic randomization was the factor which made possible the leap to verbal behavior.* That randomization takes two forms or is observable in two kinds of behavior. When a figure is distinguished from its ground, it becomes a sign, as we have seen. As a sign it elicits a response. The first stage of the response is a physiological change leading to movement of the organism, basically manipulation of the sign eliciting the response. If, however, the individual has in his repertory of responses no response appropriate to that sign, the impulse towards movement will be randomly continued. But now in human history, it is extremely common for the impulse to movement to be repressed. That is, the movement is internalized and affects internal organs rather than skeletal muscles. The result, as all the world knows, can be ulcers. In highly civilized societies it is principally only a smaller number of individuals whose behavior is at a "high cultural level"—a term to be explained in Chapter III—who can permit themselves a high degree of behavioral randomization. Such individuals are physically insulated and socially protected—artists, scientists, individuals at very high levels in social institutions, and other intellectual workers. Nevertheless, randomization, now most easily observable in animals, creates the possibility for verbal response transfer. The reason is that from the perspective of nonverbal behavior, all verbal response is inappropriate, since the response to a tree with the word "tree" does not depend upon commonalty of semiotic attributes.

The other factor, the other form of randomness of response, is somewhat more subtle and less obviously related to inappropriateness. Consider the following sequence: tree, bush, porcupine, raccoon, rock, clam, sand-grain. For each pair—tree and bush, bush and porcupine, and so on—there is partial continuity of semiotic attributes, but if we move directly from tree to sand-grain, that continuity has vanished. All that tree and sand-grain have in common is that they are both signs, and this is all a nonverbal and verbal sign have in common, and all any two verbal signs have in common, aside from aurality. This is to bring out once again the instability of semiotic behavior and to bring out for the first time the enormous increase in semiotic instability brought about by the leap from nonverbal to verbal behavior. The flight towards an illusory perfection of behavior, of paradisiacal or utopian or metaphysical or religious or scientific certainty of behavior, is first to be accounted for by the inherent instability of nonverbal sign response, but that flight is given immense impetus by the enormously increased instability of verbal behavior. Moreover, that very flight reveals another extraordinary difference between verbal and nonverbal behavior.

The flight to paradise is a negation of the inherent instability of semiosis, that is, the inherent instability of human behavior itself, an instability infinitely increased from the instability of animal behavior. Negation is to be distinguished from refusal or the avoidance response.

Animals can avoid, or refuse, but only man can negate; as Hegel penetratingly observed, there are no (verbal) negations, only alternatives. The construction of an alternative is limited to verbal behavior. Free from dependence upon commonalty of semiotic attributes, verbal behavior cuts man loose from the world. Philosophical idealism is merely a rationalization or pseudo-explanation or, more mildly, an explanatory response to this condition. Plotinus constructed the human soul by successive emanations from God. He simply reversed the direction of explanatory regress, asserting that since by definition God must be real, then the phenomenal world must be unreal. There is just enough accuracy in his description to be confusing and to offer a temptation to the flight to paradisiacal certainty. Hegel reversed Plotinus and ended his explanatory regress with the Absolute, an empty category, he said; and the consequence of the recognition of that emptiness is the realization that God is dead, a proposition he uttered long before Nietzsche. A negation, then, is an alternative. Negation is possible because a response randomly arrived at can be verbally explained, justified, and validated. Fictiveness is an attribute of both verbal and nonverbal signs, but verbal semiosis enormously, fantastically, increases the possibilities of fictiveness. It enormously, fantastically, increases the possibility of true negation, the verbal construction of alternatives. If the degree of fictiveness is sufficient, we call the result either a lie or an act of the imagination, depending upon whether we are concerned with validating or invalidating it. We even have a kind of discourse so fictive that to categorize it as a lie is judged to be inappropriate: we call it "fiction," and it is said to be a product of "the imagination." But, as we have seen, semiotic behavior is fundamentally imaginative, for response transfer, depending upon the selection of some semiotic attributes and the suppression of others, is imaginative.

Verbal behavior, then, differs from nonverbal behavior because, by means of connectives (connectives which make possible the continuation of the hierarchical categorization initiated in nonverbal behavior), it constructs explanations and because it can validate not only constructed alternatives but any random response to a nonverbal or verbal sign. We need not conclude, however, that randomness has survival value for humanity. (It could only be *known* that it does *not* have survival value; and that could be known only when there are no human beings to know it.) If from the point of view of nonverbal behavior, verbal behavior is inappropriate, then human behavior is inappropriate, biologically maladaptive. And that very well may be.

SIGN PRODUCTION

From sign response, it will now be necessary to turn to sign production and the categories of humanly produced signs. That sign production categorized as sign production is a unique human mode of semiotic behavior can be indicated simply enough by recognizing that "sign" is, before it is anything else, a word. That there are numerous, almost innumerable, substitutes for that word has already been suggested in the translation of the subordinate's remarks about his superior at the beginning of this chapter. What the word "sign" does in giving instructions for behavior can be seen clearly enough by a further translation of that same passage. "His words called my attention to his not judging my slip very important. . . . However, the tone of his voice called my attention to his being really very upset, and the expression on his face called my attention to his very real anger," and so on. A further translation is even more revealing. "His words made me aware that he did not judge my slip very important. . . . However, the tone of his voice made me aware that he was really very upset," etc. And a still further translation illuminates the problem even better. "His words made me conscious that he did not judge my slip very important, . . . However, the tone of his voice made me conscious that he was really very upset," etc. We use the word "sign," then, when we are giving instructions to respond to a particular configuration or set of configurations to the exclusion of others.

But does the second of these two translations mean that "consciousness"—about which, whatever it is, so much to-do has been made for such a very long time—is merely the human capacity to give and receive instructions to respond to a sign or set of signs to the exclusion of others? So it seems to me. To be "conscious" of the rain falling on the roof, or to be conscious of the capitalist exploitation of the proletariat is, in either case, to respond to certain configurations, the first quite simple, the second more complicated—observations controlled and validated by an extremely elaborate explanatory regress but one based, however, on the simple observation that the many people who run the machines in a factory control fewer goods and services than do the few people who give the instructions to run the machines and, higher still, the instructions that the machines should be run. To explain this observation and to validate or invalidate these behaviors, that is, the behaviors of controlling goods and services, is possible by constructing explanatory regresses in a considerable variety of quite different directions from the basic semiotic response to this difference. And those regresses can validate or invalidate the difference.

But men are said to be more than "conscious"; they are also said to be "self-conscious," and it is asserted that this is quite a marvelous phenomenon. I confess it does not seem to me so very marvelous. To begin with, the individual is a social dyad. That is, what I know about my behavior I know in the same way that I know about your behavior—by observing it. To be sure I can respond to covert verbal and nonverbal behavior, behavior "inside my head," and to stimuli (configurations, signs) which I judge to have their origin within the surface of my skin, and these configurations or signs are signs that you cannot respond to, and vice versa. However, my mode of apprehending, my mode of being conscious of, my mode of being aware of, my mode of categorizing them as signs is no different from my mode of responding to any of your behaviors, to any signs that you produce. I respond to my behavior in exactly the same manner as that in which I respond to yours. "Self-consciousness," then, seems to say no more than that I can observe myself producing behaviors which I categorize as signs. We use the word in a casual rather than a philosophical or psychological sense when we say that a person is "self-conscious," if he is, we judge, obviously uncertain and somewhat embarrassed about his behavior, if he seems to be unsure as to whether or not his behavior is appropriate. He is engaged in responding to his own sign production and attempting to judge his competency or judging that production as incompetent.

It may be illuminating here to speculate on the beginning of sign production in the infant. For a while in the 1920s and 1930s it was believed that when infants cried, it was best to ignore them. Eventually it was decided that such behavior is a mistake. Whatever the reasons given for this change of procedure—most of which seem to me rather unconvincing—there is a very good reason indeed why a child should be responded to when it cries. Signs are effective instructions when they control behavior. Indeed, as we have seen, we tend to categorize a sign as a sign when it is controlling our behavior, even if we determine not to let our behavior be controlled according to those instructions. While we are making that decision by covert or overt semiotic behavior, the sign in question continues to control our behavior. For the infant to experience the control of adults by emitting or producing signs is clearly of the highest importance in socialization. As we have seen, semiosis makes the world as something-other-than-signs inaccessible; we live within a sphere of signs, the inner wall of which is opaque. Thus, we can hardly say whether or not the infant responds to its own cry by categorizing it as a sign. On the other hand we can be fairly certain the process has begun of so categorizing one's own noise productions as signs when the infant stops crying at the approach of a parent. At what point in this development of sign production does the infant respond to discomfort by crying, that is, begin to engage in sign production? I doubt if that question can be answered. To us, trained in categorizing our behavior as sign producing, the infant is producing a sign. The knowledge of whether or not the infant makes that judgment or of when it begins to make that judgment is to us, therefore, inaccessible.

All of the infant's early signs present puzzles to the parents. It is appropriate to respond, but how? What is wrong? What steps should be taken? They are general to the highest degree; they can be signs of anything, signs that any response is appropriate. A cry is at first a sign that has scarcely risen above the level of simply being a sign, except for the attribute of an indicator of a change in the infant's condition. The first nonverbal signs that a child makes—and this seems quite free of cultural control, according to the researches of Rhoda Kellogg—are equally general, even, perhaps, more general than the cry. Initially the first nonverbal sign is simply a mark in the sand with a stick or on a piece of paper with a crayon. From these simple marks develop the paintings of a Raphael. Nevertheless, between these two kinds of signs lies an immense gulf. Even so, the cry is nearer to the stick mark than a more fundamental kind of sign, the bodily gesture. Infants are born with the capacity for bodily movement, and shortly after birth bodily movement comes under the control of others. Is this the basis for what subsequently develops: the imitation of the bodily gestures of others? Seeing bodies move, and bodily appendages move, does the infant start to move its own body and its own appendages? The cry of the infant, which after all the infant itself hears, is of a different category, for it is produced by a bodily gesture. Most mothers are convinced that an infant continues to cry, once it has started, because it hears itself crying. If this is correct, it is a recognition of how any semiotic response is established.

We can see the principle involved here by glancing not at the least sophisticated of human behaviors but at the most sophisticated, the behavior of scientists. Scientific "truth" (which had better be called merely confidence) is established by recurrence. The very principle of experimentation is that an experiment can be replicated; that is, a set of behaviors can be repeated, and the results will be the same. The repetition of a configuration is the sole source of behavioral stability. But this is not quite the case. It is rather what we judge to be the repetition. Recurrence is response transfer, as we have already seen. A scientific report of an experiment includes instructions on how the experiment was performed so that it might be repeated. The behavior of the scientist who repeats the experiment has been verbally controlled, but that control is possible only because in the laboratory the scientist has learned the appropriate behaviors by observing the recurrence of such behaviors in others and by imitating them. It is not, however, mere mimesis, or imitation. A gesture which is imitated occurs within a perceptual field. Mimesis involves a perceptual selection from that field, a categorization of the gesture. This selection indicates what makes imitated behavior possible; it is response transfer. But the gulf between simple response transfer and the transer of the perceptual attributes selected to the observing organism's own body is an enormous one. Like verbal behavior, it is an astonishing leap, and it is just as astonishing when it is repeated by a growing infant. Hence, we cannot know how that leap is made—only that it is made—by recognizing the behavioral discontinuity between what we judge to be random motion and what we judge to be imitated motion. It certainly seems to have occurred at the prehuman level. To know more we would need to assume a meta-semiotic stance, and that we cannot assume. The cry is the next human step; i.e., vocal behavior which we interpret as an indicator that the cry has become a sign to the organism emitting a cry. And that, as we have seen, can be judged to have happened only when the behavior of the emitting organism changes when the cry is responded to. Even so, that is only the first step, for such a test cannot distinguish between learned sign behavior and genetically transmitted sign behavior, such as that of bees. Rather, a second test must be applied, a test of inappropriate response, a category which subsumes what we judge to be random response. Indeed, if an infant responds only with a smile when its cry is responded to, and always manifests the same response, we begin to suspect that something is wrong with it, that it will not develop full humanity. By asserting that the cry is the next step, I do not mean that the cry necessarily follows the development of imitated gesture in the development of the infant but, rather, that it differs from gesture in the sense that it is a sign produced by the infant. The possibility must also be recognized that a child maintains crying behavior as it develops because it hears sounds produced by the adults around it.

In any case there is considerable sign production by a child before it engages in the production of persistent signs, which may be thought of as deposits of behavior, of which the stick mark is certainly one of the first. Although all children produce much the same signs and in much the same order of growing complexity and specificity, it seems unlikely that they would do so had they not observed others, both children and adults, producing persistent signs. It seems more than likely that it is based upon gestural mimesis, although certainly it not infrequently happens that an older child or an adult places some kind of marking instrument in the child's hand and moves the arm and hand to make the mark. However this comes about, it is once again an astonishing leap, and upon it is based the human production of everything that humans produce, from the simplest club to an automobile or a computer. Signs give directions for behavior for those who have learned the response appropriate to that sign. They control behavior, then, once the response has been learned. Anything that human beings make is then a sign, for made objects control behavior. The simpler tools, for example, control behavior in that there is only one way possible to hold them for effective use.

CATEGORIES OF NONVERBAL SIGNS

This analysis, however tentative (by necessity) and even unsatisfactory as it may be, at least serves the purpose of categorizing the three kinds of nonverbal signs human beings produce: the gesture, the sound, and the persistent configuration. What makes sign production possible is response transfer, for that involves a perceptual selection of a configuration and the identification of its semiotic attributes, that is, categorization and subsumption. The configuration and a selection of its semiotic attributes are thus perceptually abstracted from the perceptual field and produced by bodily movements. The gesture and the cry, or similar physiological productions, such as urine or feces, certainly seem to be semiosis at the prehuman level. The production of persistent signs, however, appears to be uniquely human. Apes who pick up sticks to burrow into an ant hill are not, in spite of the apparent behavioral similarity, involved in tool use in the human sense, for a tool is a sign that directs and controls behavior. The human use of a stick for a similar purpose is something quite different; it is the transfer to a found object, not produced by a human, of behavior learned in response to humanly produced persistent signs. The most significant factor in sign production, then, is that the organism that produces the sign by a process of semiotic selection, abstraction, and reproduction responds to the produced sign as it responded to the sign when encountered in its original perceptual field. Since mimesis and imitation and sign production are unsatisfactory terms, I propose the term "semiotic transformation." Once the behavior of semiotic transformation has been established, it is then possible for the organism to combine signs and even invent signs freely. However, this freedom in semiotic transformation is unique to human beings. It is not available to other animals. That is, sign behavior must be verbally categorized as sign behavior—must become semiotic transformation—for that freedom to be possible, for only verbal signs can subsume in the same category two or more configurations which have no perceptual attributes in common. *Thus in humans all sign behavior (that is, virtually all behavior) is ultimately dependent upon verbal behavior.* However, it is worth reemphasizing that the value of that freedom should not be exaggerated. We do not know if it is adaptationally advantageous for survival, nor can we know. For "freedom," then, a better and less value-laden term is "indeterminability" of human sign response, of human semiotic transformation, and human recombination of reproduced signs. Verbal behavior increases drastically and (in theory) uncontrollably the indeterminability of behavior. Consequently, in human behavior the role of culture, of behavioral management and control, has a proportionally increased importance, for only thus can interactional competence be maintained.

A little further elucidation of this notion may be useful. For example, it may be objected that birds build nests, and animals and reptiles dig burrows and use caves. Is this not sign behavior? In considering this question, it must first be recalled that the word "sign" is here used as the termination of an explanatory regress. It subsumes, as suggested above, all words which instruct the responder to such words to respond to a configuration or set of configurations to the exclusion of all others, some such words being "mind," "awareness," "thought," "consciousness," "imagination," "belief," "intentions," and so on, as well as their verbal and adjectival and adverbial forms. As always in verbal behavior, the word "sign" cannot transcend the opacity of the verbal, except by the analogy of the continuity of response from the verbal to the nonverbal. In the behavior of mammals, as in the behavior of rats and bears, there is clearly not the indeterminability of semiotic transformation to be observed in human behavior, although just as clearly there is semiosis. But the problem has to do with such phenomena as the building of nests by birds and bird calls and what has been designated as the dance of bees. Is this semiosis? At this point the opacity of human semiosis intervenes. "Sign" is a verbal category, by analogy extended to human nonverbal behavior and thence to the nonverbal behavior of some animals, each analogy losing some of the attributes of the preceding analogical stage. When it comes to bird calls, the analogy breaks down and becomes a mere verbal metaphor. What is missing is the vital element of randomness of behavior. The question of whether or not bird calls are to be categorized as signs, that is, as behavior learned by mimesis, cannot be answered. If birds should develop verbal behavior independently of human interference, the question could then be answered. It is just as fruitless as asking if the earth in its changing relation to the sun is engaged in semiotic behavior. Indeed there are some semiotic speculators who have pushed the concept of "sign" to such extremes that they call genetic "coding" semiotic. To do so is to lose all the value of semiotic speculation. "Sign" becomes like "God." In subsuming all configurations, it explains none.

The notion of semiotic transformation deserves further analysis. As the perceptual field of a human moves through the world, the world, I have proposed, becomes signs. The response to those signs is the production of signs by the process of semiotic transformation. This gives us a much more precise definition of the perplexing term "response" than it was possible to arrive at in the first chapter and also explains more succinctly why the stimulus eliciting a response cannot be determined. The reason is that a "response" is a "semiotic transformation." We can go even further and say that since virtually all of human behavior is sign response, involving semiotic transformation, *the most precise definition of human behavior*, the definition that most economically and succinctly presents human behavior's defining attributes, *is "semiotic transformation."* As the range of responses in much psychological experimentation suggests, each individual responds to the world uniquely; that is, each human organism has a unique mode of semiotic transformation. (The explanation for this will be offered in greater detail in Chapter IV.) The unique history of each human being is responsible for his unique categorizing structure of the world as signs. Psychological experimentation can and does narrow the range of semiotic transformation by setting up protocols and other controls which merely reduce the range among disparate individuals, such as, "Answer yes or no." Precisely the same device is used in another theatrical situation, the courtroom.

In the action of semiotic transformation, that is, to repeat, in human behavior, three factors can be identified: attributional preservation, semiotic modality, and style. As an example of the difference between the first two, consider a drawing of a work of sculpture. Many of the attributes of the sculpture can be preserved in the drawing: the outlines from the point of view of the draftsman, the shadow, indicated by cross-hatching or some other mode of shading, the discernible lines within the external configuration or outline, such as the line of the nose in a three-quarter view, the color, and so on. However, the semiotic modality of the drawing is two-dimensional, rather than three. The draftsman cannot make a drawing which preserves all the configurational attributes of the outline as one walks around the sculpture or moves it. The drawing can preserve only some of the attributes of the texture, only some of the attributes of light and shadow. The semiotic modality, then, limits attributional preservation and at the same time adds semiotic factors which are attributes of that modality—not only two-dimensionality, but also the hardness or softness of the pencil, and indeed all of the modal attributes characteristic of that modality. Semiotic transformation from the nonverbal into the verbal involves all the attributes of linguistic behavior. As for the third factor, a copy of a Leonardo by Rubens looks more like a Rubens than it does a Leonardo. Under the subsumptional category of "style" can be listed such explanatory terms as "imagination," "perceptual uniqueness," "structure," "taste," "intelligence," and so on, that is, all of the factors, genetic in origin or learned, which are the product of that individual's unique history. It is not too much to say that every individual uses even semiotic modality in a unique way, in his unique style. What cannot be accounted for by attributional preservation and semiotic modality, what is added to those two factors, is "style," which can just as well be called the "semiotic additional." The ultimate explanation for that additional, or "stylistic," factor in semiotic transformation is the capacity of the brain to produce random responses and the capacity of the individual to control that randomness in unique ways.

Finally, each of these three factors—attributional preservation, semiotic modality, and style—varies independently from the variability of the other two. Thus what is judged by conventional protocols to be the overdetermination or neglect of attributes of the semiotic modality is a matter of style—that is, the degree of preservation of the attributes of that which is transformed. It is, then, this enormous complexity of semiotic transformation which makes the determination of anything more particular than "stimulus field" impossible and which prevents the determination of "a stimulus."

REGULATORY AND PERFORMATORY SEMIOSIS

There is a category of signs which though not unique to human beings has been immensely elaborated by humans. These are signs that are usually accounted for as expressions of emotions. "Emotional expression" has been a catchall term used to terminate explanations of behavior at a very low explanatory level. Yet an individual can produce a sign of anger without being angry, just as Tchaikowsky could write the last movement of his Sixth Symphony, usually judged to be sad, or tragic, or dreary, or neurotic, when he was feeling more cheerful than he had ever felt in his life. To begin to untangle all this we must first have clearly before us what is being subsumed by the word "emotion," what it is that the word directs us to respond to.

Any stimulus received by the sensorium has a consequence somewhere in the physiology. If the autonomic nervous system is sufficiently stimulated so that the consequences become a configuration—like butterflies in the stomach—it becomes a sign, and it is categorized as an emotion. It is hardly necessary to point out the great verbal confusion that attempts to deal with this phenomenon. Such signs are sometimes called the result of an emotional disturbance which produces such signs. This is at once to hypostatize "emotion," to raise it to a high level of explanatory regress, and to conceal what is going on.

One consequence is that overtly produced signs of emotion are believed to be expressions of emotion, so that an "anger sign" is supposed to be the concomitant of the emotion. On the contrary, the production of the anger sign is the consequence of responding to the emotion as a sign—but as a sign of what? That is, what is the appropriate way of responding to—what should be looked for in obedience to—the instruction "an emotion is a sign of _____?"

We may begin by observing that all behavior is aggressive. The claim that the foundation of behavior is the manipulation of the environment at least recognizes and underlines this aggressive character. But more deeply than that, even the categorization of a sign, even the perception of a figure against its ground, is aggressive, is a modification of the perceptual field. Metaphorically it too is manipulatory aggression. Aggression may be conceived of metaphorically as a flow of energy, like water through a garden hose. It can be interrupted, it can flow in spurts, it can flow smoothly, it can be increased to overcome an obstacle, it can be reduced when the obstacle cannot be overcome, it can be cut off. We have in fact all kinds of adjectives to subsume our judgments of the quantitative and qualitative attributes of aggression: passionate, gentle, uneasy, unpredictable, angry, happy, and so on. It is sufficient to point out that emotion—a disturbance of the autonomic nervous system the consequences of which are responded to semiotically—is itself a consequence of aggression, that is, of all behavior. Any emotion is a sign of the relative flow of aggression.

Some readers may be a little startled and recalcitrant at this use of "aggression," generally employed in a pejorative sense, although not long ago many employers advertised for "aggressive young men," a use coherent with *Webster's Third*, "marked by driving forceful energy, ambition, or initiative." Webster also defines "aggressive" as "tending or able to utilize a variety of habitats: able to encroach on occupied areas: variable and adaptable aggression used of organisms and taxa." For "aggressive" Webster offers the following: "3:a a form of psychobiologic energy, either innate or arising in response to or intensified by frustration, which may be manifested by... (5) healthy self-assertiveness or a drive to accomplishment or to mastery esp. of skills." (The antecedent of "which" is "energy," not "frustration.") From this, the prefix "psycho" (in psychobiologic) may be dismissed, for reasons already discussed, but "frustration" is worth considering for a moment. Ordinarily, it is subsumed by an explanatory regress terminated by such a word as "psyche" (as misleading a term in giving directions for observing behavior as the word "mind"). In order to desubjectify the notion of "frustration," instead of it I shall use "hindrance"—to subsume any interference with the activity of the human organism, *with the qualification that such activity is always and inevitably hindered*. Humans like to think of themselves as free, but "freedom" is a verbal construct to which there is no complete behavioral equivalent. If we ascribe to any human's activity the word "free," we do so only by ignoring whatever hinders that activity. For semiotically controlled organisms, such as human beings, the fundamental hindrance is the eternal possibility that any configuration can be categorized in a theoretically unlimited number of ways, that is, can be so responded to. If there were an immanent link between configuration and response such that the perceptual attributes of the configuration determined the response, then the use of the term "aggression" would be inappropriate. It is precisely because semiotic meaning is not immanent that the semiotically controlled organism must be aggressive in imposing appropriateness of response, whether upon himself or upon another.

Hence I am not to be understood as proposing that behavior "really is" aggressive, for we cannot say what anything "really is." Rather, it is more analytically useful to have a unidimensional term for the quality of behavior, since a polarized terminology ("aggressive/passive" or "dominant/submissive") has created in psychology and psychiatry inextricable confusions. Psychology sometimes attempts to make a distinction between "aggression" and "aggressiveness" (a distinction which *Webster's Third* does not recognize), but such a distinction is obviously a moral distinction between "aggression-to-be-approved-of" and "aggression-not-to-be-approved-of." Psychiatry talks about "passive-aggressive behavior." But all passive behavior is aggressive. A human being is never passive; when he appears to be so, he is controlling his own behavior in response to semiotic instructions. He is controlling, then, the *level* of his aggression. Even when a human behaves randomly, he is necessarily hindered by the protocols of behavioral control, and an effort is made, if only by himself, to place that randomization once again under the control of those protocols. But those protocols are themselves verbal and nonverbal signs the response to which is best understood as aggressive.

Finally, the very indeterminability of human sign response, of semiotic transformation, requires the human organism to determine that response—aggressively. And that indeterminability requires cultural control, that is, controls by others; aggression requires counteraggression. And that counteraggression is responsible for the fact that aggression is to be understood as occurring along a continuum of aggression, or levels. *All behavior is aggressive, but the aggression is always at a particular level.*

It is generally said that emotional expressions are signs of emotion, are externalizations of internal conditions, or more precisely are observable signs of nonobservable conditions. But this I believe to be in error. Let us glance back at the irony between Smith's denigrating remark to Jones and the friendliness of his tone. If Jones responds in the ordinary manner only to the words, he will indulge in a sudden spurt of aggression. He may or may not perceive the configuration of a physiological change in himself. He may behave according to the protocol of aggressive attack on the occasion of an insult without in fact experiencing any consequence of an activation of the autonomic nervous system to the level of observability. On the other hand, Smith's friendly tone was an instruction *not* to respond to the denigration of the remark, to behave according to the protocol that it was a joking insult, not an insult at all but an ironic way of being friendly. If Jones responds to the tone, then his aggression is controlled, subdued, perhaps even lessened from a previous state. Smith, in short, is employing a very common behavioral protocol which, if effective, regulates Jones's aggression. Hence what we usually call overt signs of emotion, or expressions of emotion, are nothing of the sort. They regulate aggression; that is, they regulate emotion. I shall call them, therefore, regulatory signs. They are signs that give instructions on regulating the flow or level of energy, or aggression.

The arts, particularly the nonverbal arts, are highly instructive for investigating and considering regulatory signs. Indeed, to call the arts expressions of the emotions is commonplace, though a verbal phenomenon of only the last few hundred years. This is a most inadequate definition, as we shall see farther on, and moreover insofar as the arts are "expressive," they are concerned with detaching regulatory signs from the normal semiotic environment and making free constructions of them, that is, with the indeterminability of semiotic transformation.

Since dance is the art concerned with gesture (with muscular movements which if completed would be engaged in manipulating the environment and sometimes are), it is useful to begin with that, particularly with the semiotic systems of the great American dancer Martha Graham, justly called the Michelangelo of dance.

Graham's basic system consists of two continua between two kinds of gesture. The first kind is a continuum between maintaining without motion a position on the stage and moving with the greatest rapidity possible about the stage, across it, around it, into it, to the footlights. The second kind is a continuum between a position of shrinking the trunk and the arms and legs into the smallest possible space and extending the full range of the body into the largest possible space. The ultimate point of both continua—movement and bodily expansion—is the leap. The significance of the leap may be defined at once: it is unhindered aggression. It is to be noted, however, that it may be a leap of desperation or of ecstasy, both of which must be determined by other signs. The ecstatic leap is obviously free from all hindrance to aggression. The desperate leap can be recognized from a dramatic situation; the character, faced with total hindrance of some terrifying threat or object or character, leaps, perhaps, to his death. It is nevertheless an avoidance leap that frees him from the hindrance of whatever is interfering with that aggression.

Certain common expressions are helpful to understand Graham's semiotic transformations. One hears such metaphorical statements as "He has fallen back upon himself," "He has turned away from others and towards himself," "He is highly withdrawn," and even, "His stance is that of complete disengagement from the situation." But also there are such statements as "He is fully engaged in his task" and "He is quite free in the way he deals with other people." In understanding Graham's signs, one finds it instructive that the first step toward breaking through the conventions of classical ballet was made by Isadora Duncan, who was contemporaneous with those artists in other fields, particularly painting, who abandoned configurational signs—those with perceptual-semiotic attributes preserved from configurations of the phenomenal world—in favor of increasing interest in regulatory signs. This direction in developing the dance, or rather in taking it back to the most fundamental semiosis of bodily gesture, culminated in the work of Graham. Hence, when Graham reduced herself to the smallest possible space, and assumed an almost embryonic posture, she was concerned in signifying a withdrawal from aggressive engagement with the environment, a complete "turning in upon oneself." In one extraordinary dance, "Dark Meadow," she went further. First she spread a great strip of black cloth upon the stage and then rolled herself up inside of it, as if in a cocoon, until at length on the stage appeared but a black cloth bundle absolutely still. Then movement was observable, the bundle unrolled itself, she emerged, and there followed a dance made up of increasingly rapid penetrations into all parts of the stage, moving to a climax of great leaps. That is, after the "spiritual death" of the organism (its incapacity to engage at all with the environment), there followed an exploration of the environment, culminating in triumphant ecstatic leaps, the unhindered release of aggression. The point of the dance, the regulatory instructions to the audience, was that if one is afflicted with an incapacity to deal effectively and freely with a situation, it is a useful strategy to withdraw totally from it and to husband one's resources of aggression until one judges them to be restored to their full power, and then to emerge. Or, to put it another way, a problem that seems to be totally resistant to attempts to solve it can frequently be solved if one disengages from it, turns one's back on it, forgets it, and then tackles it again, a pattern anyone engaged in problem solving of any kind will confirm. Other signs in the dance indicated that Graham was using aspects of Jungian ideology and recommending a retreat into the "unconscious" as a way of renewing one's capacity for aggressive energy release and engagement.

Others of these regulatory signs—verticality, height, and horizontality—may be found in a number of the arts, including the dance, but they are most easily understood in architecture and painting. In his striking autobiography, *Memories, Dreams, Reflections*, Carl Jung relates the building of his country retreat, Bollingen, which was accessible only by water. He had planned a central tower, higher than the two towers at either end of the facade. He was not able to build it, however, until his father died. One's own home, particularly if it is a retreat or vacation home, disengaged from one's ordinary modes of manipulating the environment, is a building in which one has the greatest freedom (degree of uncontrolled indeterminability of semiotic transformation) in producing signs that regulate one's aggressiveness. It is where one can be most freely aggressive (although if it is also a family home that freedom is constantly hindered). Bollingen was clearly a place in which Jung had to consider no one else's wishes, at least in the general design of it. Even so, he was not free to build his central tower; he was not free to regulate his behavior by the central high tower sign until his father died. Clearly, both verticality and height are signs that regulate the level of aggression. As one example of the latter, in Versailles during the Old Regime, no house could be built with a roof higher than the level of the Marble Court, directly below the king's bedchamber, and the center of the whole palace. That is, only the king was permitted a higher level of aggression than anyone else. On the other hand, the spreading horizontality of the vast building was a regulatory indicator that the royal aggression was limited and controlled. Thus, royal thrones are always on a dais, as teacher's chairs once were, the regulatory direction being that to the individual with superior environmental control is reserved the right to initiate action.

A particularly delightful example is to be found in the first Kinsey report. A young man was accustomed, before he dressed to go out, to standing in front of a mirror and producing a good firm erection. Having done so, he judged he was able to go out and face the world successfully. Indeed, a better regulatory sign of aggressive energy and manipulatory power than the erect penis can scarcely be imagined. It is, of course, the perfect sign for machismo, the unimpeded release of aggression and manipulatory expansion. The Hindu worship of the lingam, especially by Indian women, is not at all sexual, just as Hinduism claims. It is the Indian female respect for the aggressive male power to control the environment for the benefit of men and women alike. In Jung's case, it is to be noticed that as a European he had been surrounded by towers all his life, particularly in churches and castles. Before the modern period, cathedral towers were invariably the highest objects, as well as the most vertical, in Europe. They were a regulatory instruction that unimpeded aggressive energy is reserved to God, an instruction that man must place limits on his own aggression. A custom in Philadelphia, that no building should be built higher than the soles of William Penn's feet on top of the City Hall tower, was a regulatory sign that the individual's energy release was subordinate to the interests and welfare of the city as a whole. Thus for Jung his tower was a regulatory sign, a self-instruction, that he no longer need subordinate his individual aggressiveness to his father, at least insofar as his intellectual efforts were involved, i.e., his activities as private citizen and independent thinker. Hence one need not agree that his decision to build his tower was in fact caused by the death of his father. More probably he judged himself about that time sufficiently competent in his profession not to hinder himself with verbal controls incoherent with the explanation of behavior he had chosen to develop. In that case his father was a regulatory sign for him that subsumed all the regulatory signs in his culture which, he judged, inhibited the indeterminability of the semiotic transformations of his intellectual life. On the other hand, horizontality is an instruction to subordinate aggression to the aggression of others, as the verbal instruction "I've got to take it lying down" makes perfectly clear. The individual turns his aggression against himself. Architecture, then, is not frozen music. Rather, since its source is gesture, a better metaphor is frozen dance. Likewise, steeples and towers are not symbols of the phallus, as one hears so often; rather, all three are parallel signs of unhindered aggression.

Colors are also regulatory signs. (For such purposes black and white are conveniently categorized as colors, for all systematized and conventionalized color semiosis uses them. The color continuum runs from black through purple, violet, indigo, blue, green, red, orange, yellow, to white.) The more "disturbed" and "withdrawn" the child, the more frequently it uses blues, purples, and blacks—that is, the more its aggression is under severe control and takes the form of refusing to respond, of using its aggression to control its response to others. (Children called "autistic" are quite probably simply refusing to respond.) As the child gradually returns to "normal" behavior, that is, to normative aggressive interaction with the environment and other humans, it begins to use more reds, oranges, and especially yellow, as it arrives at "psychological health." This suggests that color as semiosis regulates the level of aggression toward the environment, including other individuals. And it is a commonplace that individuals we call "withdrawn" are marked by an extreme limitation or contraction of environmental engagement. It certainly seems to be the case that in hospitals patients in rooms painted green or blue get well more slowly than those in yellow rooms. Such colors are instructions: "Don't get well." The use of black can illustrate the subtlety of this kind of behavioral control. It seems at first glance incoherent that both mourners at funerals and those members of motorcycle gangs (of which Hell's Angels are the most famous) wear black. Yet there is a common element. For both, black is an instruction that neither the Angel nor the mourner—for quite different reasons—will accept the aggressive control of others. Control is perceived as hindrance to aggression. Traditionally, villains, characters who reject social protocols, are dressed in black. The mourning costume also has this same aspect, for a different reason; as a regulation of others it is an assertion that grief is so great, environmental disengagement is so great, that the individual is not capable of engagement. Black does not express mourning; it sustains it. The motorcycle of the Angel, its capacity for great speed, on the other hand, is a sign that efforts at control will be resisted with a high degree of aggression, for speed in any activity evokes a high level of aggression. The black leather and the motorcycle are designed to terrify, but as self-instructions they operate in such a way that the Angels have no choice but to rush about terrifying people, reserving aggression for themselves—hence the divine attribute of their name, "Angel." (Behavior validated by such words as "God," "State," "Nature," "Liberty," "Justice," and so on, is granted as much unhindered aggression as is necessary to carry out the assignment so validated.) On the other end of the color continuum the white of the bride's dress is a regulatory sign that no hindrance will be offered to the aggression of the groom. White is the color of innocence, of a social ignorance of how to hinder the aggression of others, i.e., of acceptance of control as guidance.

As an indication of the role of color semiosis in painting it is significant that, in the nineteenth century, landscape painting became the dominant genre, culminating in the abstract painting of the twentieth century, which emerged from it. For culturally complex reasons the innovative nineteenth-century painter, the Romantic, was interested in intellectual and artistic aggression free from the control and impedance of socially validated behavioral protocols. Landscape was a genre that provided the possibility of the greatest freedom in the use and disposition of color, as well as other visual regulatory signs derived from gesture, such as verticality. "History painting," the subject matter of which required the presentation of specific humans in specific places, with all the appurtenances of costume, architecture, and other "props," was much more confining in this respect. Skies, trees, lakes, cows, and clouds can be disposed with great freedom. Thus in the 1880s what had been Impressionism entered a new phase, one in which the color became so important that the scene presented was degraded from subject to motif.

For precisely the same reason music became the dominating and eventually the model art of the nineteenth century, so that, as Pater said, all art tended to approach the condition of music, and various abstract painters of the twentieth century have identified their paintings as "visual music." What we call "up" and "down" in music is an increase in vibrations per second of bodies of air or of various kinds of strings. Such vibrations are precisely the way vocal tones are produced, and music is based entirely on an abstraction of tone from linguistic behavior. Once tone had been separate from verbalization, virtually infinite freedom of treatment became possible, far more various than the human voice is capable of, though for many people singing remains the most "expressive" of all musical sounds. Basing his conclusion on extensive research into the conventional associations of words and music, Deryck Cooke identifies the up-and-down of pitch with out-and-in and away-and-back from the self. The objection to his work that music does not have meaning is easily overcome. First, no sign "has" meaning, and the objections to the meaningfulness of music invariably amount to the assertion that only words can have meaning or that verbal meaning is the only possible meaning, clearly an absurdity. Indeed, no one but a few aestheticians and their misled followers among composers have ever believed for a moment that music is meaningless. Second, the meaningfulness of music can easily be demonstrated. If you ask a number of people to generate verbal responses to the conclusion to Beethoven's Fifth Symphony, they might call it triumphant, or ecstatic, or decisive, or energetic, but no one will call it sad, or gloomy, or despondent, or neurotic. In other words, verbal responses to music invariably fall into families of response, verbalisms ordinarily quite easily subsumed under a verbal category, as indeed so do verbal responses to words. Because of verbal metaphor, however, verbal responses to words fall into a wider range of categories, often quite discontinuous categories, than do verbal responses to music, a point that supports Mendelssohn's claim that the meanings of music are more precise than the meanings of words. Cooke, to be sure, depends upon an inner-outer dichotomy of self-and-other. Such hypostatizations are not, I think, acceptable and, as is to be expected, are based upon an expressive theory of what I believe are better understood as signs regulatory of the level of aggression. Nevertheless, all of Cooke's observations are quite easily translated into the vocabulary used here and which, I think, successfully subsumes and explains his terminology.

Music has other semiotic systems than pitch. Volume is a regulatory sign of aggressive level, as is tempo, a regulatory sign music shares with the dance and with acting. Tone, abstracted from the voice into various instruments, is like gesture and color in presenting regulatory signs of hindrance or lack of hindrance to aggression. To talk about the "colors" of instruments is to be justifiably metaphorical. With these variables of regulatory semiosis—pitch, volume, tempo, and tone— music at the high level of Western culture has almost infinite resources for regulatory semiosis. It is no accident that Romantic symphonies, beginning with Beethoven's Fifth Symphony, particularly the last movement, combine with high pitch, great volume, fast tempo, and piercing tone to create enormously powerful redundant regulatory signs which present the instructions to raise to new heights the level of asocial aggression. The major-minor dichotomy, unique to European music and found there only within the past five hundred years, is a regulatory semiotic system concerned with the interpretation of the regulatory control of aggression as either guidance (major) or hin- drance (minor). It has long been a puzzle—since minor is said to mean "sadness"—that Gluck's Orfeo laments Eurydice in the major. But the major here is quite appropriate, because it informs us that Orfeo is interpreting this new loss of Eurydice not as a hindrance to his love for her but as a situation which will impose on him a guidance, an aggres- sive guidance, to recovering her. Similarly, visions of heaven in music are invariably dominated by female choirs and high-pitched instruments—high violins, brilliant trumpets and woodwinds, and so on—all these instruments playing at the upper extremes of their ranges, usually with low volume in a slow tempo, and always in the major. This vision of Heaven, or union with the Godhead, like all visions of deity, is a regulatory sign of a low level of aggression combined with full acceptance of control as guidance. In the secular equivalent of all this, at the end of Wagner's *Tristan und Isolde*, the heroine sings at the extreme upper range of her pitch and becomes one with the *Welt-All* to the point of total loss of personality, or self-consciousness, or self- hood. Every trace of "will"—the perception of control as hindrance—has disappeared. Passages in music called "seductive" invariably go down in the major—an instruction to lower the level of aggression and to accept that lowering as guidance. But in Wagner's *Ring* the motif for Wotan's spear—on which are graven the runes of *Verträge* (Wotan's treaties or contracts which give him power)—goes straight down in the minor: control is a matter of power and force.

Any configuration in the world has those attributes which can function as regulatory signs—height, depth (or visual recession), color, size, volume, sound, and so on. Color alone is abstracted from the perception of the world. All other regulatory signs are abstracted from the body and its movements and gestures. For this reason color is the least controllable in its regulatory significance, the most difficult to categorize under the terminology proposed here. And for the same reason, color is most easily stabilized as the nonverbal equivalent of words, that is, as will be discussed shortly, as emblems. Blue is Mary's color; red, the color of courage; green, the color of hope; and so on. A thorough and transcultural study of color as regulatory semiosis has scarcely been done, nor even a study of color as emblematic semiosis.

The attribute of signs other than regulatory is generally recognized as "information," that is, the instructions on the category of appropriate response. A perceptual field is filled with information according to the learned ability of the perceiver to respond to the richness or poverty of the informational aspect of its signs. Commonly, such information is said to be the material for something called "communication." Successful "communication" depends upon two factors, the capacity of the individual receiving the communication to respond appropriately to the informational aspect of signs and the capacity of the communicator to employ those semiotic protocols which control randomness of response, usually referred to as ambiguity. In the poetry of Wallace Stevens, for example, an uncertainty of the antecedents of pronouns is the primary factor in the difficulty of responding—that is, of understanding his work. But since the protocols of poetry permit and even, at a high cultural level, tend to demand communicational difficulty, that device of his is not considered a fault. It is, however, considered a fault in expository prose; and in spoken verbal interchange, the demand for the antecedence of a pronoun is anything but infrequent. It is clear from this that the individual receiving the communication must also be familiar with the protocols of control, that is, what in Chapter I was called the procedural aspect of verbalization. From this point of view the difference between "What did he say" and "How did he say it" disappears. "Information" and "communication,'' then, I believe to be inadequate terms for indicating the behavior involved. Rather, turning to the proposal that both verbal and nonverbal signs are normative, *all informational signs can be understood as instructions for behavior controlled by protocols*—that is, to adopt a metaphor from the theater, *as instructions for a performance.*

I propose, then, the term ''performatory aspect'' as coordinate with ''regulatory aspect.'' The performatory aspect gives instructions on what is to be done; the regulatory aspect gives instructions on the level of aggression with which the behavior is to be done. A descriptive statement, such as, ''That meadow is brown from the drought,'' is an instruction to perform looking at the meadow and to explain its color, to the exclusion of other behavior or performances. The peculiar advantage of written language, stripped of tone, is that verbalization can be reduced to its performatory aspect and freed of its regulatory aspect (or, rather, almost free, for a sentence of unusual length is a regulatory instruction to raise the level of interpretational aggression). There is, in fact, a general tendency to call verbalization ''poetic'' to the degree to which regulatory signs are present, such as unusually high degree of sound similarity or of regularity of alternation of stressed and unstressed syllables (rhythm). The explanation, of course, is that poetry is the mode of verbal behavior which makes the fullest use of regulatory semiosis.

As we have seen, it is a characteristic of the arts that they make rich and constant use of regulatory semiois. Thus, it has been claimed that the arts are ''expressions of the emotions,'' that they are made up exclusively of regulatory signs. Obviously, this is not the case. Even music may present performatory signs. In *The Marriage of Figaro* Mozart uses hunting horns to indicate cuckoldry, stag's horns being an ancient emblem of the cuckold. In the second act of *Tristan* Wagner presents in the orchestra a semiotic transformation of the sound of hunting horns with high attributional preservation but with no indication of cuckoldry, and then converts these sounds into a semiotic transformation of the sound of a brook, though with a somewhat lower level of attributional preservation. Clearly, both present both performatory and regulatory signs. The latter give instructions on the aggressional aspects appropriate or inappropriate to the kind of situation indicated by the former. Thus it is hardly an exaggeration to say that tragedy is concerned with aggressive inappropriateness, i.e., the hindrance to aggression is justified, and that comedy is concerned with aggressive appropriateness (a clearing away of hindrance). In the former the aggression has a destructive consequence and in the latter a fortunate one (destructive and fortunate at least for the character whose aggression is the play's primary concern). This simultaneous and interacting use of informational and regulatory signs is not the only attribute of the arts, however, as we shall see later, nor indeed the most important.

Nevertheless, the arts as a means of maintaining the cultural protocols governing aggression are of great importance. It seems probable that regulatory signs are prehuman, although in animals they appear to occur only in gestures and vocal sounds. If that is the case, the leap to exploiting the regulatory possibilities of all signs was one of the great leaps into humanity. Be that as it may, one thing is obvious: to maintain existence men must respond appropriately to the performatory aspect of configurations. A man must know that if it rains, he is likely to get wet unless he seeks shelter and that getting wet might be dangerous for his health. But to maintain interactive existence, aggression must be regulated. The ingenuity of human beings in using any sign for that purpose, and in abstracting from signs their regulatory aspect, and in semiotically transforming those attributes in humanly produced signs is as impressive as it appears to be inexhaustible. Like words, regulatory signs, since they are doubly fictive, are capable of infinite development and combination and also, of particular interest, are capable of semiotic transformation: that is, they are capable of responding to one modality of regulatory signs, such as music, by producing signs in another modality, such as the dance. For these reasons words which explanatorily subsume regulatory signs—words such as "gentle," "violent," "relaxed," "angry," "tender," and so on—can be responded to by semiotic transformation into music, and similarly music can be responded to by semiotic transformation into the regulatory verbal sign modality, and the result falls within a certain range of conventional response, or verbal families. Further, complex sign structures can be produced in which the original sign can be presented simultaneously with an ironic transformation. A Charles Ives can set a hymn so that the validity of the religious verbal behavior is called into question, the regulatory aspects being ironically appropriate to the performatory words and the regulatory semiosis of the words. A hymn that directs a smooth flow of controlled aggression can be so set that the music gives directions for an interrupted flow of powerful but impeded aggression.

This notion of semiotic transformation is of some help in understanding emotion itself, as defined above. The first thing to be noticed about emotion is that it can be evoked by an "act of will." The individual can give himself instructions to produce the emotion. Likewise, works of art can do so, as well as political rhetoric and sports, to give but a few of a wide range of possible examples. Since the time of Diderot the most effective way of acting has been constantly discussed. Should the actor produce only gestural and evanescent regulatory signs, or should he also "feel" the appropriate emotion while doing so? The latter position is usually justified by explanatory regressive appeal to "nature," or "instinct," or "the unconscious." But actually the very question indicates that the actor can so manipulate himself that he can produce "at will" what he judges to be an appropriate emotion. Obviously, emotions, not merely for the actor but for everybody, are regulatory signs that can be at once covert and gestural. The production of such gestural regulatory signs, that is, emotions, is a matter of semiotic transformation, the response to verbal or other regulatory signs, by producing regulatory signs in the modality of covert gestures. To feel an emotion, then, or a feeling state (to use the two most popular terms for this perception as configuration of the consequence of stimulus to the autonomic nervous system) is an example of semiotic transformation, which the semiotic transformation of regulatory signs from one modality into another is a special case.

One example of how regulatory signs work and also how they are subsumed by verbal signs is particularly instructive, as well as amusing. It is the distinction between "masculine" and "feminine," the distinction which some factions of Women's Liberation are bent upon obliterating, though it is reasonable to predict only very partial success; but not because of the natural superiority or inferiority of men or women, or even their equality, but for quite different reasons. I have already suggested that "machismo" or masculine superiority is a matter of unimpeded aggression, that verticality and height are regulatory signs of these two aspects of aggression and that men come equipped with a distinguishing bit of anatomy the perceptual attributes of which are remarkably dense and suitable to be responded to as a regulatory sign. It is not surprising, then, that in music an ascending melodic line, one characterized by a more or less steady increase in sonic vibrations per second, is traditionally called masculine and that a descending line is called feminine. Likewise, horizontality tends to be called feminine—possibly the reason for "Mother Earth"—and verticality masculine. Indeed, Erik Erikson has observed that boy children playing with blocks tend to build towers, while girl children tend to build horizontal enclosures. This is convincing enough, or would be, were it not for the fact that girl children just learning to play with blocks will in fact pile them up. This suggests that the phenomenon Erikson observed takes place after children have learned to control their behavior by the masculine-feminine distinction.

Kinsey's young man in front of a mirror, gaining confidence by looking at his erection, gives us a clue here. This clearly has nothing to do with sexual behavior nor even with the differentiation between male and female. Moreover, there are societies, though rare, in which women do all the tasks that in our culture men do, while the men stay home, take care of the children, and spend their free time in adorning themselves with makeup and costume. In such societies the men control their behavior according to the regulatory and performatory semiosis which controls female behavior in most other societies. This negation of the norm, or more precisely this alternative to the statistical norm, suggests again that the masculine-feminine distinction is not biologically based, nor even necessarily based, let alone justified, by the larger frame and heavier skeletal muscles of men. In some societies, or in some culture groups within a society, the tasks requiring greater strength are done by women, even though men maintain a powerful machismo.

(In addition, it is worth observing how the distinction is maintained by explanatory-validational regressions, especially at the present time, in response to the agitation of the Women's Liberation propaganda. More conservative regressions explain and justify both the distinction and masculine domination and superiority by an explanation which terminates with the word "God," while modern explanations terminate with the word "Nature," a term as suspect as "God," as we have already seen, for both assume the impossible meta-semiotic stance.)

The distinction, therefore, is best understood as a regulatory distinction maintained by innumerable regulatory signs, verbal and nonverbal. I have already suggested that the explanation for regulatory signs is to be found in the necessity for controlling aggression if predictability and interaction among members of the species are to be maintained. It is usually assumed that passivity is the negation of aggression, but this cannot be the case if, as I have maintained, all behavior is necessarily aggressive. Rather, what we subsume by "passivity" are behaviors in which aspects of aggression are hindered by the action of the individual said to be passive. Passivity is observable only in hierarchical situations, that is, interactional situations—including an individual's interaction with himself—in which the individual's aggression occupies a lower place on the continua of aggressive energy release and aggressive engagement than does the aggression of the individual with whom the passive individual is interacting and to whom he is responding. Women passive when interacting with their husbands are not infrequently highly aggressive when interacting with other women. Indeed, it is my observation that women not infrequently are more aggressive than a man would be when they are interacting with strangers, especially those in some kind of bureaucratic position. Or as a friend of mine put it, "If women are to be liberated, they must learn some manners." Passivity, then, is subdued or impeded aggression, and indeed in noting degrees of passivity we recognize this. All this is equally true of the terms "dominance" and "submission," and "masculinity" and "femininity." If interaction is to take place smoothly, there must be protocols of behavior which regulate degrees of aggression in hierarchical situations, and all situations are hierarchical in which the interaction is initiated by a single individual, that is, virtually all situations. Innumerable regulatory signs control degrees of aggression, and an indefinable number of these are subsumed by the words "masculine" and "feminine." It is quite possible that the erectility of the penis is a sufficient as well as a parsimonious explanation for subsuming hierarchical degrees of aggression by the terms "masculine" and "feminine." In the next chapter we shall see how the individual in the passive, submissive, feminine position undermines aggression, dominance, and masculinity and inverts the hierarchical relationship. The lesson of this is that Women's Liberation will simply create more men, in the sense that "masculinity" is a social role governed by regulatory signs of a high level of aggression.

SOME SEMIOTIC TERMS

It may be useful here to propose distinctions among five words, all of which are characterized by a high degree of polysemy and semantic instability: "sign," "symbol," "emblem," "emotion," and "feeling." To begin with the last pair, "emotion" is often used to indicate a strong feeling; on the other hand, it would be more usual to say, "I feel marvelous today," than, "I am in a splendid emotional state today," though the latter, such is the penetration of psychiatric terminology into the general culture, would be only a little odd, whereas a hundred years ago it would have been very odd indeed. Thus, "I feel marvelous today" is tantamount to the assertion that I feel as if there were no hindrance between myself as an organism and any level of aggression I might decide to be appropriate. A not infrequently encountered metaphor for "I feel marvelous" appears to be "I feel as if I could embrace the world," a sign of a judgment of the possibility of freedom from hindrance.

As for the other three, they are constantly used interchangeably. Nevertheless there is a semantic tendency to use "sign" when one's interest is in the performatory aspect of signs, and "symbol," particularly nowadays, when one is interested in the regulatory aspect. Until about 1800, however, and a little later, "symbol" meant "emblem," either a performatory sign or a regulatory sign which had a conventionally stabilized verbal equivalent. Thus, a lion might be an emblem of courage, and the color gold of nobility, or, more generally, great value. Today, instead of "emblem" we are likely to use "sign." while symbol tends to be reserved for regulatory signs. (The explanation for this, historically, is the nineteenth-century identification of regulatory signs as expressive signs, the separation of aggression (as self-expression) from social protocol (leading to the judgment of music as the model art), and the establishment of such aggression as an independent behavioral variable for and by those individuals whose primary interest was significant innovation and cultural transcendence, the Romantics.) Moreover, when we examine the situations in which the word "symbol" is used, the fundamental meaning of the term is readily recognized. We use the word when we are indicating that two or more different responses to the same sign are appropriate. And this definition can subsume all cases.

INTERPRETATION

The interaction of the hierarchy of explanation and of the control of aggression emerges in the interpretation of signs, verbal and nonverbal. It is best to take as an example a very ordinary interpretational event, rather than the difficult and complex problems of interpretation at a high cultural level, the sort of problem that ordinarily gives rise to efforts to establish a theory of interpretation—a hermeneutic. Interpretation at that level, no matter how complex, must have mundane interpretational behavior as its historical origin and as its theoretical base.

A customer, let us say, enters a restaurant and sits down at a table; the waiter approaches; the customer asks for a cup of coffee; the waiter brings it. What is the waiter's behavior such that the customer judges the waiter's response appropriate to the customer's request? It is by no means idle to point out that waiter does not bring the America Cup filled with unroasted coffee beans; nor does he wander off and start petting the restaurant cat. His behavior is neither bizarre nor random, but it perfectly well could be either. Philosophers of science and some scientists, particularly in the social sciences, are now fashionably fond of asking, "What is the methodology of this study or research?" What, then, is the hermeneutic methodology of the waiter? Two factors can be immediately recognized. The waiter has received a request for coffee innumerable times; and he has responded appropriately in this and no doubt other restaurants. The importance of the second factor can be underscored by supposing that waiter and steady customer meet at the beach when both are on vacation. Should the customer be so bizarre as to ask for coffee, it is unlikely that he would get it. Or, on the other hand, the waiter might go and buy him a cup of coffee and take it to him. In the latter case, the waiter's response would be ironic, humorously inappropriate, for the waiter would be aware of the ironic inappropriateness of his behavior. Or, back in the restaurant, the waiter might say, "I'm sorry, sir. I can't get you a cup of coffee, because it is 11 A.M., and at this very moment all the waiters in the city are going on strike."

All this, obviously, is to spell out what has long been recognized as interpreting according to "context" of "situation." But the waiter's methodology can be put much more precisely. What his hermeneutic methodology amounts to is this: *He has perceptually disengaged an analogically determined recurrent semiotic pattern from an analogically determined series of semiotic matrices.* He has analogically determined that this request for coffee is sufficiently similar to other requests for coffee to justify a response transfer; and he has subsumed that determination by a determination that restaurant-table-customer is one of a series of complex sign configurations that instructs him to respond to the request by getting the coffee. The semiotic matrix, then, is at a higher hierarchical level than the semiotic pattern. The matrix controls the interpretation—and hence the response—to the pattern. But, of course, the matrix does not do anything, nor does the pattern. It is the waiter who does the controlling; he controls his own behavior.

Two conclusions may be drawn from this. *All interpretation is hierarchical*, identical with the structure of explanation. The effort of interpretation is to identify appropriately the semiotic matrix which controlled the behavior of the individual who generated the utterance to which the interpreter of that utterance is responding. But, since there is, as we have seen, no immanent connection between any two hierarchical levels of explanation-interpretation, the control of pattern by matrix leaves the way open to error, irony, reinterpretation, and particularly to questions about the "intention" of the generator of the semiotic pattern in question. The statement about intention in the previous chapter can now be put more precisely: when we ask about the intention of a speaker, we are asking about what matrix is appropriate for controlling our interpretation. A somewhat more sophisticated example may be observed by considering the semiotic pattern "The moon is made of green cheese." If we encounter this sentence in a philosophical work, we will, if we are familiar with philosophical discourse, recognize it as a commonplace exemplum in the rhetoric of philosophy. But if we encounter it in a scientific treatise on astronomy, our interpretation will be far different. We may be faced with a hermeneutic puzzle. Is the author being serious? That is, does he really mean that the moon is indeed made of green cheese? Is he being ironic? Is he being bizarre? Is it, perhaps, a joke by the compositor of the type, impatient with the text he is setting?

The second conclusion about interpretation is this: *All interpretation is historical*. Response transfer, which is what interpretation and the control of interpretation consists of, takes place over time, as the very word "transfer" indicates. That is why the words "recurrent" and "series" are in the above formula. As we have seen, the foundation of human behavior—its "essence"—is semiotic transformation. The problem of the "arrow of time" reduces itself to the fact that such transformation takes what we call "time" within a world made doubly opaque by verbal and nonverbal semiosis. The waiter responded appropriately to the request for a cup of coffee because he had *previously* responded to that semiotic pattern in that semiotic matrix and *because his response had been judged appropriate*. The historical character of interpretation is recognized in ordinary language by such words as "always," "never," "rarely," "sometimes," and "occasionally," and "probably," "possibly," and "perhaps."

What is ordinarily called "historical interpretation" in the hermeneutics of literary and other research amounts to the chronological arrangement of a series of documents (and sometimes artifacts, as in archaeological and paleontological research). Ordinary interpretation is obviously the model for the historical interpretation of documents and artifacts, but there is a profound difference between the two; in the latter the documents and artifacts are coexistent with the interpreter. On the other hand, the historical hermeneuticist controls his ordering of his documents and artifacts by such words as "time" and "history"; and he controls his selection of those documents by an ideology derived from his encounters with other documents and artifacts and, above all, from his encounters with the tradition of such selection as interpreted from the documentary discourses of his predecessors. Thus, though his ordering and selection of documents and his examination of them differs from the behavior of the waiter (since the waiter's pattern and matrices have ceased to exist), his interpretation of them is identical with the waiter's, for it is dependent upon his previous interpretations of patterns and matrices (analogically determined), and these are interpretations which no longer exist. All interpretation, then, is response transfer from no longer existing pattern-matrix complexes. *Uncertainty is the condition of interpretation and, therefore, the condition of semiotic transformation—the condition, that is, of behavior itself.*

EXPLANATION AND THE NONVERBAL

We are now in a position to put together the conclusion to Chapter I and the account of nonverbal signs and the relation of the nonverbal to the verbal in the present chapter. Chapter I concluded with an explanation of verbal behavior as explanatory regression, accomplished by subsumption of words by other words but qualified by the fact that since meaning is not immanent, then there is no immanent connection between the various levels of such a regress.

It should now be apparent that it is possible to state what explanatory verbal regressions explain: they explain nonverbal signs.

Moreover, the hierarchy of explanation descends down into or pene-trates the nonverbal. Subsumption begins with the categorization of a configuration as a sign and continues with the transfer of response from one sign to another on the basis of identity of some semiotic attributes, that is, continues by means of categorial subsumption. Verbal signs subsume the perceptual categories created by response transfer, but freely, that is, independent of any continuity of semiotic attributes from the nonverbal to the verbal, except for the attribute of semiosis, of being a sign.

Further, all signs can have, and perhaps do have, a dual aspect or bifurcation of function, the performatory and the regulatory: instruc-tions on how to respond and how to regulate the degree of aggression to be released in the response. Sign production, which I have described as semiotic transformation, selects signs and semiotic attributes and produces their semiotic equivalents, either transitorily, as in gesture and sounds, or persistently, as in lasting objects. The semiotic trans-formation, since it is ultimately under the control of verbal directions, has the freedom of structuring which is the characteristic of verbal behavior, except for the capacity to construct explanation. Since that freedom does obtain, however, it provides the opportunity for random response and hence the raw material for innovation.

Words randomly strung together cannot be responded to: the pro-tocols governing explanatory subsumption and connectives have to be observed, though if they are observed, randomly included nouns can be responded to as metaphor, though some ingenuity is required to do so. Musical notes, however, randomly strung together, can be per-ceived as a melody, though the individual whose perceptions are too tightly controlled by existent protocols for melody may not be able to do so. I can make a melodic gestalt or configuration of any series of tones randomly struck on a piano, though my piano teacher, far better musically trained, cannot. This capacity of nonverbal semiotic trans-formation for free and even random semiotic structuring is of the highest importance, for it can undermine the nonimmanent subsump-tions which link the verbal to the nonverbal. Finally, although we can get out of the magic and often opaque sphere of words with the aid of the subsuming word "sign," we cannot get out of the more magical and completely opaque, hollow sphere of nonverbal signs. *All human semiotic behavior is semiotic transformation.* Hence, we cannot de-termine either the point at which sign behavior emerged in the history of the species or the point at which it emerges in an infant living in the present.

MYTHOLOGY AND SCIENCE

An example of how all this works can be found in two words which are ordinarily considered to be contrastive or negational of each other: "mythology" and "science." It is usually affirmed that an explanation is either mythological, a pseudo-explanation, or it is scientific, a true explanation. An example may be found in the nineteenth-century controversy over lightning rods. After Franklin had drawn lightning from the heavens, the lightning conductor or lightning rod, first used in the eighteenth century on ships, began to be applied to buildings. The theological objection to this practice was very fierce indeed, for the theological explanation of a near miss or a hit by lightning, whether of trees, cattle, people, or buildings, was that it was a sign from God that the individual whose property was thus damaged or destroyed or who himself or a relation was hit and burned or killed, was guilty of sin. It was a warning or a punishment. Lightning was subsumed under the general category of "signs of warning and/or punishment from God," and the explanation of lightning was thus "theological," literally "subsumed under the word 'God.' " It instructed the individual who accepted it that he ought to respond to a hit or near-hit by lightning as he responded to any other sign to which the appropriate response was a recognition of the omnipresence of deity and of his own sinfulness. The sign, lightning, was thus subsumed under the words "God" and "sinfulness," the attributes of which in Christian theology are the omnipotence, omniscience and omnibenevolence of God, and the omnipresence of sinfulness in all men. Any unpredicted threat or potential and otherwise inexplicable danger could be (and, with great frequency, was) a warning message from deity or a punishing message, always a warning to others, while any escape from such threat or danger was similarly interpreted as a sign of God's benevolence. Indeed, for some members of today's society all this is still the case. The appropriate response to lightning was a recognition of one's sinfulness, and the appropriate response to escape from its threat was a recognition of the benevolence of deity in warning you when he was capable of punishing you.

It followed that to substitute a scientific explanation for a theological explanation meant a negation of the theological explanation. Two consequences of this were foreseen by believers and theologians. What was judged to be observable evidence of the omniscience, omnipotence, and omnibenevolence of God was removed from that category. Control of behavior by that explanatory validation of what theology judged to be good and bad behavior would thus be both lessened and weakened. A more serious consequence was that if lightning were removed from subsumption by theological explanation, then other such signs could also be removed, and thus the negation of the behavior appropriate to such signs could be extended to all such signs, as indeed it has been for what is now probably the majority of the population, including believing Christians. Moreover, only one category of divine signs consisted of signs of warning. If the attribute of divinity were removed from danger and threat signs, then the attribute of divinity could be removed from all signs of divinity, such as the sun, the perfection of adaptation of plants to soil, and so on. The effect of this disappearance of the category of divine sign could, it was believed—and the belief was correct—mean the disappearance of any response to the word "God" except to categorize it as an example of the more general term "mythology," or pseudo-explanation and pseudo-belief. Even before this negational process was terminated, even worse things, according to the theologians, would happen. If the religious response to certain natural signs, such as lightning, were removed from the culture, then social control would be impossible, for, it was asserted, the only justification and validation for making a distinction between good and bad behavior was the evidence of divine awareness of that difference and of divine sign behavior that supported that distinction. Since, by theological definition, all men inherited original sin, or the proclivity for bad behavior, the removal of theological explanation would mean the disappearance of social control over bad behavior, and the necessary consequence would unavoidably be that all human behavior would be vicious. Statements that no one who did not believe in God is capable of moral behavior were ubiquitous in the nineteenth century, and they are by no means uncommon now. Thus it was reasoned that the spread of scientific explanation of natural signs necessarily entailed the disappearance of the distinction between good and bad behavior with the result that all behavior would be bad.

The argument over lightning rods, then, though to us trivial and absurd, was to the theologically minded quite the contrary. It undoubtedly contributed to what has been called the disappearance of God—

though that event had been announced by Hegel early in the nineteenth century—but also made more room for the development of alternative explanations of social control, a process well under way in the eighteenth century. Moreover, the quarrel was as important to science as it was to theology. The scientific explanation was that lightning was caused by natural phenomena—that is, lightning was a sign of some kind of meteorological change which could be subsumed under explanatory systems for electricity. But "cause" here means merely "a sign of," that is, an instruction that one ought to respond to lightning as one already has responded to other unanticipated events, either by proffering a scientific explanation, rather than a theological one, or by a response of indifference, so long as no damage was done, or by taking active defensive measures against lightning, such as installing a lightning rod on one's house. The scientific mode of verbal response and nonverbal behavioral response was transferred from one category of signs and extended to another. But this meant the negation of the validity of an existing categorization. The assertion was that the attributes of the sign configuration "lightning" are analogically inter- changeable with the attributes of other phenomena already under the control of scientific explanation, such as the contraction of a frog's legs when a current from an electric battery is applied to the nervous system of a decapitated frog. When it is realized that these attributes are themselves verbal, that is, verbal semiotic transformations to non- verbal signs, then it is obvious that the structure of theological explana- tion is analogically categorizable with the structure of scientific expla- nation. Two kinds of rhetoric (i.e., verbal overdetermination governed by procedural rules) known as "science" and "theology" are both subsumed by the more regressive explanatory word, "explanation" itself.

This was not always thought to be the case. First, until about 1840, the word "science" was applied to theological explanation, and the expressions "the science of theology" or "theological science" were culturally conventionalized and validated. Any explanatory rhetoric believed to be held together by a set of culturally validated procedural rules, or logic, was judged to be a science. It is this older response to the word "science" that was and is responsible for categorizing Marx- ism as a science. Marx's claim that his theories were scientific was under the cultural control of this use of the word. In the 1840s the use of the word was limited in England and the United States to approximately its modern sense that no explanation can be justly called scientific unless it is modifiable by and confirmed by the kind of nonverbal behavior called "experimental." Second, it was believed that the task of science was to discover the laws of the universe, that is, the observable world of nature. What survived from theology and from the older meaning of "science" was the attribute of finality, or permanent stability of explanation. Thus, by metaphor the appropriate response to a law (a configuration of words that must be obeyed by human beings) was extended to a law of nature which was no more than a verbal configuration that the universe must obey. Already in the 1870s Charles Darwin was writing that scientific law is only a mental convenience, and in the last decades of the century Ludwig Boltzmann was lecturing in Vienna on "the hypothetical character of all our knowledge"; or, as I would put it, on the verbal character of all explanatory behavior. (The best explanation of anything is after all only an explanation, only verbal behavior.) What Boltzmann's position amounts to is that the attributes of scientific explanation and mythological (theological) explanation are such that the analogical similarities undermine the legal metaphor for scientific explanation and therefore undermine the finality or permanent stability of scientific explanation. Hence, "mythology" and "science" are not negations of each other. Rather, when an explanation is invalidated, it is relegated to the category of mythology, but it does not follow that it was not an explanation to begin with.

To understand more fully this explanatory identity of mythology and science, it is useful to explore the character of mythology itself. An example may be found in, at first glance, an unlikely source, Plato's Theory of Ideas. Plato observed that the attributes of an idea (that is, a categorial term, since all terms are categorial) did not correspond to the attributes of any configuration which the idea subsumed. It followed, he concluded, that the ideas of the mind were not derived from the configurations of the phenomenal world but must have another source. Nor could that source be the individual mind itself, since all human beings have the same ideas. The ideas in the mind did not, then, arise directly from interaction with the phenomenal world. The explanatory system available to him was mythology. That is, he asserted, the ideas have a transcendental, or nonnatural, nonhuman, hence divine, origin. Mythology, then, is the negation of the natural. Plato's assertion that only the ideas are real is perfectly sound, if by "real" we understand "that which controls what men do." Hence the "real" is ultimately "divine," for it is not derived from "nature," the world to which men respond by imposing ideas upon it. Hegel was really the first to resolve this problem by proposing that the source of the ideas is the "*Geist*," which is best translated today by the word "culture," in the anthropological sense of that word, and he made an equally important step by proposing that *Geist* is marked by historical modification.

We can complete Plato's acute observations, then, by stating that the "ideas" (categorial terms, phrases, propositions, and discourses) are words and that the use of words is learned behavior, learned from other humans, and that the behavior thus learned changes as it is learned. Mythology, then, is an explanation which recognizes that the source of individual human behavior is the negation of the natural. Mythology is an explanation and validation of behavior thus recognized. As explanation, mythology can even be recognized as a more primitive form of modern cultural anthropology. (That is why cultural anthropologists are so fascinated by mythology—and so perplexed by it. In attempting to understand mythology, they are attempting to understand their own foundations, at once theoretical and historical.)

This recategorization of a scientific explanation into the status of mythology can be seen more clearly by examining an explanation which once had scientific status but has been abandoned by science, that is, removed to the category of mythology. The phlogiston theory and its history shows this process of recategorization very well, a process of changing the response to the word itself and also the response to certain observable phenomena. The complete entry in *Webster's Third* is as follows:

> a theory in 18th-century chemistry disproved by Lavoisier: every combustible substance is a compound of phlogiston and the phenomena of combustion are due to the liberation of phlogiston with the other constituents left as a residue (the *phlogiston theory* thus provided a general explanation of the chemical processes of oxidation and reduction: oxidation was taken to be the liberation of phlogiston, and reduction combination with phlogiston—Linus Pauling).

Lavoisier conducted experiments which involved the extremely careful weighing of substances before and after oxidation and reduction. "He proved that in all cases of combustion there is a combination of oxygen with the substance burned.'' He thus discovered oxygen and founded modern chemistry. He offered a new explanation and a new terminology, and these verbal innovations displaced the old phlogiston theory. What had been accepted as a true explanation suddenly became a pseudo-explanation. Since then, the word ''oxygen'' has come to subsume statements about atoms and molecules. The response to the word ''oxygen'' now excludes certain experimental behaviors, but also prescribes certain others. At an earlier period, however, it merely excluded certain behaviors but prescribed no others. The development of atomic and molecular physics made it possible to respond to the word with innovative experimental behaviors.

The history of science is marked by the frequent occurrence of such words as ''phlogiston,'' words that suddenly become mythological words. Nevertheless, it would be a mistake to conclude that no scientific explanation ought to be culturally validated, as some commentators have too hastily concluded. To accept such a proposition as Boltzmann's ''hypothetical character of all knowledge'' is not to deny that some hypotheses are better than others. It is unquestionable that science has given men much greater control over nature, though even this, as we shall see, requires a serious qualification. This meaning of knowledge, on the other hand, would not be acceptable to old-fashioned theologians and other mythologists. To them the test of knowledge is moral certainty or, to be a little more precise, unhindered explanatory aggression. Clearly the Boltzmannian use of ''knowledge'' is to be interpreted as ''scientific knowledge,'' and it depends upon the explanation that the only valid knowledge is scientific knowledge.

A farmer in an undeveloped country, untouched by modern agricultural methods, scientifically derived, certainly can be said to have a considerable knowledge of what soil and what weather conditions are most productive of certain crops. He certainly can predict verbally the probable outcome of his farming behaviors, and he can predict what events will falsify his predictions, such as too much rain. But is his behavior appropriately to be responded to by the term ''science?'' The word ''science,'' derived from the Latin *scire*, ''to know,'' simply means, if we take into account only its derivation, ''knowing.'' But the phrase ''scientific knowledge'' or ''knowing knowledge'' obviously asserts that there is a special category of knowing behavior which has attributes not be located in other categories, such as knowing how to spell a word correctly or knowing how to play the piano. To decide whether or not our farmer's behavior is to be appropriately named "scientific," we must turn to the history of science.

What happened is simple enough, but its consequences have been tremendous. "Scientific science" (to extend and make quite clear the only apparent redundancy in "scientific knowledge") involves two behaviors, verbal and nonverbal. These are usually known as theory and experiment, but theory, as we have seen, is another word for a complex and deep explanatory regress, while experiment is something that everyone does all the time, when, for example, one sticks a few toes into a lake to see if it is too cold for swimming. By the end of the sixteenth century, explanation had a long and complicated history. European culture had developed an extremely rich and complex explanatory tradition in its study and development of Aristotelian logic and in its effort to reconcile logically two quite different explanatory systems, the Christian and the Platonistic. Furthermore, the attempt to reconcile the Christian and the Platonistic explanations of the world, in spite of the fact that both terminated with the word "God," had created a situation in which the possibility of alternative explanations was always present. Inspired, it would seem, by a minor branch of Platonistic explanation, Copernicus, faced with the impossibility of reconciling the mathematical data about the movement of the planets about the earth, proposed the alternative explanation that they moved about the sun and that the earth itself was a planet, a moving and celestial body the orbit of which around the sun was on the same plane as the already identified planets. The importance of his alternative explanation for the future of science lay in his decision to propose an alternative explanation because of observations. That on the old system prediction of planetary motion was highly unreliable and that on the new system it was infinitely more reliable was less important than the linking of a prediction to an explanation and the derivation of subsumed propositions from that theory—propositions which in turn made it possible to make predictions. The result was the decisions of Galileo and Bacon that truth-value should not be assigned to a proposition if it was logically coherent with the propositions from which it was derived—but if and only if the proposition directly (or through intermediary subsumed propositions) permitted a prediction of the consequences of nonverbal behavior. The epistemological explanation and justification for this was a simple empiricism, that is, that nonverbal behavior and the configurations manipulated by that behavior and the configurations that issued from that manipulation dictated nonverbal and verbal responses. (Or, that the meaning of such signs was immanent. Likewise, the original validation for the construction of explanation was logic, which again depended upon the assumption that the relation between the various levels of explanatory regression was immanent.) In the whole sweep of science, from the observed configuration to the termination of the explanation, it was assumed—for a long time without serious questioning—that all the levels of regression from observed configuration to explanatory determination were necessarily, determinedly, and immanently related—from the categorization of the configuration as sign to the innovation of a new response to that sign, to the construction of innovative nonverbal signs (i.e., the total experimental behavior itself), to the terminology which was the verbal response to the final stage of nonverbal or experimental behavior, through the various levels of explanatory subsumption, to the final goal of explanatory termination.

What had happened was simple enough. The age-old tradition of experimental manipulation of observables for the sake of prediction was linked firmly with the very ancient tradition of explanatory constructions. That linking was the behavioral innovation which marked the emergence of scientific science, or scientific knowledge, or, simply, science, as the word is used today. For fewer than three centuries this magnificent pattern of verbal and nonverbal behaviors remained almost unchallenged, though a few philosophers here and there had their doubts. It took a Boltzmann and his pupils to blow it up, though for most practicing scientists today it is a behavioral structure that has not been disturbed. They do not know what has happened to it. (We have already seen in the phlogiston theory what can happen to scientific explanations; they can be metamorphosed into mythologies.) The notion of scientific proof has evaporated, at least for sophisticated scientists, few as they are. The notion of the crucial experiment, the experiment that would prove a theory incontrovertibly, has likewise been abandoned. The distinctions among scientific law, theory, and hypothesis have been collapsed into hypotheses, and the analogical similarity of scientific explanation to all explanation has been revealed. But perhaps the most important intellectual consequence of modern science is not to show how, as was once thought, a scientific theory is proved, but how it is undermined. Karl Popper maintains that no theory can be proved; it can only be disproved. But I do not believe this to be the case. The history of science shows not so much that theories are disproved but, rather, that they are abandoned. The phlogiston theory was not disproved; it was abandoned in favor of an alternative theory, the oxygen theory.

Lavoisier proposed an alternative response to the phenomena of combustion, of oxidation and reduction, but he proposed both a non-verbal response and a verbal response. It was his nonverbal response that was crucial. As we have seen, he weighed substances before and after combustion with extreme care. What Lavoisier did, once he decided that the phlogiston theory was incapable of successfully subsuming the observables, was to undermine the theory by producing new data which the theory was even more inadequate at subsuming. And this is the classic behavioral paradigm of science.

It is necessary to ask, therefore, what aspect of human behavior makes such a paradigm possible. It is the human capacity to innovate responses to observables for which conventionalized and validated responses already exist. And that in turn is made possible by the brain's capacity to produce nonverbal random responses to nonverbal signs.

We do not have any exact account of what Lavoisier did in his experiments, but we can observe scientists today when they find themselves in the same situation, a situation in which the conventionalized nonverbal behavioral responses to a scientific theory do not produce the results predicted by the sentence or sentences at the extreme lower pole of the explanatory polarity. They scratch their heads; they pull their beards (if they have beards); they try various mathematical formulas on their blackboards; they put together scientific instruments in novel ways, hoping that something will come of it. They engage, in short, in random behavior until they are able to respond to the signs they are manipulating in such a way that the results of their manipulation seem promising. And the judgment that the results are promising is "intuitive," as all linking of separate behaviors is "intuitive," that is, inexplicable, unpredictable, and uncontrollable by conventionalized behaviors, verbal or nonverbal. In short, they randomize their behavior, and the key to that randomization is again scientific instruments.

SCIENCE, THE MODEL FOR "KNOWING"

Any scientific experiment or collection of observables invariably results in the generation of more data than the scientist actually uses. All
perception is selective, and the interest of modifying a theory or constructing a new one controls, for the scientist, that very perceptual
process, as can be seen in the neglect of the phenomenon of radiation
until the Curies responded to it innovatively. Radiation was the consequence of certain experiments, but before the Curies it had not been
responded to, since the interest behind the experiment had no place for
that observable. Likewise, in the nineteenth century more paleontological material was collected than paleontologists have yet taken account
of, explained, or responded to. Further, an observable which is the
consequence of a scientific experiment is one that is predicted; the
observable is a sign; hence, other responses are possible which are in
fact not engaged in. For these reasons it follows that even if a scientific
experiment is judged successful, there is invariably a residue of data
which is unresponded to and a range of possible responses which are
not made. Thus, the consequences of any scientific experiment are
invariably in part unpredicted and unpredictable and, therefore, uncontrollable. We currently have several obvious examples of this. The
invention of aerosol cans was a consequence of scientific knowledge,
but no one engaged in the experiments or the application of the theory
and its commercialization imagined that the use of millions of one kind
of such a can could so damage the ozone belt that a greater amount of
solar radiation would reach the surface of the earth, with the probably
enormous increase in the incidence of cancer. Nor when vinyl was
developed, one of the most remarkable and useful products of science,
did anyone imagine that the manufacture of vinyl would be extremely
deleterious to the health of the workmen who make that plastic.

The whole ecological crisis is the result of the unpredictable and
uncontrollable consequences of scientific experiment, made possible
by scientific instruments. It is the necessary consequence of science's
original assumption that a response to an observable under scientific
control is dictated by the immanent meanings of that observable rather
than the contrary assumption that science, like everything else, depends on the response to a configuration as a sign and therefore on the
selection of one possible response among an indefinably large number
of possible responses. It is not merely true that psychological
laboratories are, as we saw in Chapter I, appropriately categorized with

theaters. It is the case that all scientific laboratories are theaters in that by semiotic transformation they separate a sign from its sign or stimulus field and thus create a new stimulus field, a sign situation to which certain responses or classes of responses have been conventionalized.

An example of all this occurred in the autumn of 1974 with the discovery of the **J** particle. The account in *Newsweek* (Dec. 2, 1974, p. 87) brings out the behavior important from the present point of view.

> The discoveries of the new particle were as fortuitous as many of the great scientific findings of the past. . . . One group . . . detected the particle during a routine experiment. . . . The other team . . . came across the particle quite by accident . . . ; indeed, only when [the leader of the first group] compared notes with the [other group] did they realize they had discovered the same particle and recognize its importance.

"Routine experiment" is an instructive phrase, for it suggests that it was quite possible that the **J** particle, which "splits asunder just 100 billionths of a billionth of a second after it forms," might very possibly have appeared before in other routine experiments, but that no one responded to its presence. Furthermore, although the discovery may be of the highest importance in developing a unified field theory (an explanation in physics which has existed for some time but which no physicist has been able to confirm, that is, use to control his behavior to obtain results he categorizes as predicted), neither group recognized immediately its importance. Significantly, only when the physicists compared notes, only when social support was forthcoming, did they recognize the explanatory potentiality of the discovery. The explanation for that failure probably is the explanatory limbo, close to mythology, in which the unified field theory has existed ever since it was proposed. But the fact that they did recognize that potentiality when they compared notes is equally instructive.

The discovery of the **J** particle is an excellent instance of the fact that scientific instruments produce unanticipated and often neglected data. In this case, however, the instruments and the observable sign producers on the instruments have become so refined that not observing the configuration is much more unlikely than is the case with cruder instruments. This is why physics is usually thought of as the model science. What the experimenters responded to, then, were certain instrumentally produced signs. These signs they responded to at the level of configuration, the first level of sign response and categorization. Initially they could not go beyond that to a categorization of the configuration. They were unable to respond to it, aside from recording it and making notes about it. Only when members of the two teams compared their responses to the mathematical verbal notes were they able to make a categorial response. Once made, however, and the results published, one of the teams in a very short time announced "the discovery" of a second particle similar to the new one. The possibility has arisen of discovering a whole class of particles hitherto unknown. Yet it must always be remembered that "particle" here is metaphorical. What have been discovered are instrumentally produced signs. And the unified field theory has not been confirmed; only the possibility of confirmation has arisen. What has not yet happened is the construction of a regression of subsuming statements up to the very high level of that theory, which will then become, if it happens, a termination to the statements about **J** and other particles.

As I have suggested, what has made this possible is the brain's capacity for randomness of response. Randomness of response is the raw material from which innovative responses are constructed. Physics is now at the point—it was not always so—in which random responses are considerably less likely to occur than they were earlier in its history. And by innovative response is meant a response which is itself recognized as a distinct configuration but only because it can be analogically categorized with already existing response configurations. Thus, the discovery of the **J** particle was possible only because numerous particles had been discovered by physicists since World War II. The behavioral configuration of particle discovery was already well established, as is indicated by the rapidity with which the members of one team discovered another similar particle in such a short time. The instrumentally produced sign was first, then, categorized as the evidence for a hitherto unidentified particle but only because such signs were already categorized as instances of the general category, "particle sign." Both teams did this, but only when a member of each team met and consulted did the innovative response take place; only then were the attributes of each particle sign subsumed into a single category, a new kind of particle, with the possibility that it might provide a link "in the search for a unified field theory."

The category having been established, it was responded to by uttering sentences derived from an available explanatory system. Whether that particular procedural overdetermination was appropriate remains to be seen. In any case this is a splendid example of how an innovating sign response—"a new particle"—is explained by employing an already existent explanation. The structure of the behavioral sequence is identical with that of a medieval theologian who interprets as a direct sign from God the fact that lightning has hit a wicked king. And the analogy between the two is made the more striking by the fact that the link between the categorization and the theory occurred only when members of each team talked to the other. Two medieval theologians observing from different places the lightning strike the wicked king would have at once agreed on how to make an interpretative response to it. In the discovery of the **J** particle we have an instance of cultural convergence. It was not a random event that the two physicists agreed on the interpretation of the independent discoveries, nor is it random that the two discoveries were made almost simultaneously. When they made their discoveries, the two teams were culturally prepared and were obeying culturally conventionalized and validated behavioral instructions; and the team leaders were doing exactly the same thing when they talked and agreed on how to interpret their data. What is evident in this situation is the physicists' interest in limiting and in channeling response which threatened to be an occasion for randomness of response, and equally evident is how their channeling behavior was in turn channeled by their culture.

CONCLUSION

How this channeling takes place is obviously the next step in this inquiry. Here the present inquiry into the bridge between the verbal and the nonverbal may be concluded by frankly recognizing that scientific knowledge, or knowing, is the model for understanding that bridge, and in this example we find the whole process from configuration recognition to terminating explanation in a condition of incompletion and ongoing formation. It is quite possible, indeed, that these experiments may completely undermine the general field theory. Stranger things have happened in science. Currently, however, the terminating field theory is controlling and channeling the behavior of this particular kind of physicist. The example is especially instructive, then, because it shows the reciprocal or dialectical relationship between configurational categorization, the first stage or level of sign response, and the ultimate level, the termination of the explanatory regress. The regress controls the nonverbal behavior, while the nonverbal behavior modifies the regress—for even if the general field theory is not undermined, it will certainly be modified but only if the convergent responses of the physicists in question are socially validated by other physicists as appropriate verbal responses to the experiments in question.

Science, then, is the most complete model of the semiotic hierarchy from configuration to the termination of an explanatory regress. The completeness is indicated by the immense control over nonverbal, nonhumanly produced signs which modern science has developed, but because, as in this instance, unpredictable consequences are made possible by scientific instruments, the residue of scientific discovery may very well destroy us all or destroy civilization as we know it and reduce men again to a simple food-gathering state. This possibility makes it all the more crucial to understand the control of human behavior, i.e., How does behavior control behavior—a question which for some time has been examined with the aid of the directional categories "society" and "culture," categories of the utmost vagueness. To reduce, if possible, that vagueness, and to introduce clarity about these words instead of the current confusion, will be the object of the next chapter.

III

CULTURE AND SOCIAL INSTITUTIONS

THE CULTURE OF HOMO SCIENTIFICUS

For human beings, the world consists of signs, and it is impossible for human beings to consider the world, or themselves, from a meta-semiotic point of view or position. The world is an immense tapestry of innumerable threads, emerging and disappearing in the presentation and evanishment of indefinably innumerable designs, and human beings themselves form some of those same threads and patterns. We are figures in the tapestry we observe, and respond to, and manipulate. The old notion that the world is an illusion is sound, for no sign (configuration) dictates our responses. But it is sound only up to a point, because the physical character of the world limits the range of our responses. We can do lots of things with water, but as yet we have no way to build a skyscraper out of it, though the possibility has its charms; nor can we walk on it without doing something either to ourselves or to the water. Or to use another notion, the world is Idea, our Idea, but it is also Reality, Actuality, Factuality. The mind transcends the world, but then it does not transcend the world. Plato's *demiourgos* did not create the reality he set about ordering; he set about ordering a chaos, a recognition that human behavior works on material that is really there. Or, to put it in somewhat newer terms, the world is object, and man is subject, and the subject is different from the object but, nevertheless, somehow the same.

These various attempts to define our relation to the world are, we must always remember, themselves but words; they are but verbal behavior, and therefore they are fictive and normative. And the ultimate aim of all of them is to tell us how we *ought* to respond to the world: either to free ourselves from maya or illusion (the result of which seems to be the disappearance of that which creates and is victim of maya, man himself); or to find and settle upon the *true* ideas, those that reveal the reality itself; or to find a way of aligning subject and object, so that, in more modern terms, the response is always and invariably appropriate to the sign. Only rarely, as with a Boltzmann or with a Vaihinger, do we find an acceptance of an irresolvable tension between subject and object, and even with them there is thrust to resolve it. Even in post-Boltzmannian science there is a continuous and ongoing effort to settle once for all what a science truly is and what is or is not a true science. But as we have seen, a science is simply the most complete exploitation of the hierarchy of sign response and or- ganization from the mere configuration to the terminating explanation. There is no radical difference between science and any behavioral sequence in which response to the verbal is modified by the nonverbal. Men have always engaged in experiment, just as they have always engaged in explanation. And no known social group, no matter how simple or primitive, is without behavioral sequences in which experi- ment and explanation are placed in dialectical relation one to the other.

Yet Auguste Comte was clearly on the right track when he saw human intellectual history as moving from the mythological and reli- gious stages through the metaphysical and on to the scientific or "positivistic" (as he called it). But his position is unacceptable in its identification of this movement with the movement of human behavior through history, for he was describing not the movement or evolution of the mind but, rather, the evolution or movement of high explanatory regress. It is only the extraordinary success of modern science and the tendency of intellectuals—those whose competencies are in the ma- nipulation of the rhetoric of high explanatory regresses—to identify their activity as the paradigm or true model of thought and the essence of human behavior that led him and others to neglect the obvious point that men have always, lacking any choice in the matter, engaged in experiment. Still, scientific explanation has displaced the mythologi- cal, religious, and metaphysical at high cultural levels; and it has become the regnant explanatory regress, giving men an immense power in the manipulation of signs not produced by humans—what might be called, safely enough now, "natural" signs. Above all, sci- ence, because of its very explanatory sophistication, has made possible the development of alternative responses and innovative responses to these signs. Once an explanation has emerged, it can and does operate independently, or rather human beings can and do manipulate the rhetoric of explanation without reference to nonverbal signs, without placing explanation in a dialectic with natural signs, without modifying it by experiment. Unfortunately, they usually prefer to.

A good modern term for that modification is "feedback," and the principle of science is that no explanation—or theory—is to be accepted unless it is supported by feedback. The first stage of modern science was the belief, carried over from religion and metaphysics (to be Comtean for a moment), that feedback stabilized explanation. We are now—or at least a few scientists are now—in the second stage, in which that belief, itself an explanation, has been modified, so that experimental feedback is conceived of as continuously modifying the theoretical-explanatory structure of science. The aim of the truly modern scientists is not to stabilize explanation but to exploit its inherent instability, an instability that arises from the fact that the meaning of that explanation is not immanent but is a matter of response. This development has made two insights possible: one, that experiment is not something that was suddenly discovered a few hundred years ago and led to the outbreak of modern science but rather that experiment is an attribute of the category "man," that nonexperimenting humanity cannot even be imagined; and two, that if explanatory meaning is not immanent, and since there is agreement and likewise disagreement on any explanatory meaning, the explanation for the agreement must be found elsewhere than in the explanation itself. It must be under social and cultural control. But what are we talking about when we use the terms "society" and "culture"?

From this point of view we can again see that the attempts (referred to above) to decide what kind of behavior is truly scientific, or what kind of explanation (i.e., explanatory behavior) is truly science, are normative attempts; they are attempts to say what science *ought* to be. They are thus remarkably similar to attempts to say what art is, attempts which on examination turn out to be efforts to establish, once and for all, what art *ought* to be. A study of the history of aesthetics shows that theories of aesthetics are invariably based upon what is accepted as art by those whose high explanatory competence is in the rhetoric of talking about art. Moreover, theories of aesthetics always select as their examples a current distinction between good art and bad art and also a distinction between art and nonart, and the two distinctions are commonly confused, one with the other. The consequence is that theories of aesthetics are always explanatory justifications for what is currently accepted as both art and good art. Moreover, the ultimate explanatory justification for those theories is invariably derived from an explanatory regress that has not been built by responses to art at all. Rather it has been built by responses to "nature," or by responses to religion, or (most generally) by responses to the manipulation of the rhetorics of explanation which are manipulated without reference to "natural" signs but only with reference to already existent verbal signs, particularly those of high explanatory verbalizations. In short, the ultimate justifications for theories of aesthetics are under the control of high explanatory regressions which have nothing to do with art. Exactly the same processes of rhetorical manipulation may be found in contemporary discussions of what a science really is and what really is a science. The appeal of such speculations is not to an observation of what scientists actually do, in the whole range of their activity as scientists, but rather to explanatory utterances not derived from any such observation. Science, in short, has not been scientifically investigated but only verbally responded to and, hence, under the control of explanations which precede in time those responses. Were science really investigated in terms of human behavior, it would become at once obvious what was pointed out above—that it is only an elaboration, though an immense elaboration, of what is virtually a defining attribute of human behavior, the linking by control and feedback of experiment and explanation. The reason for this is that sign response is a fundamental attribute of human behavior, though not a defining attribute, since at least some animals engage in semiotic behavior— and some of their sign behavior can be incorporated in human sign behavior—and that explanatory response *is* a defining attribute, made possible only by the subsumptive powers of language.

It follows that the linking of behavior-modification-by-response-to-nonverbal-signs to behavior-modification-by-verbal-explanatory-signs is itself a defining attribute of the category "man." Man is inadequately defined as the tool-using animal, or even as the language-using animal, but most adequately defined as the scientific animal. Such a definition brings out most clearly that the effort of theorists of science, in any case a normative effort since it is a verbal effort, is an effort to separate scientific behavior from all other behavior. But its defining attribute is more accurately understood as a defining attribute of man. Hence, the effort to ascribe to science a unique place in human effort is no more than a normative effort. It is an effort to control what ought to be called scientific; it is an effort to stabilize the use of the term, to make the idea correspond to the reality, to make the subject isomorphic with the object. Today to call something or some behavior "scientific" is to confer very high status, very great value. The effort to create stable theories of science, therefore, is obviously an effort to maintain that high status by limiting severely its application.

This consideration leads to a very odd conclusion. For some time there has been a branch of philosophy known as Philosophy of Science. And a couple of decades ago it was fashionable among radical and innovative philosophers (the Logical Positivists) to insist that the only philosophy possible is the Philosophy of Science, all other philosophies being merely metaphysics, i.e. bad poetry—a statement that indicates not the faintest comprehension of poetry. However, if men have always engaged in experiment and explanation and linked the two, and if science is merely the most elaborate and sophisticated mode of this behavior, then on the one hand it is true that the only philosophy is the Philosophy of Science, but it also follows on the other hand that there is no such category as "science." That is, there is no such conjunctive category as science, a special class of behaviors marked by attributes found in no other class of behaviors. Science is not a conjunctive category but a disjunctive category, and Philosophy of Science is revealed as a typical normative effort on the part of philosophers to control behavior at the highest possible explanatory level. As we shall see, Philosophy of Science is an ideology; it is not in itself scientific, for it does not link experiment and explanation.

If instead of simply responding as best we can to that abstract, hypostatized, and highly regressive word "science," we invent and use another word, "sciencing," we can use that latter term as a direction for observing what scientists actually do, and this is particularly true if we look at the scientific establishment. As an example, consider Marschack's contribution to paleontology. Any number of paleontologists had observed those markings on bones which he became curious about and started studying, but no establishment paleontologists became sufficiently curious to try to innovate a response to them. Why not? The science of paleontology is maintained the way any other science is, by publication and by conferences and by more intimate interaction in laboratories and studies, by informal or corridor talk at meetings, by letters, by dissemination of elaborate verbal responses to selected individuals before publication. It is true, as the case of the discovery of the J particle shows, that such interaction can result

in innovative responses, but it is equally true—and indeed far truer—
that most of the verbal behavior is a repetition of "what is already
known"—that is, exemplary sentences and the fragments of theory
that explain those sentences. Sciencing in any scientific field is a social
institution, and the bulk of energy output in the behavior controlled by
any social institution is spent in maintaining that social institution so
that that behavior can be controlled. And this requires a continuous
reiteration of the rhetoric employed in that institution. Any modification of that rhetoric requires the displacement or abandonment of some
segment of that rhetoric, and it is never possible to predict exactly how
much of that rhetoric may be eventually displaced, abandoned, turned
into mythology. Since meaning (even scientific meaning) is not immanent, a continuous repetition of meanings is the strategy by which the
rhetoric and the institution are preserved and kept viable. Any innnova-
tion which threatens that rhetoric in fact threatens the institution and
threatens the validity of its behavioral processes, i.e., the frequent
interaction and reiteration of the institution's rhetoric.

The principle of behavior involved here becomes clear if we take a
very simple social institution, one that ordinarily involves almost no
verbal behavior, an urban bus. The driver and the passengers comprise
a temporary institution, one in which, moreover, the personnel is constantly changing as passengers get off and on. The behavioral protocols
or rules of bus behavior are simple. The basic requirement is that the
passengers do not talk to each other or at the most exchange a few
commonplaces about the weather or shopping. Occasionally temporary
friendships are struck up, and one can talk, to be sure, to a companion.
But the verbal behavior is always in a low tone. If someone suddenly
starts talking to himself in a very loud tone, the rest of the passengers
are thrown into near panic. First of all, since the oddball has violated
one social protocol, who knows what other protocols of public behavior he may violate? But that is not all. Unable to predict the
oddball's behavior, the passengers are unable to predict their own
behavior. The protocol having been violated, they do not know how to
respond to the innovative behavior. Since the protocol is well established, the oddball's behavior is immediately judged as deviant. The
consequence is that the aggressive state of the passengers is suddenly
altered from one of reasonable comfort to one of fairly high anxiety,
the result of impedance. And that anxiety is allayed only if the oddball
violates no other behavioral protocols, or, to put it differently, only if
he supports the rest of the bus protocols by controlling his behavior

according to their demands. Innovative behavior is tolerable (even if it is judged deviant, i.e., neither to be justified nor validated) if it is accompanied by a reiteration of the behavior (whether verbal, nonverbal, or both) which maintains the institution to which that behavior is pertinent.

If we apply this principle to the verbal tapestry of sciencing and of humanistic scholarship as well, several strategies are visible by which sciencing institutions are maintained. When an editor of a scientific journal or a scientific publishing house receives a manuscript submitted for publication, the first test he applies is whether or not the paper has been presented in the approved and highly standardized structure of such papers. The second test is to decide whether or not the paper shows a mastery or at least a competence in the rhetoric of that science, a matter of procedural overdetermination. And the third important test is whether or not the paper has sufficient citations and includes a bibliography for those citations. For scholarly papers in the humanities the citation protocol is different. Footnotes are demanded, rather than citations within the text. I know of more than one instance in which otherwise excellent scholarly papers were rejected because there were no (or not enough) footnotes; and more than once the text had to be needlessly and even pointlessly altered in order to provide an excuse and an occasion for adding footnotes. As with the oddball on the bus, the deviance is acceptable if the rest of the protocol is scrupulously obeyed. Moreover, to obey a behavioral protocol is to produce a sign that normatively gives instructions for obeying it. Hence, in scientific and scholarly papers citations introduce and direct attention to reiterations of the discipline's rhetoric. They are signs that give instructions for obeying the discipline's protocols, both in themselves and in what they refer to. The paper is acceptable only if, in spite of innovation or deviance, there are plentiful signs that it really does not disturb the patterns of that discipline's verbal tapestry. And such reiteration goes by the name of "proof." Only after these tests of reiterative over-determination have been passed is the editor willing to consider whether or not the innovative proposition in the paper—there is rarely more than one—should be called "creative" or "deviant," whether it should be validated or invalidated. Though he does not have the power of final validation, he has the power of initial invalidation.

From the opening of this chapter there is one reiterated word which the reader can scarcely have missed, and that word is "control." In sciencing and in scholaring and in bus riding we have seen instances of

social institutions (interlocking behavioral patterns which control behavior) and the behavioral means by which such institutions are maintained: the reiteration of the verbal and nonverbal semiotic rhetoric of
those institutions themselves. With these as examples it is now necessary to look more closely at the behavior involved, to discover its basic
units, its interactional organization, and its strategies for maintenance.

THE BRAIN'S RANDOMNESS

Two great questions have hung about the examination of human behavior for over a hundred years: What is culture? and What is society?
What distinction can be made between the two, if any? And which is
prior? From what has been proposed so far it seems reasonable to
conclude that the basic unit of human behavior is sign response, *not* the
individual organism. Sign response is not genetically transmitted, and
therefore it must be learned, and it follows that it must be taught.
Teaching, whether of arithmetic or of philosophy, uses various
strategies to narrow the response of the student to a given sign so that
he responds in a way that is culturally and socially judged, at the time
of the teaching behavior, to be appropriate. What that phrase "culturally and socially judged" conceals must for the moment be postponed,
though in that lies the crux of the matter. How does the teacher *know*
that the desired response is indeed currently judged to be appropriate?
Putting that deadly question aside, it may further be observed that in
the early stage of the teaching process the answers of the learner tend to
be judged inappropriate. But this leads to two further observations.
One, the inappropriate answers tend to be unpredictable—almost anything. That is, they are random. Two, insofar as the student gives any
answer, he is behaving appropriately, for the requirements of the first
stage of learning anything, merely giving an answer (whether verbally
or nonverbally) is the most important matter. Or it would be, were it
not for an even more important condition of teaching: that is, whether
the student answers or not, the first requirement is that he remain in the
teaching situation. In the first grades, simply to sit still, no matter what
happens, is the first thing the student must learn, if he has not learned it
in his home. If he is an adult and is trying to learn to play tennis, he can
scarcely learn if in a fit of petulance he leaves the court and his teacher.
In that adult situation he himself imposes upon himself the requirement
of remaining in a situation in which for the time being he is failing.
And failure is an essential mode of behavior in any learning process. In

the childish situation that requirement of merely remaining is imposed externally; and if the child violates it, he is *forced* to remain, and punishment of some sort may be administered. In the adult situation of learning tennis the punishment is either the refusal of the teacher to give further instruction or the sacrifice of the money which is being paid to him. In either case the punishment, though self-administered, is the form of deprivation, either instructional or instructional and economic. And what punishment and deprivation have in common is the infliction of pain, either immediate or postponed—that is, threatened or predicted within an undefined range of probability. Thus, at the very root of the teaching situation lies the imposition of force, the first use of which is to keep the student in the learning situation. This needs to be looked at more closely.

The basic unit of human behavior is the sign response, but the meaning of a sign is not immanent in the sign: it does not dictate the response. This is what an analysis of the teaching situation makes very clear. What the teacher does is to get the student to produce responses, any responses; the teacher then selects one response, that judged appropriate, by employing various strategies, which can be reduced to two, force and seduction (as we have seen in Chapter I, in the consideration of how behavior is altered by pain and bribery). The raw material of learning, then, is the production of random responses, a principle we have already seen in considering how the child learns to grasp. But it has also been suggested in Chapter II that in scientific activity, the same principle is to be observed—that is, the randomization of behavior as the necessary precondition for scientific innovation. Thus, randomness of responses is not only the precondition for undermining complex explanatory behavior, but it is also the precondition for learning anything, and the two situations are identical; the scientist, by randomizing his behavior, creates the conditions necessary for his learning a new response which he judges to be an appropriate one. He is his own teacher. The interactional process between teacher and student and between the scientist and himself is identical in both cases. The fact that in the one case two people are involved and in the other but one person is unimportant or, rather, very important: the relation between teacher and student is dyadic situation and so is the relation between the scientist and himself. He may be a biological individual, but in learning innovative sign behavior, he is a semiotic dyad. For it must be remembered that though the student may be learning a behavior well established in his culture and his society, he is learning a behavior that is innovative to him. The identity of the two situations is further brought out if we consider that the scientist dyad also uses force and seduction. He makes himself continue his activity until he arrives at a promising result, and having done so, he rewards himself by self-praise. And he uses seduction upon himself. If he keeps at his task, he can have a martini at the end of his working day, and that seductive reward is kept before him by his own covert behavior. Moreover, since man is best understood as *homo scientificus*, the same factors may be observed in all learning situations: the response to be learned is innovative to the human organism engaged in the learning activity; and the factors that are the precondition of the learning are the production of response, the production of random response, and the selection or validation of one of those random responses.

I propose, then, that the genetically transmitted behavior that makes semiotic behavior possible is the brain's capacity to produce random responses. This is the fundamental condition of human behavior. For exemplificatory purposes this phenomenon may be considered from several points of view. In an earlier book, *Art and Pornography*, I proposed that to the degree to which any behavior pattern is poorly transmitted, to that degree there will be a spread of deviancy from the culturally defined norm. What I was specifically concerned with then was sexual deviancy. In our society the transmission to the young of validated patterns of sexual behavior is particularly sloppy, and indeed the effort to use the schools for transmitting it more successfully is constantly resisted, with the odd result that an almost unbelievable portion of pregnant teenagers do not know how the pregnancy came about. If premarital teenage pregnancy is to be categorized as a deviancy (as it certainly is, no matter what its incidence), here is a particularly obvious example of what I have called the "delta effect": the spread of deviancy. To illustrate this point further, I pointed out that college teaching, particularly in the humanities, is not something in itself that is ever taught. Indeed, almost nothing is actually known about it. The consequence is an enormous spread, or delta, of individual teaching styles. Condemned to innovate, the individual has no way of determining his teaching behavior. Another example may be found in the current situation of the arts at the high cultural level. The traditional conception of art, that is, the traditional directions for how to be an artist and what an artist ought to do, have been undermined for complex cultural reasons. The consequence is an enormous delta of what is now called art. A work of art has become anything that a self-designated artist designates as a work of art. The most amusing result is the attempt of art critics to give great significance to objects to which it is extremely difficult to respond to in any way, except possibly boredom. (The brilliant Andy Warhol has recognized this situation better than anyone.)

Another way of looking at the problem of randomness of response is from the point of view of evolutionary theory (admittedly unsatisfactory but still the best explanation we have for the phenomenon of the nonexistence of human remains and artifacts below certain geological levels). If we arrange existing animals along a continuum of increasingly complex nervous-system and brain organization, what is apparent is the increasing capacity for randomness of behavior as we move along the continuum from the poorest to the richest nervous systems and brains. As I suggested in Chapter II, from the point of view of evolutionary theory, this increasing randomness has a survival value. Within a given species the behavior of individuals varies along a continuum from behavior which varies little from the genetically transmitted behavior to individuals whose behavior varies considerably. The latter tend to be less well integrated in the interactional behavior of the species; they are fringe individuals. The theory of adaptation suggests that when the situation to which a species is highly adapted undergoes severe change, the best-adapted individuals are precisely those which do not survive and produce offspring, while the fringe individuals, those least well adapted, are those of which *some* can survive and produce offspring in the changed situation. Thus the brain's potentiality for the production of random responses is evolutionarily selected for survival. As evolutionary development increases and more complex organisms come into existence, a result of that randomness, the brain's potentiality for randomness accumulates and increases with each emerging species.

Such an explanation must, of course, be considered speculative and is presented here primarily for exemplificatory purposes, indeed to illustrate how an explanation is constructed from a subsuming theory which did not at one time take into consideration that which is being explained. Still, it is worth pointing out that modern evolutionary theory, neo-Darwinism, is highly statistical and that Darwin himself, though somewhat dimly, made it reasonably clear that accident, or

chance, or randomness played a very important part in what he originally called the origin of species (meaning their emergence from already existing species—a term that is more successful in indicating
what Darwin's accomplishment was than the term "evolution," which
he at first did not use).

The brain's capacity to produce random responses, then, is the
termination of the explanatory construct of human behavior I am pro-
posing. That randomness is the cause (using "cause" in its usual subsumptive way) of the indetermination in human behavior of response to
any given stimulus and the cause, indeed, of the impossibility of locating any stimulus. And that in turn, subsumes, or is the "cause" of, the
delta effect. Obviously, however, the vast bulk of human behavior is
not random. Or, more precisely, it is random within tolerable limits,
limits tolerable for successful interaction. The problem that emerges is
how human behavior is channeled.

THE CHANNELING OF RESPONSE

The beginnings of the channeling of response are observable in the
learning-teaching situation, and this will also give us a clue as to how a
response is maintained. It is not sufficient, obviously, simply to assert
that the memory maintains response. For one thing, there is no such
entity or faculty as the memory; there is only "remembering," and the
attempt to model brain memory on the structure of the computer, and
hence to assert that the brain has a memory bank, has been misleading.
To be sure, the stimulation by an electrode of a carefully limited
segment of the brain will produce a covert image or memory which the
individual with that brain may not have produced overtly for many
years. However, there is no reason to think that the brain has stored
every stimulus it has ever perceived, for there is no way to discover
whether it has or not. To do so there would have to be a record of all
the stimuli an individual brain has received in the course of its existence, and that is obviously impossible. Let us assume that all
stimuli are stored, to continue that metaphor, but that only some are
accessible. As to what makes them accessible, what brings them out of
storage, the electrode probings make one thing reasonably clear: the
brain produces a remembering when it receives a stimulus. On the
other hand, it does not always produce the remembering response
which is demanded. The teaching situation makes it clear that only the
constant reiteration of a demand in a particular setting can produce the

demanded response at the beginning of a learning process. Further, if the demand is not continually made, the probabilities of producing the demanded behavior are lessened. The memory, psychologists tell us, fades; and indeed it does. After twenty years of not reading a language which one has spent some years in learning, one is in a way worse off than after only a year or two of study. Languages are generally taught in a certain order, but after a good many years what one has learned first is mixed up with idiomatic subtleties one has learned much later. Assuming there is an advantage to the order in which a language is learned—a somewhat dubious proposition—when one turns to it again, that advantage is lost. What one can remember has been affected by the randomness of remembering, the randomness which is so characteristic of all the brain's activities. Only the constant use of a language makes it possible to sustain the behavioral responses appropriate to reading that language.

Remembering is unreliable, then, and any explanation of the channeling of behavior, maintaining it through long periods of time, cannot be subsumed by the explanatory term "remembering." Some other factor must be at work. What that factor really is has been suggested by the reiteration which is necessary to establish a response. As an example, consider so simple and commonplace a sign as a stop sign at an intersection of two streets. Stop signs have multiplied enormously as automobiles have multiplied. When automobiles first came into sufficient use to start bumping into each other, it became obvious to most drivers—not all—that if they entered a main street from a street of lesser importance, it would be wise to stop, or at least to slow down. Now if the memory were reliable, it would be quite sufficient to learn that it is legally required to stop at such intersections. But, clearly, stop signs have multiplied at least as rapidly as automobiles and probably, one suspects, much faster. The driving public must continuously be reminded to stop. Moreover, once the pattern of putting up stop signs at such intersections became common, a new problem arose. What should one do at an intersection in which it is not immediately apparent that only one street is the main street, not to speak of intersections in which both streets are lightly traveled, but traveled enough to make right of way at intersections problematic? Continuous instructions having been given for one kind of intersection, they became increasingly necessary at all intersections, for such instructions became expected. Moreover, even such constant instructions are not sufficient. It is also necessary to have random policing, to arrest people unpredictably for going through stop signs. Moreover, the arrest and giving the ticket have behind them the threat of force, deprivation of resources in the form of a fine and, if the fine is not paid, imprisonment.

Further, another lesson may be derived from this example. If one encounters a stop sign on an open highway, deep in the countryside, with no intersection visible and no possibility of a hill or trees or bushes concealing an intersection, what should one do? What is the appropriate response? Thus, the stop sign is not an isolated sign but, like all signs, is part of a situation. And we see the same phenomenon as that of the learning-teaching situation in the classroom. Such a stop sign in its odd situation presents two conflicting sets of instructions. The resultant behavior would be random: some drivers would stop, some would slow down, some would continue. In the first two response circumstances if another car were close behind, the probabilities for a collision would be high.

This same principle of conflicting responses can be understood clearly by examining another traffic situation. In the 1930s an attempt was made to establish a special rule for traveling on North Broad Street in Philadelphia. During the morning and evening rush hours the rule was that instead of stopping for a yellow light, which was delayed, one should continue. In spite of the fact that a sign presenting verbal instructions to this effect was placed on a traffic island at every intersection, the plan, designed to speed up traffic during rush hours, was a total failure. Everywhere elsc in Philadelphia, and in the entire country, one was required legally to stop if the light turned yellow before one entered the intersection. Only on North Broad Street and only during these hours was that requirement different. The attempt required two entirely different responses to be made to the same sign. The requirement to stop was overwhelmingly more frequent than the requirement to continue. The success of the plan required an absolute reliability of memory, since the instructional signs could not always be seen if the traffic were heavy and one were in the wrong lane; and it depended upon every driver's remembering to look for and obey all special instructional signs. The result, of course, was an immense slowing down of traffic because of the frequency of rear-end collisions, that is, of random or unpredicted and unpredictable responses.

These three examples show *fairly successful, totally unsuccessful, and predominantly unsuccessful* ways of channeling behavior. The first lesson to be drawn is the explanation for channeling. As the frequency of accidents in all three examples indicates (a frequency that increases as one moves from the comparatively successful to the totally unsuccessful), the adaptational necessity for channeling behavior is smoothness, or predictability, of interaction among organisms. This can be even more clearly grasped if one looks down on the floor of a railway terminal, such as New York's Grand Central, during the busiest times of the day. One wonders why everybody does not end up in a struggling mass in the middle of the floor. What is actually happening is that each individual is constantly making a semiotic interpretation of the probable movements of the individuals whose paths he might cross. Some collisions, of course, do take place, but on the whole those interpretations of "intention" are reliable. Smoothness of interaction depends upon the continuous presentation of signs in specific situations, for the appropriateness of the response depends not only on the principal sign but also on the subordinate signs to be observed in that situation.

This leads to the second lesson: since remembering is unreliable, since it is the consequence of the brain's capacity to produce random responses, and of the fact that it will produce random responses if left to itself, learned behavior can be maintained and made reliable only by the constant reiteration of instructions for behavior.

To this principle I shall give the name "cultural redundancy."

POLICING

But redundancy alone is not sufficient. The third lesson, policing—that is, force—is the ultimate sanction for maintaining response behavior. And to be effective, it must be unpredictable. Economic deprivation, imprisonment, the infliction of pain, and killing are the ultimate sanctions for the validation of any semiotic link between sign and meaning, and obviously the validation for the first three is to be found in the fourth. The infliction of death is the behavioral strategy for sustaining any such validation. It is a shibboleth of liberal thinking that no man should be executed for an opinion, but in fact no man is ever executed or murdered for any other reason. The popularity of murder, especially in this country, is sufficient evidence. Husbands and wives kill each other because of their mates' responses to the semiotic redundancy systems of the validated marriage situation, responses which they judge to be violations of marriage. Men kill for money because money in sufficiently large amounts confers status; that is, it validates the individual's opinion that his existence has value. "I am" is at once the most fictive and the most normative of statements. In most cases suicide is not dissimilar, for the self-directions leading to suicide are frequently assertions that others will be "sorry when I am gone"; that is, they will, the suicide believes, recognize that "I am valuable." Descartes' famous statement, "I think, therefore I am," can be appropriately translated into, "This organism engages in covert semiotic behavior, therefore I exist as a metaphysical entity." It is a transparent nonsequitur, intuitively controlled by the cultural redundancy of the value of individuals and disguised by logic, as logic always disguises intuitive movements from one utterance, or behavioral sequence, to the next. When men kill for food, their behavior is controlled by the opinion that life is worth living—their lives in particular. All religions can be appropriately interpreted as cultural redundancies that life is worth the trouble it takes to live it. The constant reiteration in Western culture, a reiteration ordinarily initiated for the individual when he is of very tender age, that "Christ died for all men," is a cultural redundancy that asserts that the individual ought to ascribe value to himself and ought to maintain the opinion that his life is worth living. Consequently, suicide is accounted a sin, though in other cultures suicide is the ultimate method, validated by the culture and maintained by cultural redundancy, of asserting your own value and the value of existence. Nevertheless, even in the West at times of wars and revolutions the opinion that the individual life is valuable is abandoned for some other opinion—that all men are brothers, for instance, an opinion validated by massive killings of those same brothers. Considering the fact that at least in our society most murders are intrafamilial, the metaphor of the brotherhood of all men is not ill-chosen nor inappropriate. Sartre said that a man lives in a world dominated by the most murderous of all species, man; and the explanation and justification for his remark (though it is not true) is to be found in the conventionality of the link between sign and meaning, between semiotic stimulus and response.

Sartre exaggerates, though, because clearly there is far less killing than there might be. Though it is the case that the only ultimate way to get rid of an opinion that you wish to invalidate is to kill everybody who holds it, it is equally the case that only at times of severe crisis is that ultimate sanction resorted to—at times when the terminations of two explanatory regresses cannot be subsumed under a more regressive termination. The Chinese cultural revolution of a few years ago is a case in point. At the very highest level of Chinese government there was a conflict between those redundancies explained and justified by the terminating word "Confucius" and those explained and justified by the terminating word "Marx." More regressive explanatory terminations were culturally available for both words, but these were the most widely used explanatory terminations. Mao was of the opinion that Chinese society, in spite of the efforts of himself and his immediate staff and followers, was not moving in the direction dictated by "Marx" or at least not moving fast enough. That he was quite right is indicated by the fact that a primary way of spreading "Marxist" values was through the famous Little Red Book. For thousands of years the dominating redundancy system of Chinese culture had been Confucian slogans; and every attempt was made to replace these with Maoist slogans. Chinese society and culture were extraordinary stable, for the principal instruction of the Confucian slogans had been the maintenance of social stability at all costs. That instruction was maintained by the other main redundancy system of Chinese culture, Taoism, the instruction to maintain a stability of aggressive relation between the individual and the "natural" world. That remarkable Chinese stability was the dominating hindrance to the innovating instructions brought into the culture by Mao. To combat the Confucian redundancy, therefore, its same rhetorical form had to be used, the constantly reiterated slogan. However, the introduction of the innovating slogans could only be accomplished by the use of force; so China was swept by extraordinary turmoil. No one knows how many people were killed. And at the same time there was a wholesale destruction of redundancies linked to those Confucian slogans and likewise responsible for maintaining Confucian social stability: the nonverbal redundancies linked to the Confucian slogans, such as statues, pictures, other works of art, and books, not so much for what was printed in them but for their simple existence as redundancy signs. Precisely the same thing happened in Florence when Savonarola dedicated the city to Christ and persuaded the citizens to burn pictures, statues, books, and other objects of human vanity, all elements of the redundancy systems which sustained the secular values Savonarola wished to displace. But when he failed, he was killed for his own opinions.

These episodes indicate the links between economic deprivation, imprisonment, torture, and killing—for all four were used by the followers of both Mao and Savonarola, as well as by the leaders of the

American, French, Russian, and Hitlerian revolutions—and the redundancy systems of verbal validational explanations and their nonverbal exemplifications. Now that things have settled down in China, it is obvious that Mao's desired end, a condition of permanent revolution, was not accomplished, nor could it have been. Judging by fairly recent reports, Chinese society is if anything more stable than ever, and the explanation is to be found in what outsiders have called "cultural impoverishment." What is happening in the reopened universities is a displacement of almost all previous explanatory redundancies by Maoist redundancies. Moreover, these redundancies are maintained by what appears to be a policy of rotating all intellectual workers between their intellectual work and work in the fields, alongside the peasants. It is evident that the intellectual worker has no choice in the matter. Refusal is met, and always can be met, with the application of the ultimate sanctions: economic deprivation, imprisonment, torture, and death. Explanatory innovation is, it would seem, maintained only in science and engineering, two behavioral systems that have always been under the control of more regressive validational explanations, a control which it is very easy to enforce. All this is easy enough to understand if we remember that Marxism and Christianity are alike, and like all other religions, in that they maintain the value of the individual life (except for those lives which verbally and nonverbally negate the explanatory and validational redundancies of those systems).

A culture is stable, it appears to follow, to the degree that the ultimate sanctions of physical force are obviated, or postponed, or circumvented. Circumvention, for example, is a commonplace in the manipulation of legal sanctions. The uniform, draconian application of legal sentences, in both meanings of the word, creates a situation in which the ultimate sanctions must be increasingly relied upon, and this in itself leads to instability, since if the ultimate sanctions are ineffective, no other possibilities remain. A special case, or exemplification, of the principle of legal circumvention is bribery, a consequence of an incoherence of redundancy systems, an attribute of all legal systems. Since taxation, for example, involves economic deprivation, and since the taxing power's rhetoric of justification for what is always judged as punitive by some individuals is never completely effective—for no such rhetoric can be, given the capacity of the brain for randomness— every taxation system is particularly open to bribery, and probably all taxation systems are always characterized by some bribery. Hence there is the governmental rhetoric, only partially effective, that the taxation system is immune to bribery, hence also the outcry when it is discovered, as it was with the Nixon administration, that the taxation system is actually being used for punitive purposes, since this merely confirms the opinion of a great many that taxes punish them for something of which they are not guilty, except for being alive. Since a common opinion is that one indeed has no right to be alive, is guilty of being alive (a consequence of the random negation of religious rhetoric that every one has a right to be alive), then a great many people are always ready to judge that any economic deprivation, especially that of taxes, is punitive. The outcry against that punitive interpretation is thus an attempt to negate the opinion that one is guilty of being alive.

SACRIFICE

An interesting example of the hierarchical link between redundancy systems and the ultimate sanctions (themselves redundancy systems) is to be found in the almost universal practice of religious sacrifice. I have suggested that the ultimate purpose of religious redundancy is the validation of individual lives, since for the individual everything depends upon the fictive and normative assertion of his own value. This seems incoherent with religious sacrifice, a case of economic deprivation. But religious centers have as purposes subsumptive to their prime purposes the dissemination of the redundancy systems of normative instructions for behavior. Less technically, they tell people how to be good, how to achieve validation, how to obviate the application of the ultimate sanctions of semiotic behavior. To sacrifice an economic good, then, is to affirm the hierarchical position of those instructions over one's own behavior by limiting one's potentiality for aggression. It is the social dyad's application to himself of an ultimate sanction of the rhetoric of validation. If a man deprives himself of economic resources, he asserts to himself the hierarchical validity of that rhetoric; just as when a man is imprisoned for theft, the governmental power asserts to the thief that the antitheft redundancy systems are not to be violated, but also, it is maintained, and correctly, that the punitive sanction asserts to others that it is to be maintained. Thus, an ultimate sanction not only punishes but also is itself a sign in a redundancy system of the culture. Capital punishment is argued against because it does not discourage people from committing murder, and it is argued for because it does. Both arguments are obviously correct: no redundancy system is or can be completely effective, in part because of the incoherency with each other of various redundancy systems—our culture includes strong redundancies in favor of killing other people— in part because of the always existent actuality of randomness of response (including negation and in part because the incoherence gives rise to randomness). The deterrent effect of capital punishment cannot be known, since it involves a contrafactual conditional; on the other hand, the deterrent effect on most people of traffic policing does limit the amount of speeding. By analogy (all we have to go on) the deterrent effect of capital punishment appears probable. But, of course, no deterrent effect can be completely effective, for the ultimate sanctions do not immediately maintain the link between sign and response but do so only mediately, for these sanctions maintain only the *validation* of that link. And anyone can negate (construct an alternative to) any validation.

Two other examples of sacrifice will show this connection between the ultimate redundancies and the redundancies which they sanction. In a great many cultures a rite of moving from adolescence to adulthood consists of fasting (economic deprivation), self-imposed separation from the social group in a small area or place (imprisonment), and the self-infliction of pain (torture). (Hiawatha performs all of these behavioral patterns.) The consequence of this ritual is an illumination, a conviction of the value of the individual's existence so long as it is subordinate to the validity of the regnant instructional utterances (moral values) of the culture. This is ordinarily interpreted as a divine illumination, even as the God's possession of the individual. Without that illumination or possession it is judged that the ritual has not been successful, and probably rightly so, for such illumination certainly serves to maintain the effectiveness of the nonverbal religious signs in the culture the individual responds to the rest of his life. (This is an instance of the selective use of memory to be found in any learning-teaching situation.) Similarly, self-conversion of the criminal on the way to the scaffold is by no means uncommon, and torture by others not infrequently brings about a lasting reversal of opinion, religious and moral.

In this cluster of ultimate sanctions the separation from the social group is not be underestimated. In virtually any culture the redundancies can be seen to be incoherent or even to have a negative relation one to another. For example, in our culture there are two mutually incoherent and highly frequent instructions: "A man has to depend upon himself," and "A man should be a part of a team." In baseball, as in certain other sports, these two apparent contradictions are subsumed in a redundancy ritual in which the individual controls his behavior alternately by both redundancies and in which the spectator rehearses the aggressive states appropriate to both and responds to the signs which exemplify both redundancies. The separation from the group does something similar, but something which is at the same time very different. By removing himself from the group, a man removes himself from exposure to the incoherencies and contradictions of the group's redundancies. His task, thus isolated, is to produce covert verbal and nonverbal signs which exemplify the dominant or terminally regressive redundancies of his culture and are themselves often enough the terminating words of his culture's validating explanations. Thus, it is a very old practice in Christianity to combine meditation upon a particular saint (a nonverbal sign of a particular moral value or redundancy), with fasting and self-flagellation—self-torture.

A second example, human sacrifice, is more puzzling. The most striking instance of massive human sacrifice is to be found in the indigenous pre-Conquest Meso-American cultures. The Aztecs seem to have carried it out more consistently and on a larger scale than did the Mayas or any of the other cultures. The humans they sacrificed were prisoners of war. What is puzzling about this is that economic self-deprivation characteristic of sacrifice seems to be absent, even though it is easily understood as a redundancy system for, and ultimate validation of, the Aztec validating explanations and the divine images and temples which exemplified those explanations. Aztec warfare, as is the usual case with warfare at that level of cultural development, had as its object the capture of prisoners. Indeed, it seems to be the case that the reason Cortez defeated the Aztecs so easily is that the Aztecs were unable to modify their mode of making war from capturing sacrificial victims to the more highly developed system of defeating the enemy, rendering him helpless against the imposition of cultural demands. Other cultures, however, such as Egypt or those of the ancient Near East, put their captives to work. They made economic use of them. They were used for economic enhancement, not economic deprivation. We can scarcely know when and how the Aztecs began to sacrifice all of their prisoners, but it is significant that in other indigenous Meso-American cultures war captives were used for economic enhancement. From this point of view the Aztecs did indeed use human sacrifice as economic self-deprivation for the purposes of redundant ultimate validation of hierarchically subordinate or subsumed redundancies. (And certainly by the time Cortez arrived, the Aztecs were already in economic difficulties and threatened with economic collapse of their very recently built city of Tenochtitlán because of the rapid depopulation of the valley of Mexico. Cortez or no, the Tenochtitlán cultural center would probably have collapsed anyway. As it was, the Aztecs were threatened by immediate neighbors, such as Cholula, whom they had never defeated and who, quite reasonably, aided Cortez in the destruction of Tenochtitlán. All this is perfectly congruent with and analogous to the medieval theory of the Christian church that the God-given task of the secular arm—the emperiors, kings, princes, and the rest of the feudal establishment—was to be the executioner of those who had transgressed against the validated instructions of the church or who, as heretics, had denied their validity.)

ULTIMATE VERBAL REDUNDANCIES

Below the level of the ultimate sanctions, and different from religious behavior, is another kind of verbal sanctioning, a rhetoric which increases quantitatively as the religious sanctions of lower level redundancy systems quantitavely decrease. These are such terms as "natural" and "reasonable" or "rational," and "logical." Such terms assert that the semiotic link between stimulus field and response depends upon the immanent meaning of the sign and the dictation by that sign of the response, and they are constantly used to terminate arguments about the preferability of alternative meanings and performances. It is not surprising, and it is most instructive, that the rhetoric of philosophers should depend so completely upon the sanction of such terms and why they are both so suspicious of the term "intuitive" and at the same time made so uneasy by it. "Intuition" is a term used to sanction the link between two utterances when "natural" and "rational" and "logical" will not do the trick. Readers who care to look up the article "Intuition" in *The Encyclopaedia of Philosophy* will find it, from this point of view, deliciously comic. To give but a sample: "philosophers have found it puzzling that one can have knowledge, and thus justified belief, without having made oneself aware through the process of inference of any justification for this belief," or, more precisely, without having gone through a conventionally validated sequence of verbal behaviors. What happens behaviorally is that "the process of inference" is itself sanctioned by the logical rules governing inference (not that, of course, there is any universal agreement among professional and sophisticated philosophers on exactly what those rules are or, rather, to bring out what they themselves conceal, what they ought to be). It may be asked what the ultimate sanctions of force are that control the high-level redundancy sanctions of philosophy. And the answer lies in the fact that philosophers grant the honorific term "valid philosophy" only to philosophical discourses that come into existence in a society marked by freedom, that is, a society in which the state does not attempt to establish ultimate control over the vagaries of philosophers. Contemporary philosophers tend to grant that term to Marxist philosophy, though grudgingly, if it is produced in the West, but not if it is produced in Russia, where a violation of the state-validated sanctioning terms for philosophy is punished by what the medieval church called the secular arm—at once policemen, judge, and jury. (Russia is a country notably deficient in redundancies which obviate, postpone, or circumvent the ultimate sanctions of force, except for bribery, and has been for centuries. Communism has not changed Russia one whit, except to impoverish the culture by increasing the coherency of the various redundancies and thus increase that deficiency.)

This situation, moreover, brings out one of the difficulties, one of the paradoxes (the, perhaps, intolerable paradoxes) of hierarchical explanation as an adaptational strategy. One of the most important of cultural activities is the resolution of redundancy incoherences, as in baseball and philosophy, and if terminal sanctioning redundancies cannot be reconciled, a cultural crisis arises; revolution is not infrequently the consequence. As an example, consider the sanctioning redundancies at work in the French Revolution. Put with excessive simplicity, but no greater simple-mindedness than it was often enough put at the time, the traditional explanatory validation was that the production and distribution of goods and services was properly controlled by a social system established by God and currently in existence, but the revolutionary explanation was that the production and distribution of goods and services was properly a product of Nature (always capitalized), but which the tyrannous deceptiveness of the traditional explanation had perverted. Burke, the Englishman, held a middle position: it was a natural product, but it had been developing since the beginning of time (since 4004 B.C., when God, according to Ussher, created the world) so organically (observe the sanctioning metaphor) that to interfere with it would bring about disaster. While it is true that the interference which Burke so dreaded did bring about a great many disasters, it is equally true that most Europeans and Americans live more satisfactory lives as a result of the French Revolution.

But this improvement of the condition of most men in the West cannot be entirely accounted for by the French Revolution—or anything else—and is not really to the point. For the point is the introduction of a redundancy system into the culture but not the complete displacement of the old redundancies. The result is that both continue to exist without a reconciliation of their incoherence. A similar instance may be found in a topic discussed above—the displacement of religious explanation by scientific explanation. But that displacement has affected only some of the individuals in the culture and, indeed, only a small part of the total population. It is, however, a crucial part, for in its control are the more remote regressions of various explanatory systems. At this high level, science has displaced religion, and that displacement affects the lives of those for whom religious and religiously sanctioned redundancies have not been displaced.

These are but two examples of what has happened in the culture of the West in the course of the last four or five hundred years. It has experienced an increasingly rapid rate of increase of introduction of innovating redundancies, not infrequently accompanied by high-level explanatory regresses. More recently this situation, complex enough, has been made more complex by the introduction of redundancy systems from outside of the West, notably from Asia. The present difficulties of the West may arise, then, from exactly the opposite condition that has prevailed so long in Russia. Even before Communism, the redundancy systems of Russia and their validating explanations were unusually simple by Western standards, and that simplicity was intensified by the coming of Communism. Moreover, in the nineteenth century the introduction of Western explanatory systems into so unusually simple a situation of cultural redundancies created incoherences of extraordinary and unavoidable sharpness. Severe cultural crisis was the result, together with an increase of the exploitation of the ultimate sanctions of physical force. The consequence was a series of revolutions and attempted revolutions until, after the particularly abortive revolution of 1905, the revolution managed by Lenin terminated the revolutionary period. (It is instructive that the redundancies of Communism have been to a considerable degree maintained by exactly the same nonverbal redundancy that maintained the redundancies of czarism. The continuous display of religious icons was followed by the equally constant display of political icons, pictures, and statues of Marx, Lenin, and, for a time, Stalin. As in China, the form of maintaining redundancies has not been altered, nor from the present point of view would it be possible to alter it.)

In the West, however, there was an entirely different situation. The incoherence between Christian explanation and neo-Platonist explanation had obtained for a long time, as we have seen, before the scientific revolution. Even before Protestantism there were innumerable sects, each with a differing interpretation of Christianity. There were even a great many ways of being a monk. All of this led to a condition of toleration of explanatory redundancies. The religious crisis which swept the West and resulted in wholesale slaughter and the separation of Protestantism from Catholicism involved the highest levels of explanatory regress, while the corresponding crisis in Russia, that of the Old Believers in the seventeenth century, by no means reached such remote levels of explanation and was in fact contained by the autocracy with relative ease. Unlike Russia, the West had a number of centers (independent governments) for applying ultimate sanctions. Those intellectuals who introduced innovating explanations and their accompanying redundancies could always flee to another country. (The Dutch Republic became the favorite place of refuge.) Furthermore, Protestantism itself split into a variety of sects, in each of which the explanatory incoherence with other sects reached a fairly high regressive level. Though it seems doubtful that the scientific revolution would not have taken place without the explanatory revolution for the first time successfully innovated by Luther in religious explanation— previous attempts having failed—it does not seem entirely accidental that that revolution followed Luther's and was most successful in the Protestant countries. All of these factors led to a toleration of innovation (itself enshrined in a widespread redundancy system) and created the conditions for a complex interaction of incoherent redundancies such as no other culture area has ever experienced, an incoherence that is now spreading throughout the world. For example, is the inability of economists to give the government binding advice in the current eco-

nomic difficulties not a consequence of the multiplicity of economic
explanations now available? In the 1930s there were fewer such explanations, mainly that of classical economists and that of Keynes. The
latter descended, strangely enough, from the economic speculations of
Ruskin.

The question therefore arises as to whether or not an increase in the
number of a culture's explanatory redundancies as well as an increase
in redundancies deficient in high-level explanation (such as, for example, those of the counterbusiness of organized crime) may reach an
intolerable and adaptationally destructive level. This possibility arises
from the fact, as we have seen, that exposure to incoherencies in
situations in which mere social protocol requires response breeds randomness of response.

The quantitative increase in redundancy systems increases, therefore, the probability of random response. And randomness of response
undermines explanatory systems, and in their ruin comes the abandonment of the redundancies they sanction.

An example may be found in the recent history of the unfortunate
African tribe, the Ik. They were forced by the government to leave
their hunting grounds and to turn from a hunting economy to an agricultural economy. The result (since they knew little about agriculture
and since there were neither redundancies nor explanations nor gods to
validate agriculture) was that the incoherence between the validity of
the "tribe" and the validity of the "individual"—an incoherence that
exists in every society and is a constant threat to social stability—
became so marked that economic activity was completely randomized.
Hence, most of the validating explanations and religious semiotics of
the tribe were undermined. Each individual was reduced to a purely
experimental interaction with "natural" signs. The result was an indifference of each individual to the welfare of anybody else, and the
indifference to the sufferings and deaths of others itself became a
redundancy system, maintained by the constant exposure to such suffering and death, signs to which the appropriate response became utter
indifference.

However, the undermining of the redundancies that still were in a
condition of maintenance at the time of the tribe's forced change of
culture was not the only factor. They were also removed from the
redundancy systems provided by the hunting of animals and of those of
their traditional living area. The impact of this cultural impoverishment

can be understood if we observe the analogy with those individuals in our culture who feel "at a loss," or desolated, merely on removing from a familiar environment to a distant and unfamiliar one. They feel as if their world had been laid waste; they become empty and almost incapable of action. Such a response is extremely common even in a culture in which the redundancy systems have not been damaged. The desolation visited upon a tribe in which all members experienced the same response, in which the redundancy systems of the tribe, not merely an individual, were abandoned is easy enough to imagine.

Redundancy systems, then, maintain not only patterns of behavior but behavior itself. In the absence of redundancy systems the meaningfulness of existence—the ability to respond at all, let alone competently—is lost, or certainly can be.

A similar example may be found in a rapidly spreading behavioral pattern to be found among large numbers of the young people from the early 1950s to the present. These alienated young (or beatniks, dropouts, or hippies, as they have variously been called) reveal in their very rhetoric what happened to them. The "hypocrisy" of the society, of the adult world, was their explanatory validation. Such a term is merely a normative rhetoric for redundancy incoherence. What they called hypocrisy was the universal incoherence between the redundancies which assert the value of the "individual" and the redundancies which assert the value of the "society." There seems to be no way to reconcile this incoherence in any actual society, though such a reconciliation is the vision of all utopias. Even the frequent use of the ultimate sanctions can only suppress the incoherence; it cannot resolve it. Possibly the explanation for this remarkable youth movement, remarkable for its scale more than for anything else, is to be found in the affluence of the United States, an affluence which made possible and brought about a qualitative spread of the redundancies of the validity of the individual and thus sharpened the incoherence with the redundancies of the validity of the society. Whatever the explanation, the results were consistent with what has been proposed here. The incoherence thus perceived led to a randomness of behavior. The typical result was wandering all over the country. However, the beatnik stage maintained a great many redundancies, particularly those of art. The randomness, however, produced a further undermining of these redundancies, and the hippie stage was, thus, far more culturally impoverished and less purposeful than its predecessor. When the hippies set about an attempt to resolve the incoherence between social and individual redundancies by establishing living areas of an unusually high population density, in which the redundancy system asserted the social value of an unusually high interaction rate together with a complete individual permissiveness, the rhetoric used revolved around the word "love." The hippie group differed thus from the Ik in that indifference to others in the group did not become the redundancy system; on the contrary, concern for others was the predominating redundancy. Likewise, in contrast to the Ik, there was a corresponding lack of concern by the individual for himself. Thus, the two groups, hippie and Ik, for the same reasons, undermining and negating the explanatory redundancies, developed systems of symmetrical contrast. The explanation is not difficult to arrive at. The Ik had an economic problem, maintaining life; the hippies were an economically parasitic group, having never developed an economy that was self-supportive, though there were a few ineffective attempts to do so. The Ik are probably disappearing because their culture was severely damaged and in great part destroyed. The hippies are disappearing because their culture developed controls over the distribution of goods and services but not control over economic production.

"CULTURE" DEFINED

The word "culture" directs us to respond to those semiotic, directive redundancy systems in response to which behavior is controlled and patterns of behavior are maintained through time.

A culture group is any group of humans which maintains semiotic responses by means of the redundancy systems which control their behavior. With such a group the redundancy systems ("system" is used here in a loose sense) may be responded to as coherent, incoherent, or unrelated. A culture group is judged to be related or unrelated to another culture group depending upon whether the two are or are not judged to be subsumed by a single category.

Thus, a business corporation may have a redundancy system, such as its control of the rituals of retirement, which makes it appropriate to put it in a different category from that of a business corporation with no retirement rituals. The two corporations may have identical organizational structures, however; and that would make it appropriate to put them in the same category. In the same way a village in France may be culturally different from another village twenty miles away, but the two may also share redundancy systems not to be found across a provincial boundary. In the first, the villagers belong to different cultures; in the second, they belong to the same culture.

Finally, since they metamorphose the world into signs, human beings have extremely little genetically transmitted behavior, if any, though of that we cannot be certain. To do almost anything at all they must respond to signs, and signs are transmitted and sustained by culture. Thus, the basic definition of culture is "those semiotic redundancy systems which maintain not merely behavior patterns but human behavior itself."

Human beings have turned themselves into humanly sustained semiotic systems for initiating, learning, and maintaining behavior. Since that behavior must be learned, it is not merely behavior; it is performance.

The simplest and most appropriate determination of what "human culture" subsumes is the initiation and maintenance of human performance.

Culture, however, has serious weaknesses. It is constantly threatened with disintegration, with undermining, with impoverishment. Culture channels behavior through time, but it also produces the delta effect of deviance. The reasons for this we have already seen: ineffectively channeled teaching and learning; culture incoherence; the fact that the validity of any sign can be verbally negated; the negative feedback or undermining effect of randomness of behavior (the consequence of the first three); and innovation (the consequence of the fourth). Hence, culture is not only constantly threatened with disintegration; it is in fact constantly disintegrating, though it is likewise constantly being renewed by the introduction of innovative redundancies. But even this renewal, as was suggested in the discussion of the quantitatively increasing complexity of Western culture, may itself be disintegrative. In many culture circles, after all, "innovation" is an abusive term; it is, as Jeremy Bentham would have said, "dyslogistic," or pejorative. As we have seen, any innovation can threaten the integrity of an interlocking set of redundancy systems, since the meaning of those redundancies, consisting of observable signs and their conventionalized responses, is not immanent. The negation of one sign can spread to all related signs in a system and in those systems with which it interlocks. The question arises, therefore, What maintains culture?, if culture (i.e., semiotic redundancy systems) maintains performance, and if culture is constantly threatened with disintegration.

We have already seen some of the answer: the validation of culture by naked force, naked physical compulsion, the sanctions of economic deprivation, imprisonment, torture, and killing. But we have not considered how that force is put into action, how it controls behavior. The answer to that question is obviously "society," but such an answer is entirely too vague for any comprehension of human behavior, even though it is constantly used to terminate explanatory regresses. If it is asked, What observable does the word direct me to look for?, I am at a loss in the effort to respond with any conceivably appropriate performance. However, if it is asked, What is verbally subsumed by the word "society"?, certainly one appropriate answer would be: social institutions.

SOCIAL INSTITUTIONS:
1. TEACHING-LEARNING INSTITUTIONS

The problem is to understand, if possible, what we are directing ourselves to observe when we use the phrase "social institution." As an example I shall begin with "family," which Webster, in defining "institution," calls the "fundamental institution" and which, in defining "family" itself, calls the "Basic biosocial unit," comprising parents and children. (Both of these definitions are dubious, but they will do for the present purpose.) Banal as it may be, the first thing to be noted about the family, thus defined, is that its task is in initiating and maintaining behavior in children. From this point of view it is a teaching-learning institution, and in advanced societies that task is continued by schools. To be sure, this teaching-learning task is true of any institution, such as a business corporation or a government bureaucracy or a male hunting group, in which the recruit is taught the behaviors peculiar to that institution. However, a teaching-learning institution may be defined as one which teaches cultural redundancies to be used outside of that institution, that is, in other institutions. Seen in this way, the family is indeed the fundamental social institution, at least in societies other than the most primitive.

In the early months of the infant's life, much of parental teaching is devoted to the basic problem of transmitting cultural redundancies: the getting and keeping of the attention of the child, which amounts to maintaining his readiness to respond to his trainer's signs to the exclusion of other stimuli, the first and fundamental condition of initiating and maintaining cultural redundancy. After that, the selection from random behavior can proceed. What is really going on here, however, becomes apparent if we examine the sanctions used in the family, the sanctions which validate the teacher's instructions. They are the ultimate sanctions: economic deprivation ("Young man, you're going to bed without any supper"); social separation by imprisonment ("Go to your room and stay there until you're ready to behave yourself"); torture ("This is going to hurt me more than it hurts you"); and killing. The incidence of the latter is still sufficient to arouse public attention, control, and punishment, nor was it too long ago that even in our society the right of a father to kill a severely recalcitrant child was unquestioned. It was one of the redundancy systems of family control. Likewise, legal limitations on the amount of torture a parent can inflict upon a child have only recently been put into effect. As we have seen, the response to nonverbal signs is under the control of verbal signs, while the redundancy systems of verbal signs are under the control of validation by the ultimate sanctions.

This is worth examining from the beginning of the inculcation of redundancy systems. I have suggested that the only alternatives to the ultimate sanctions of force are the various modes of seduction. It is instructive that the first step in teaching the child, the getting of its attention and the maintaining of it (that is, maintaining the readiness to respond) is accomplished not by force but by economic seduction, or feeding; and it is equally instructive that the second step involves the use of force, that is, regulating the times of feeding, or economic deprivation. It is not surprising, then, that human beings are so responsive to control by seduction, since that is the first means of social control experienced and since it is very soon thereafter intertwined inextricably with force. The next step reverses this order, however, and force precedes seduction. (But, it could be maintained that force precedes seduction even in feeding, since force is used to hold the infant in the feeding position and to insert the feeding instrument, whether breast or bottle, into the child's mouth and to keep it there.)

As soon as the child engages in behavior not validated by the social redundancy systems, he is doing something considered undesirable by the parent; and perhaps it is dangerous to the child himself. Since the child cannot yet respond to verbal instructions or is not yet sufficiently competent in them, an ultimate sanction in the simplest sense is used: the child is picked up and deposited elsewhere. Perhaps it is cuddled; force is compensated for by seduction. One of the redundancy systems to which parents are constantly exposed is the virtue of patience. The child must be forcefully though gently restrained, or interfered with, or removed repeatedly. The redundancy systems of force available to parents are obvious. The next step is the introduction of control by nonverbal signs: toys and feeding devices, highchairs, spoons, and so on. Here again, seduction plays a highly important part, and once again control by removing toys or food intertwines force and seduction. It needs to be pointed out that the playing with toys is not a behavior genetically transmitted. Children are instructed in how to respond to toys, and the instruction is accompanied by numerous nonverbal gestural signs of approval and assurance. Thereby arises a difficulty, for the child immediately starts categorizing everything manipulable as a toy and must be instructed by the application of force that the toy response is inappropriate for some objects. This is among the first and most important lessons in categorization, for it discriminates between signs which may be used for seductive purposes and those which may not be.

The particular character of seduction and the redundancies by which it is maintained need to be understood before the next stage, that of linguistic control, is examined, for linguistic behavior, consisting of both verbal and nonverbal linguistic signs, is all-important in maintaining the redundancies of force and seduction. These two may be thought of as two modes of behavioral control, and their relation is highly symmetrical. Religious sacrifices are also called gifts to the gods; and kings, in whom the ultimate validation of sanction by force reposes, are also instruments of social generosity. That which corresponds in seductive redundancies to economic deprivation is economic gain without energy loss—the gift, the present. Consequently, in initiating socially validated behavior patterns and redundancies, the giving of presents and the ritualization of giving presents, as on birthdays and at Christmas, is central. From this point of view whether the child is given many presents or very few, often or only rarely, makes little difference, so long as gratitudinal behavior is elicited and marked by an initial hindrance to aggression of such a character that future controllability is probable. In the same way, imprisonment has its symmetry in an increased freedom, both of behavior and of permission, to go beyond the ordinary boundaries of day-to-day existence. In English public schools the presence of an important visitor, a bishop or a duke, was traditionally marked by a half-day without studies and of freedom to wander in the area. The sharp removal from social interaction has its symmetry in the freedom from hierarchical control, the freedom (as is not the ordinary circumstance) to interact with one's own peer group. Torture likewise has its symmetry in the offering of pleasure. With children as with adults this merely amounts to an increase in frequency and duration of a sensation they have already been taught to recognize as a pleasure, such as certain foods or certain physical activities. This is a segment of that redundancy system of pleasure giving of which the withholding and offering of sexual pleasure is so important a part in adult life and is so useful for the purposes of social management. The symmetrical opposite to the infliction of death is more subtle but also present, for it is to be found in such rituals as baptism (especially after the years of infancy), birthday celebrations, religious confirmations, bar-mitzvahs, and the like. Killing is the most effective method of social control, at least as far as the victim is concerned, but its most important task in the redundancy systems of force is its effect upon others. It is a nonverbal sign that the individual killed or executed is without value, both individual and social. Consequently, pronouncements of judicial execution are invariably accompanied by explanations as to exactly why the individual to be executed has no value. The ascription of value to the individual is the most effective device of seduction. Christianity, in its generosity, usually leaves the final ascription of value to God, though it makes an exception in the case of heretics, but such generosity is best understood as part of the redundancy system of all religions, the ascription of individual value. Celebrations in which the child is the center of the ritual are devices for ascribing value to the child in his own eyes and in those of others. (The ritual of Christian baptism is particularly instructive here, for it recognizes that the child has a "soul," and the word can thus be understood as ascription to an individual of the attribute of value.)

By the time the child begins to learn to use language and to respond to verbal instructions, he is already under the control of the nonverbal redundancy sanctions of force and seduction, including the most subtle and important of all, approval, or the ascription to him by his parent of value. The learning of language opens him up to the full effect of explanation, and one of the most important things he learns is to ask *why*, annoying as this so frequently is to everybody in the vicinity. Verbal instructions are now supported and validated by explanations, and the character of *homo scientificus* is established; the burnt child

dreads the fire because he "knows it hurts." There is no great difficulty in observing how the normal child begins to explore and experiment with all manner of available objects and how that behavior enters
into a dialectic with the instructions and explanations of the parent.
The child begins to be "rational" when he can begin to generate his
own explanations, and since verbal behavior is replete with explanatory sentences, this entry into the cultural redundancies does not take
long to get under way. Increasingly, beginning with the seventeenth
century, child-rearing has been affected by the development of modern
science, at least among the more educated classes. It began to be
realized, though without adequately understanding why, that children
can be reasoned with—and that long before adolescence they can be
appealed to by such words as "rational," "reasonable," "natural,"
and even (in time) "logical." The place of such terms in the redundancy systems of sanction of behavior by seduction is now clear
enough. They are the direct descendants, as it were, of giving the child
toys and unexpected treats and presents. Verbal behavior in general is
gradually substituted for nonverbal behavior in the teaching of cultural
redundancies and in behavioral management and control, and increasingly the intrafamilial behavior becomes primarily linguistic. If the
youngster is now permitted to argue, his future competence in manipulating the rhetorics of the redundancy systems of his culture is
supported and facilitated. Nevertheless, arguments are still settled by
authority, and sometimes by force (at least until the child is no longer
small and weak enough to be controlled by force). Even so, he will
often submit to it long after it is no longer physiologically necessary for
him to do so.

This brings out the hierarchical structure of the family. No matter
how complex the family verbal behavior becomes, the primary source
of explanation and validation, as well as justification, remains the
parent, while the verbal behavior of the child is of more exemplary
character. (As he grows older, however, his request for authoritative
explanation and validation requires a higher and higher explanatory
regress.) Thus, it is apparent that the hierarchical relationship of parents to children is identical with the hierarchical structure of explanation. The parents quite literally subsume the child in the sense that the
parent is continuously engaged in transferring the child's response
from one stimulus to another, as the transfer of response to a gradually
increased variety of foods, or the transference of the play behavior

from soft stuffed animals to something as elaborate as Erector sets. After all, even during the preverbal stage of the child, parental behavior is in great part controlled by verbal redundancies and by resolving redundancy incoherencies affecting the control of the child's behavior, either between the parents or by the authority of the male, so long as that authority is itself a segment of a redundancy system. Thus the hierarchical structure of the family institution is not "merely identical" with the explanatory regress from configuration to explanatory termination, supported by the sanctions of seduction and force; it is such an explanatory regress. And this same hierarchical structure is to be found in the subsequent learning-teaching institutions the individual may enter: primary school, secondary school, college, scouting, technical training institutions, and prisons (although in these last the hierarchical learning-teaching institution is not under the control of the prison staff but under that of hierarchical structure of the prisoners, a structure in which force and seduction, as principles of teaching appropriate response-transfer, are peculiarly easy to observe).

INSTITUTIONS AS EXPLANATIONS

All this is also true of all social institutions. It is not merely that verbal behavior within an institution uses explanatory regress; the verbal behavior within an institution *is* a hierarchical regress. This is the explanation for the hierarchical structure of institutions, no matter how long their span of life, and this phenomenon can be observed in very small institutions as well as in very large ones. The smallest is that of the individual, who is socially a dyad, responding to his behavior just as he responds to the behavior of others, and controlling his unmediated behavior by a hierarchy of verbal mediations. In all institutions, the higher level monitors the behavior of the lower and controls it by direction, or else permits behavior which is judged to be successfully under the control of the redundancy systems in operation in the institution, or even permits behavior judged to be productively random. In the same way the individual either permits his behavior to go uncorrected, or he corrects it. Either he constantly gives himself instructions, or he acts spontaneously (that is, under the control of cultural redundancy systems without overt instructions) or randomly. In any case explanation, justification, and validation, regress to as high a level towards terminal regression as is judged desirable. To be sure, this is a process difficult to control, and both single and multi-individual institutions are often marked by either an insufficient explanatory regress or too regressive an explanation. One of the subtle tasks in bringing up children into active participation in, and control by, redundancy systems is providing explanations no more regressive than the child can respond to or (to put it loosely) can understand.

However, if the higher level judges the lower to be performing inadequately or inappropriately or randomly in an unproductive way, then sanctions of various stringency are applied. In multi-individual institutions the individual, if he does not accept correction and control, is dismissed, imprisoned, tortured, or killed. It is to be noted that it is not so much an individual that is receiving the ultimate sanction but, rather, a behavior. A man is imprisoned for theft only because a quantitatively minor segment of his total behavior is judged to be deviant. Likewise, a man is executed for murder, not because of his total behavior, but because of a pattern of behavior statistically insignificant in the totality of a lifetime of performance under the effective control of the cultural redundancies. In the same way an individual, as an institution, will extirpate a pattern of his own behavior by similar sanctions. He may judge that he drinks too much and in the effort to terminate his alcoholism so severely limits himself financially that he has no disposable income which he can use for drinking. Or he may separate himself from all social interaction in which drinking takes place. If his vice is overeating, he may torture himself by going hungry; and from this point of view the problem of public self-flagellation in a good many cultures (or private self-flagellation in religious disciplines) is quite transparent. Or he may commit suicide, thus applying to himself the most stringent of the ultimate sanctions. As with stringent multi-individual institutions, the individual institution is concerned not with killing a person but with killing a mode of behavior.

This identification of the individual and social institution (categorizing them both as instances of explanatory regress) makes it possible to extend the notion of man as *homo scientificus* to social institutions. Consider a scientist whose behavior is controlled by a scientific theory, an elaborate explanatory regress. The frontier of his verbal behavior is reached when he engages in experimentation. Whether the theory in question controls the behavior of a single scientist or of a group of scientists working together in a scientific institution makes no difference. The very fact that science has moved from individualized behavior to scientific team behavior indicates the identity of the process in question. The constant factor is the theory, the explanatory regress. And for this reason a number of scientists can work independently of each other, controlling their individual behavior by the same theory. Once again the constant factor is the verbal behavior. In the same way all institutions—again, explanatory regresses—are marked by a frontier, beyond which lies the semiotic material they are endeavoring to subsume and to control. The frontier consists of the lowest level of exemplifications in any explanatory regress. That semiotic material may itself be verbal human behavior, as in teaching a child to talk; or it may be nonverbal human behavior, as teaching someone to run a lathe; or it may be the world of signs which have not been produced by humans, the "natural" world.

From this point of view it is apparent that if science, the fullest form of the link between experiment and explanation, is the model for "knowing," then science is also the model for institutions in their fullest form. And it becomes further apparent that "knowing" is a question not of that pseudo-entity, the "mind," a ghost which by now I hope the reader no longer sees, but is a matter of social institutions. The infamous epistemological problem is not a problem of the relation of the "mind" to the "world," or even of the individual organism to its environment, but of social institutions to what lies beyond their exemplificatory frontiers.

The structure of "knowledge" is the structure of semiotic transformation, of culture which maintains that semiotic behavior, of redundancy systems which maintain culture, and of social institutions which maintain redundancies.

SOCIAL INSTITUTIONS: 2. VALUE INSTITUTIONS

So far I have used various terms—"force," "seduction," "value," "competency," "ascription of value"—without making either them or their interdependence as lucid as is necessary. I have used them tentatively, but what they involve needs to be clarified in order to make clear the importance of a kind of institution which both logically and in terms of life experience precedes the individual's entry into other institutions and does much, if not quite everything, to maintain the individual's behavior in such institutions: economic, governmental, and ideological institutions.

What, then, are we directing our attention to when we speak of the "value" of an individual? It is easily observable from infancy onwards that we are constantly being judged on our competency. At first this is done nonverbally, by the removal of some object in which the individual is not yet trained to be competent in handling or by the actual correction of the performance. This nonverbal judgment of competency can be found as early as suckling and is very obvious in the transition to bottle feeding. Verbal judgments (initially ''no'' or ''good baby'') are gradually introduced. The child begins to be successfully socialized or cultured when it becomes a social dyad and judges its own performance, often done initially by words learned from parents, that is, by semiotic transformation. At first these judgments must to the child be highly generalized in that it is as yet impossible to provide verbal explanations as to what competency is and what will make his behavior competent or incompetent. Judgments of value, then, are gradually made more specific by judgments of competency, but at the same time the more general judgment of value is not abandoned. Rather, the judgments of competence are subsumed by judgments of value. Thus, general judgments of value become ascriptions of value which subsume judgments of competency. This pattern is maintained to the end of life. It we ascribe value to an individual, if we say he is a good man, and if we are asked *why*, we respond by uttering judgments of competency: ''He's a good provider, he's faithful to his wife, he doesn't get drunk very often, he loves his children, and he's kept the same job for twenty years.'' Furthermore, in childhood the ascription of value is already separated from judgments of competence. The parent will take his child upon his lap, cuddle it, and say, ''You're a good boy,'' or ''You're the nicest boy in the whole world.'' Moreover, the child is itself trained in the ascription of value to others. ''Who do you love?'' ''Daddy!'' Thus, from an early age ascription of value subsumes judgments of competency, and likewise each can be presented independently of the other. Ascription of negative value is related in the same way to judgments of incompetency. (Henceforward, this may be assumed when the terms ''ascription of value'' and ''judgments of competency'' are used.) What has been established is an explanatory regress, and like all explanatory regresses the connection between the two levels is not immanent and is, therefore, unstable. Moreover, that inherent instability of explanatory hierarchy is compounded by the fact that an individual is constantly judged competent in one mode of behavior but incompetent in another. This inherent instability is responded to as all semiotic instability is responded to: the effort is made to stabilize it. One has but to listen to people to observe what an enormous proportion of their utterance is devoted directly or indirectly, obviously or subtly, to the attempt to stabilize the value of others, to be sure, but principally to stabilize the value of themselves.

The importance of value ascription and its centrality in behavior management emerges clearly from an experiment made some three decades ago at the Columbia University Teacher's College. Two groups of eight-year-olds were carefully tested at the beginning of the school year. One group was constantly subjected to judgments of competence, both verbally and in written grade reports. The other group was praised to the skies, no matter how well or poorly they performed. At the end of the school year tests were once again administered; the group that was indiscriminately praised had learned more than the group the competence of which was constantly judged. The first lesson to be drawn from this is that if individuals are told they are inferior, if the value-ascription language is negative and denigrating (or incoherent), they adjust their performance to that judgment by becoming less competent. Studies of black children have clearly shown that since they are informed by all kinds of cultural signs that they are of inferior value, they will obligingly respond by learning less, by producing the incompetence of performance which can exemplify the negative value ascription. One lesson to be learned from this is that people, it appears, pretty much do what you tell them to do and respond to judgments accordingly. A second lesson is even more instructive. It is clear that the ascription of value is one of the most useful semiotic means of behavioral management. The rhetorics of that management are the rhetorics of praise—which one might as well call seduction or flattery—and the rhetorics of insult, or denigration. As the old adage has it, "you can catch more flies with honey than with vinegar." On the other hand, it must not be neglected that some individuals respond to the rhetoric of value denigration by improving their exemplificatory competences. It is always the job of the hierarchically superior to implement his social management by experimenting upon his subordinates in order to determine which rhetoric is the more effective for which individuals. This improvement of performance by responding to negative value ascription is possible, of course, because of a verbal capacity, the production of alternative semiotic transformation: or, "I'll show that son-of-a-bitch what I'm made of." That is, self-ascription of value can be accomplished by negating and violating the

semiotic instructions to which the individual is responding. (This is of
the first importance for understanding the problem of cultural vandalism, a problem to be considered in Chapter IV.)

These rhetorics of value ascription—flattery and denigration—
deserve further examination, since they are crucial to social management and control, that is, to all interactional behavior, including the
interaction of the individual with himself. As we have seen, force is the
ultimate validation for the response to any sign. But when it fails, there
is no other recourse—hence, the inconceivable importance of rhetorical control by flattery and denigration. If an individual is executed for
murder, what is validated is the link between a sign and both its
appropriate performatory and regulatory responses: the individual
murdered did not fall in the category of individuals whom it is appropriate to kill, and insofar as that individual was a hindrance to the
aggression of the murderer, he failed to control either's aggression
appropriately. But since the deterrence effect of execution is probable,
but the degree of the deterrence is unknowable (apart from the fact that
it is not 100 percent), social control depends upon rhetoric, which
because of negation is not itself capable of total control, no matter how
frequent the redundancies. (And certainly "Thou shalt not kill" is a
very frequent redundancy.)

The first level of rhetorical control, then, short of the administration
of the ultimate sanctions, is the rhetoric of threat. The rhetoric of
denigration is the next lower level of the rhetoric of force. "You are
bad and therefore you must be punished," yields to the milder form,
"You are worthless, without human value, incompetent in your performances of ascription of value to others, and therefore what happens
to you can be of no importance to anyone." It is interesting that
incompetence in ascribing value is one of the most common denigratory statements about certain individuals, particularly in a society with a
highly redundant egalitarian ideology. The negation of that latter
statement is obvious: "You are a very worthy individual, and therefore
what happens to you is of importance to everyone." The rhetoric of
flattery, or seduction, is thus a negation of the primary rhetoric of
denigration. A higher level is "You are good and therefore you must
be rewarded" (that is, granted a nonverbal sign of value, just as
punishment is a nonverbal sign of negative value). Medals, pro-
motions, income increases, crowns, special costumes—the possibilities are endless—are thus the negation of the nonverbal applica-

tion of the ultimate sanctions. In short, because of the instability of value ascription, human individuals are tremendously susceptible to the rhetorics of value ascription, flattery, and denigration. It is worth noting, too, that in a hierarchical relation, both are used. A superior manages his subordinates by constant praise, while a wife can quite easily subdue her husband by inflicting innumerable and subtle pinpricks of denigration. Both flattery (or seduction) and denigration can reverse the degree of aggressive control in a hierarchical situation, even though the signs of that hierarchy remain unchanged. Slaves, servants, and wives can be the actual rulers of households without their masters ever becoming aware of what has happened to them.

What the above brings out is that the self-ascription of value and the ascription of value to others is not merely the same kind of behavior but is indeed the selfsame behavior. This comes out obviously enough in such a manifestation of social management by slogans as is to be found in sentences such as, "Love thy neighbor as thy self," or "Do unto others as you would be done by," or Kant's categorical imperative: "Always act as if your action were the right action for all men." The reason for the identity of the two kinds of value ascription is again the fact that the individual is a social dyad. The general term that subsumes these various rhetorical techniques of social management is "agape," or social love. Agape, like all other kinds of behavior, is maintained by redundancy. The institutional maintenance of agape I shall turn to in a moment, but at this point it is useful to explore a little further the semiotic strategies by which the individual maintains agape apart from social institutions—that is, by which the individual *is* a social institution, in this case a value institution which redundantly maintains agape.

The term which subsumes these strategies is "value ascription to nonhuman signs." The simplest and semiotically most primitive way this is done is to ascribe value to animals and to certain configurations with a particular kind of semiotic attribute, namely, behavioral randomization. The anthropomorphization of trees when they are moving randomly under the force of a breeze or a wind is almost irresistible. An absolutely calm body of water is unlikely to be anthropomorphized, but as soon as movement becomes random, anthropomorphization and the ascription of value almost always occur. The fascination that fires and fountains have is of the same sort. Hence, when a fountain goes through a cycle of performance, a cycle mechanically or electronically controlled, its anthropomorphization because of randomness tends to disappear. As for animals, it is obvious that the kind of domesticated animals that are kept as pets serve as redundancy signs for the maintenance of agape, not only because their randomness makes it easy to ascribe value to them, but also, and most importantly, because they have long since been absorbed into human culture by being trained to ascribe value on demand.

The instance of the mechanically cycled fountain, moreover, reveals another redundancy for maintaining agape: the category of "the beautiful." The "beautiful" is a category of signs, the regulatory semiotic attributes of which offer no hindrance to the release of perceptual aggression. In English, though not in all other Indo-European languages, it is possible and appropriate to say, "I really loved that painting." In modern times, mostly at a high cultural level, "beauty" has displaced religion. As we shall see, religious institutions are value institutions which stabilize the ascription of value both to self and to others. In the eighteenth century at a very high level of culture the explanatory regressions of Christianity were increasingly undermined and lost their explanatory power. It was not surprising, therefore, that late in the seventeenth century Lord Shaftesbury, a deist proposed a new kind of religion and a new kind of rhetoric of value ascription and stabilization of it by transferring his religious responses to the "natural world," perceiving in "Nature" the attributes hitherto ascribed to God, but insisting that in nature those attributes were in fact immanently structured by God. The point was that the behavioral attributes of agape did not need religious significance or social ritualization in order to be perceived. The individual, without such redundancy maintenance, could exercise the hitherto socialized religious behavior all by himself.

Edmund Burke pushed this displacement further, "psychologizing" the process—proposing that the attributes of agape, both those of the beautiful (regulatory signs of unimpeded perceptual aggression) and of the sublime (regulatory signs of controlled or socially limited perceptual aggression), could be perceived by the individual responding to nature without validating those signs as divine attributes. In the early nineteenth century the Romantics went further, leaving in the relation of the individual's response to nature only the ascription of value. The category of the beautiful, however, included both nature and art, so that any humanly produced evanescent or persistent sign production categorized as art automatically exhibited the attributes of the beautiful and the sublime. The Romantic, alienated as he was from the explanatory regressions still available to Burke, was left simply with the value maintenance redundancy of nature and art. By the end of the nineteenth century, for individuals at a high cultural level, only art was left as a redundancy for maintaining agape, as is indicated in Oscar Wilde's famous remark that nature imitates art—that is, that the development of innovating modes of value attribution, through the response to the categories of the semiotic attributes of the beautiful and the sublime, was accomplished by artistic behavior and its persistent consequences and that response was then transferred to "Nature." His example was Whistler's paintings and etchings of London fog. In such works Whistler had made the London fog beautiful; henceforth, it was possible to perceive actual London fog as beautiful. Thus, for a few individuals at a high cultural level, London fog entered into the redundancy system which maintains agape. This appeared a few decades later at a lower cultural level. In Edna Ferber's *So Big* the sensitive heroine, who is the recipient of a higher culture than the truck farmers whose social group she enters, astonishes them by perceiving a field of cabbages as beautiful. Her strategy in that perceptual judgment—depending upon free release of perceptual aggression in maintaining agape in her new and much cruder social milieu—is strikingly apparent. It is an interesting example of how high-cultural innovations of additions to the range of signs of agape move into a lower cultural level as that level also begins to lose its confidence in the religious stabilization of agape.

It is reasonable and justifiable to extend these observations to embrace a general theory of value, that is, of value semiosis. "Value," in this sense, is to be distinguished from "values," normative verbal redundancies about what one ought or ought not to do, a category that subsumes, as we have seen, all verbalization (since all statements are normative. There are, obviously, innumerable nonverbal emblems for such "values"). Value semiosis is quite a different mode of behavior. It is so extensive that one might as well say that the possibilities are infinite or at least that any configuration can be a value sign. A value sign can function as such for any number of people, from the entire population of a country down to a unique individual. A value sign can be either verbal or nonverbal. One of the consequences of the Enlightenment was the displacement of the word "God" by the name for a country (a "nation"). Wars between nations have taken the place of wars between religions. Ideological terms, such as "communism" or "capitalism" have, for some, displaced the name of a nation, while for others, the nation name subsumes the ideological term. The emblem of the nation has become the national flag, the desecration of which is responded to as if to a personal insult, or denigration; and the exhibition of the flag on ceremonial occasions is capable of eliciting an extraordinary emotional response, the explanation for which is that what the flag is an emblem for, the nation, subsumes the individual and therefore ascribes value to him. It is for this reason that the declaration of war arouses such enthusiasm; it is a highly aggressive assertion to the individual of his own value.

Such terms as a nation's name or its emblem are among the agape systems of any culture, perceived as separable from adjacent and nonadjacent cultures. Indeed, it can be put the other way around. *What distinguishes one culture from any other are the agape systems unique to that culture.* In public architecture, stylistic differentia are innovated as distinguishing marks of that culture. Thus the Renaissance styles of Florence and Venice are both Renaissance styles, but the differentia are agape emblems that distinguish the one culture from the other and ascribe a unique (and superior) value to the citizens of each city.

At the other end of the quantitative scale, almost every individual has unique and ordinarily private signs of his own value. We should be cautious with individuals who do not take the plastic wrappings off their lampshades or who are seriously disturbed if an ashtray is moved from its precise placement. They are individuals whose self-ascription of value is particularly unstable and who are, therefore, peculiarly sensitive to the rhetoric of denigration, or what they too easily interpret as denigration. Moving an ashtray is to them a negation of their value ascription to themselves. Because of that self-value instability, they are likely to be relatively incompetent in controlling the level of aggression appropriate (by cultural protocol) to the situation. "Ego insecurity" is more properly understood as instability of self-ascription of value, as is "identity crisis." Value signs can be linked to particular kinds of performance, that is, of competences, as well as to objects. A man may judge himself incompetent in or for sexual performance; he becomes a shoe fetishist. A woman's shoe assures him of his value, in spite of what he judges to be his sexual incompetence, and may even have the effect of making him physiologically competent by eliciting an ejaculation—just as indiscriminate praise can make children in learning institutions more competent performers.

This general theory of value, a theory that proposes value as made up of public and private agape semiosis, sheds some light on two puzzling questions: the ambiguity of economic value and the association of reward with hierarchical level in institutions. The two questions are intimately related. From one point of view the possession of a painting by Rubens has no economic value; it does nothing to support life, and can do nothing, unless one uses it for cooking or heating. Yet it might easily be worth several million dollars on the art market. Why? Some light can be shed upon this by observing the phenomenon of gift giving, which, as we have already seen, is an agape system. Until fairly recently, diplomatic encounters between rulers (or their representatives) were initiated by an exchange of objects already established as value signs and therefore appropriate for ascribing value. Such gifts established competence in agape and made possible the smooth discussion of difficulties between the two rulers. That is, the exchange was a sign that it would be inappropriate to interpret anything said in the ensuing discussions as in any sense a personal denigration or a denigration of the ruler's status and his right to hold that status, i.e., the appropriateness of his being a ruler and his competence. Nowadays the exchange of compliments has taken the place of gifts.

The "rewards" granted to individuals according to their place in a hierarchy—the higher the hierarchical level, the greater the "rewards"—are signs that ascribe value to that individual. And these value signs most generally continue to be granted in spite of his degree of competency in the performances required at that level. It is not merely that the human norm of behavior in any performance is incompetency. It is rather that the ascription of value maintains whatever competency there might be and sometimes, though certainly not always—far from it—increases that competency. But most important is the instability of value ascription. For any human being self-ascription of value and ascription of value to others can never be stabilized; value (agape) is an insatiable maw that devours whatever the object of the value ascription can manage to devour. The explanation is that value ascription depends upon redundancy, just as all behavior does. Hence, to maintain publicly the value ascription of the occupiers of the hierarchical apexes requires a steady flow of value signs, and privately for the individual at an apex a similar flow is required. The ruling aristocracy and royalty of Europe, for example, lived continuously more splendid existences as the economic resources of Europe were accumulated and as its affluence rose. Very few of these people followed Francis Bacon's advice that a noble should live in public display and private simplicity.

An important factor in this flow of "rewards," including value objects, such as paintings by Rubens, to the upper hierarchical level of social institutions arises from the condition of an institution as an explanation. As we have seen, the higher the explanatory regress, the more is subsumed but the less precise the directions for responding to any configuration subsumed by that explanation. Thus, the higher the hierarchical level in any institution, the more devastating the failure of competency and at the same time the greater the probability of incompetency. The latter is to be understood in terms of the flow of information from beyond the explanatory-institutional frontier. The growth in the splendor of the ruling classes of Europe up to the time of the French Revolution (along with the rise in prices for works of art judged appropriate as public value-ascription signs) was a necessary consequence of the impossibility of gathering the information required for competent decision making at the higher hierarchical levels of virtually all kinds of institutions, particularly governmental, ecclesiastical, and economic, but also schooling and ideological. A great slogan of the French Revolution was "The careers must go to the talented." This meant the establishment of the beginnings of modern meritocracy, by far the most important attribute of which is the removal of the glaringly incompetent individual, often enough by kicking him upstairs. (Dismissal of important personages calls too powerfully into question the competence of the individuals who appointed the incompetent.) It is not surprising—it was a necessary consequence—that what immediately followed were innovative efforts to gain information about the actual condition of the country, efforts among the first acts of the new rulers and institutionalized under the Napoleonic regime. No modern ruler lives in or with the splendor of Louis XVI (or even of Napoleon, old-fashioned in the acquisition and display of hierarchical value signs) simply *because* the modern ruler has infinitely more adequate information about the country he rules.

A general theory of value, therefore, properly directs us to look at the agape systems of behavior, and that means to look for the agape signs (ordinarily called symbols). It is hardly too much to say that the bulk of surplus economic value is devoted to maintaining the public and private agape systems and to the public and private acquisition of signs of value ascription, even to the point of interfering with economic well-being. The word that the morally indignant have for the insatiability of agape is "greed," and almost anyone is morally indignant that others possess more signs of value than himself. And the word for the display of value signs is "pride." This indignation, this ascription of greediness and pride—a rhetoric of denigration—is itself a manifestation of that insatiability. The validation of that insatiability is "sacred," the negation of pride and greed. Originally "sacred" was applied to the verbal and nonverbal value signs of religious institutions, but it has come to be applied to any value sign, public or private. It is a metaphor to say that the shoe of the shoe-fetishist is to him "sacred," but it is a justifiable metaphor; both sacred and secular value signs are subsumed by agape. The extension of "sacred" from religious to secular value signs is a further indication of the insatiability of agape. It is not surprising, then, that there are social institutions devoted to the maintenance of the individual's self-ascription of value.

These institutions, devoted to maintaining agape and stabilizing it by resolving the incoherence of self-ascriptions of value, are churches and clubs. In such institutions three easily discernible judgmental behaviors are at work. First is the fact of being a member, by virtue of which value is ascribed and stabilized; second is that the individual is constantly instructed to test himself in various kinds of competence, but especially in competence in ascription of value to self and others; third, the verbal behavior peculiar to the institution is marked by an explanatory regress which explains and validates agape, ordinarily only for members of the institution, but sometimes for all members of the human race and even all things marked by the attribute of life (as in Jainism). Clubs are first discernible in the development of the individual in late childhood. These are the kinds of clubs that groups of boys in particular originate. (These are not, of course, spontaneously generated but rather are maintained by the tradition of child culture, as are games learned from other children.) In these, as in all clubs and churches, membership is the sign of value, just as in the medieval church the principal source of pleasure in heaven was to be found in gazing down from the heavenly ramparts and watching the damned—the nonmembers, the excluded—suffering in hell. Entry into such clubs is frequently signified by an initiatory ritual which involves some kind of testing for competency in maintaining agape. This ritual ordinarily consists of two parts, the first denigratory, the second celebratory or seductive. In most Christian churches the child must learn the catechism and go through the humiliation of being the object of judgments of incompetency until he has learned the catechism. The celebratory ritual of communion follows. The same structure may be found in club initiation, most obvious in adolescent clubs, or fraternities and sororities, but also to be found in childhood clubs. The point of the denigratory stage is to determine whether or not the recruit can maintain both kinds of agape under the stress of fairly negative ascription of value to himself. If he can, then the celebratory rite ascribes value to him, a rite particularly marked by regulatory signs of unimpeded aggression or aggression impeded only by the social protocols of good fellowship. Such fellowship (or "brotherhood") is competence in the ascription of value to others, no matter how they may fail in value ascription, at least up to a point, usually established by "moral" boundaries or judgments.

The explanation for such institutions begins to come clearer when it is noted that they are invariably marked by meetings in a special building or at least in a special room. This place may be either a children's improvised and crudely put together clubhouse, or a fraternity house, or a church or temple, or a bar (as with the American Legion and the Veterans of Foreign Wars)—or, if all else fails, by meetings in a special place, as in a sacred grove. Frances Hodgson Burnett's quite remarkable and moving book for children can still be enjoyed by adults, so universal is its central regulatory sign, *The Secret Garden*. Here a group of children establish themselves in a walled garden unknown to and inaccessible to adults, and in that garden a crippled boy to whom negative value has been ascribed, and who is therefore incapable of agape, undergoes the experience of ascription of value to himself and becomes in consequence capable of ascription of value to others. He becomes competent in agape. The clubhouse or church is like the vacation or retreat house; it is a place in which agape for oneself and others is stabilized and validated. Children in the process of socialization are constantly exposed to judgments of competence and therefore to the problem of incoherent exemplification or support for self-ascription of value. Membership in a club resolves, at least for a time, this incoherence.

Exactly the same process can be seen in the phenomenon of various kinds of social outcasts gathering in a place theoretically open to all comers, such as a bar. An obvious example of this behavior is to be found in homosexual behavior. Homosexual bars are often explained as places in which contact for sexual purposes is easy, but that is by no means the important matter. It is rather that the contact initiated for the purpose of sexual interaction can be made without risk of negation of value ascription, or value denigration. Moreover, acceptance of a homosexual in such a bar is a sign that his homosexuality is not incoherent with his value. On the contrary, it is a sign of his value, just as the problem is often solved by the pathetic but quite understandable and justifiable claim by a homosexual that homosexuality is a sign that one is a superior individual. In the same way to the Anglican (or to the Catholic, or to the Quaker), being an exemplification of that category is a sign that one is superior, at least to the degree that one's value ascription is justified, and explanatorily validated, in a way not available to members of other sects and with a certainty similarly unavailable. The gay bar is the semiotic equivalent of a church. Further, just as the church member must justify his membership by his competence in the church's rituals, so the homosexual must justify his membership by his competence in the full range of homosexual behavior, whatever might be the current and local fashion of that behavior. Thus, the member of a social institution is constantly tested and instructed to test himself in some kind of competence, as well as competence in maintaining agape.

The attribute of club and church membership in resolving value incoherence is further indicated by the two kinds of club organization: hierarchical and egalitarian. Most religious institutions are marked by the former (the Quakers being a significant exception, though even among Quakers an inner group actually makes the economic and other decisions for the institution; thus, there is a primitive hierarchy, even though those decisions have to be confirmed by the entire group membership). Hierarchical organization constantly tests the competence of the individual in controlling aggression in hierarchical situations in other kinds of institutions, while egalitarian organization constantly tests the competence of the individual in controlling aggression in peer interaction. In this is visible once again the importance of agape in social control and management.

Club behavior, then, is a *rehearsal,* sharing that attribute with the various kinds of artistic experience and with sports, whether participatory or spectator. What I mean by rehearsal can be seen clearly by referring back to Martha Graham's dance, in which the gestures of manipulation are presented without the consummation of actual manipulation, though in later years her dances became more narrative, that is, directed towards the semiotic manipulation of others. To be sure, for the dancers themselves the behavior is not rehearsal, for they are performing within an economic institution, and their own competence is constantly being tested. Rather, it is rehearsal for the spectators. In rehearsal behavior, semiotic responses are redundantly maintained in situations in which nothing is at stake. One rehearses maintenance of self-ascription of value, for example, in a situation in which the competencies required in other institutions—teaching, economic, governmental, and ideological—are not demanded. The effect of such rehearsal is to be found in these other institutions. In them, for instance, the individual who as a social dyad maintains a redundancy of resentment—initiated in response to some judgment of value denigration or some judgment of incompetence which he interprets as value denigration—is necessarily less efficient and less competent in the performance of his tasks. Indeed, he may engage in sabotage or vandalism—examples of the maintenance of self-ascription of value through violating the behavioral protocols validated with his institution or more generally, within his society—that is, by unhindered and competent aggression. In the academic world, for example, much of the verbal behavior of faculty is devoted to inflaming each other's resentments against the administration, or against "society" for not providing them with what they judge to be appropriate economic rewards, or for not giving them sufficient respect for their superior culture and intellect—and all this in spite of the fact that higher education faculties form one of the most pampered groups in the country. That this interferes with faculty competence is, from my observations, irrefutable, if only in the amount of useful time such behavior wastes. Consequently, happiness and competence in the academic world depends principally on avoiding one's colleagues. Exactly the same phenomenon can be found in any institution, whether it is a business corporation, a family, or the military. The origin of that resentment lies in the incoherence between the competence of an individual at his particular level in the hierarchy and the superior value of individuals at higher levels which hierarchical organization automatically ascribes by lowering aggressive control. The contempt at higher levels for those hierarchically below has precisely the same origin. This pervasiveness of resentment and contempt indicates the necessity in any society for a wide variety of value institutions. Even so, the rehearsal of agape in such institutions is not sufficient to maintain competence in agape—at least in modern complex societies or, perhaps, in any society more complex than the simplest small food-gathering societies. And this phenomenon in turn reveals the irresolvable problem of value coherence and stabilization. It is no wonder that myths of heaven are so common in human culture, for only in heaven is the problem resolved, and resolved forever.

Next, the emergence of mass spectator sports has coincided with the secularization of modern culture, the gradual removal of the church to a centrifugal place. The church at the present time seems to be more engaged in maintaining self-ascription of value rather than in ascribing value to others, while spectator sports create secular saints or demigods. As we have seen, value institutions not only maintain agape; they also maintain the individual's competency in judging competence and his competency in ascribing value. The exaltation and depression that supporters of a sports team experience when their team wins or loses would be incomprehensible were it not for what we have already seen—the phenomenon of membership in a value institution. The fans of a team are members of a loose egalitarian institution, and as members they are subsumed by the hierarchically superior team. When the team wins, value based on rehearsed competency is ascribed to the entire institution, consisting of team and supporters. By the strange logic of verbal subsumption, value ascribed to a member of an institution is at once ascribed to all members of that institution. (The same phenomenon is observable when a member of a university department publishes a scientific or scholarly book.) Ascription of value by winning teams is thus identical with ascription of value by membership in a church.

Sports are thus similar to the use of the arts as value institutions. At higher cultural levels the secularization of culture has been compensated for by what might be called the "sacralization of art," so that much engagement in art behavior is clearly much like the interest in natural beauty, part of the agape redundancy system. Art, too, has its saints and demigods. The emphasis upon the artist as a redemptive figure coincided with the Romantic alienation from the ecclesiastically validated religious explanatory systems. To the artist was ascribed a prophetic function as a bringer of value to mankind. The artist tended to become of greater significance than the work of art. This attitude has by now penetrated deeply into the lower levels of culture and is what lies behind the current adolescent worship of rock musicians. (Ken Russell has ingeniously revealed this connection in his film, *Lisztomania,* in which a rock star plays the part of Franz Liszt. At the end Liszt kills Wagner-Hitler in the ruins of Berlin and flies off to heaven on a celestial spaceship in the shape of a church organ with wings. Thus the sacralization of art creates devils as well as saints.)

The secularization of culture has also been responsible for turning schools into agape-maintaining institutions, or at least for the attempt to do so. Universities and colleges began the process when they undertook to provide mass spectator sports. That is, the effect of maintaining agape within the universities and colleges and among the small elite that attended such institutions was extended to the general public. Interestingly enough, the universities took over some of the task of maintaining agape through sports at about the same time they also began to be ideological institutions by taking over research from the old scientific and humanistic academies. In this country in recent decades they have been incorporating academies for the arts and instituting such academies within the university institutional structure. The uneasiness of modern universities in the United States is due to the incoherence of attempting to be three kinds of institution—teaching-learning, value, and ideological.

It has not infrequently been wondered why human beings behave so badly, and the answer to that question is ultimately to be found in the instability of semiotic categorization, particularly in the instability of the categorization of the individual as a sign of value. Since this categorization is verbal behavior, there is no perceptual continuity from value ascription to the nonverbal. Value ascription is marked by indeterminability. (To be sure, it is equally puzzling why human beings behave so well. But the answer to that, I think, is to be found in the institutions and behavior devoted to the rehearsal and stabilization of value ascription.)

SOCIAL INSTITUTIONS: 3. ECONOMIC

Since institutions are explanatory regresses, the modification of institutional behavior is best understood on the model of the most complete experimental-explanatory system available, that of modern science. Such modification can be accomplished in two ways: by negative feedback or by modification of the explanatory system through the introduction of explanatory incoherence. Negative feedback can be examined by considering an institution other than that of the family (and this example will serve to further clarify the notion of an institution as a hierarchical explanatory regress). The task of an economic institution is to sustain and, when necessary, to modify the redundancies which support the production and distribution of goods and services.

Let us imagine a business corporation engaged in the manufacture of automatic electric toasters. The president is informed by his vice-president in charge of accounting that the profit margin has gone down as a result of increases in the cost of labor and raw materials and that the existence of the company is threatened. The vice-president in charge of production informs the president that increased productivity per man hour or per unit of invested capital is not possible. The president concludes that the only possible solution is an increase in sales. He calls in his sales vice-president and so informs him. The latter studies the geography of the company's sales distribution and considers the probability of increasing sales within that area. Because of excessive competition, he decides against that solution and concludes that the best bet is to expand the sales territory. He calls in his best regional sales manager and instructs him to that effect. The latter concludes that since sales are good in Texas and Arizona, the best possibility is to expand the sales territory into New Mexico, which is particularly attractive because of the increase in population and in per capita wealth since World War II. He assigns three of his best salesman to New Mexico. They visit various department and hardware stores and discount houses in New Mexico, and, employing the usual seductive rhetoric of salesmen, they manage to get a very encouraging set of initial orders. However, three months later on their second visit they discover to their horror that hardly a single toaster has been sold. This information is now reported back up through various levels until it reaches the vice-president in charge of sales. He has a choice of reporting this to the president or of trying another sales strategy. But the latter option can be of no help, because exactly the same advertising which has been successful elsewhere has been a failure in New Mexico. The president now summons the manager of the Research and Development section and gives him the task of providing an explanation of the failure. A sample door-to-door campaign is undertaken in order to discover the taste of middle-class New Mexicans in toaster design. The results show that toasters designed to look like adobe huts would probably be successful. This information is now fed back up through the sales manager to the president, who instructs the vice-president in charge of design to make such toasters. The latter instructs his design section to get busy. When the design is completed, he instructs his production manager to start making the new model. The process of selling these to retail outlets in New Mexico is now re-peated, and happily the toasters go like hotcakes. The profit margin is increased, and the president can once again breathe comfortably and spend a little more time on the golf course.

To consider what has happened in this archetypical myth of a busi-ness corporation is instructive. *First, it is to be noted that the entire behavior from the first warning to the president of a declining profit margin down to the initial selling of toasters to the New Mexico retail outlets is entirely verbal*, except for the physical making, packing, and shipping of the toasters (all of which are in fact under verbal control). Further, the new sales campaign is organized hierarchically, as is the verbal behavior, since it depends on causal explanation and subsump-tion. It has the characteristics of an explanatory regress, for each higher level of organization and verbal behavior is more general than the preceding one. It is a general principle of hierarchial organization, specifically stated in military doctrine, that only general and never specific instructions are given to a lower echelon, the principle being that the lower level has knowledge of its situation which is not and cannot be accessible to the next higher level. This is the very principle of explanatory regress, in which each higher level subsumes a larger category of exemplifications and nonverbal instances, but gives less precise instructions for responding to them. In the case of a salesman working a territory in which he has operated for some time, he has a predictive knowledge of the probable behavior of individual store managers quite inaccessible to the sales manager for the region in which salesman's territory is but a segment. In short, the organization of such an economic institution is an explanatory regress.

Second, the task of institutions in maintaining a culture's redun-dancy systems is here manifest. In the general redundancy system often categorized as the American Way of Life, this particular company maintains the redundancy of the desirability of automatic electric toasters in every American home. Likewise, it maintains the redundancy systems of making the justification of a manufactured article depend upon its marketability to produce a desirable profit margin. That it can produce a profit is a sufficient justification for its manufacture. Further, it maintains various other redundancy systems having to do with the behavior of workers—coordination of behavior in arriving on the job, a behavioral consequence of the industrial revolution; elimination of competition between workers in that they are paid by time spent on the job rather than on number of objects produced (a redundancy system arrived at after tremendous political struggles and by no means universal even now); the redundancy system of salary reward according to hierarchical position within the institution; and so on.

Third, this imaginary construct reveals how the behavior within an explanatory-validation institution is modified by negative feedback. The verbal behavior reaches its downward limit at the point at which the store manager places the toaster on display as a purchasable item. The fact that it is on display in a store is, of course, a sign that it is purchasable. The nonverbal behavior takes another step away from the verbal behavior when someone purchases the toaster, since this reduces his discretionary income and eliminates other possible purchases; and still another step is taken when he puts a piece of bread in it, pushes the appropriate switch, and discovers that it does or does not perform as the verbal instructions predicted that it would. An interesting case of this sort happened when steel filings were discovered in a box of baby food. Within a couple of days the efficiency of the feedback system became manifest when all boxes of that item were removed from retail stores and an investigation discovered how the filings got there. The company gave the widest possible publicity to the whole affair, thus maintaining the redundancy system of confidence in its product. The failure of prediction—that the food was safe for babies—could easily have undermined that redundancy, just as a failed scientific experiment can undermine a scientific explanation. This makes it clear enough that placing the toaster on display is equivalent to the scientific experiment and that the pitch of the salesmen to the store manager—assuming the latter does the placing himself—is the downward termination of the verbal hierarchy which began with its upward termination, the utterance of the president of the company (though above him, of course, is the board of directors who can remove him if his performance is judged incompetent). The salesman's pitch is the exemplificatory frontier of the explanatory regress which is the company. When the store manager verbally orders a number of the toasters, he is acting within his own economic institution. The failure of the public to buy the toasters is a negative feedback to the store, and the complaints of the managers and the failure to renew orders is the feedback to the company. This is an instance of the interaction of social institutions and explanatory regresses. The experiment of the company was an experiment on the behavior of store managers, an attempt to control their behavior. The relation of salesman to manager is thus the relation of two infantry soldiers engaged in personal combat. The experiment of the store is to endeavor or to control and modify the behavior of a randomly emerging group of purchasers or possible purchasers. Institutional behavior is thus modified by experimental feedback, negative or positive. If the toasters are salable, production is increased; if not, production is subject to innovation. Or if neither of these is effective, the company might go bankrupt and out of business, an example of the complete undermining of an explanatory regress, the result of the failure of said regress to control the behavior of the world that lies beyond its exemplificatory frontier.

Two further points are to be drawn from this example. The first has to do with the salesman, who is a member of the company and subject to its verbal behavior only when in the behavior of selling toasters to stores. He is not a member when he is getting drunk or watching television, even though he is on the road. That is, an institution is not an organization of individuals or of biologically separable organisms; it is an organization of behaviors. Of the total behavior of any man performing within that institution, only some of that behavior is controlled and maintained by the institution. A society is no more than the aggregate of all the institutions within that society, from the simple and temporary institution of an individual to the largest and most complex. "Society" is a word which subsumes and terminates explanations of institutions. It follows that an individual is under the control of an indefinably large number of institutions during the course of his life. Institutions maintain redundancy systems by controlling behaviors, but redundancy systems can be responded to as incoherent, as we have seen. An institution, however, is effective in its operations to the degree that it organizes into coherence the redundancy systems which are common to other institutions and which are unique to that institution for the reason that an institution is an explanatory regress. Consequently, institutions inevitably tend towards procedural over-determination of verbal behavior. Thus, the greater number of individuals in an institution, and the more complex it is, the greater the probability of the production of Standard Operating Procedures, whatever they are called. It is also a notable feature of old and large institutions that they tend to develop modalities of verbal behavior—rhetorics—peculiar to themselves (a special case of procedural over-determination).

Furthermore, since the individual can perceive incoherence, the highest level of an institution, its terminating explanatory regress, is continuously engaged in maintaining a redundancy system which subsumes and thus reconciles what can be judged as incoherence. A professor of philosophy can judge the educational mission of a university to be incoherent with maintaining mass public sports entertainment; and his university administration from time to time issues statements about sound minds in healthy bodies, or privately makes statements to the faculty about the necessity for mass sports entertainment in getting the financial support, or the political support of the general public, or of the legislature.

Yet such a resolution of an incoherence is peculiarly liable to disintegration, since for the individual only part of his life is spent under the control of a given institution (which for this reason is always endeavoring to extend its coherence to that portion of the individual's life spent outside of that institution). Thus, the redundancies of two institutions come into conflict in the individual, who therefore perceives incoherence between the controlling institution he is judging and his "personal" interests. But actually that incoherence lies between the redundancies of the controlling and judged institution and the redundancies of other institutions controlling different segments of the individual's behavior. For example, an individual may experience a conflict between the policy of a company that grants only Christian holidays and the fact that he himself is Jewish. He thus responds to this situation by judging it to be a conflict between the institutional (or public or team) interest and his private interest, even though his private interest is in fact a redundancy maintained by a religious institution.

The individual can easily respond to such a judgment of incoherence by questioning his own value, for if he sacrifices his religious competence, let us say, to his economic institution, or vice versa, in either case he is threatened by competency incoherence. Another example is the college student who perceives an incoherence between obeying the instructions of his professor and, under the control of an ideological institution, determining that, should he do so, he will be spending his time on material not worth knowing for him, and possibly for anyone, so confusedly is the material of the course presented. He is thus faced with a choice between competence as a student and competence as an intellectual; and he cannot resolve this incoherence by accepting the instructions emanating from every source in the university that the institution knows what is good for him. This kind of situation reveals the importance of value institutions in maintaining the self-ascription of value through rehearsal. Further, institutions make use of activities not continuous with their primary task, whether it be educational, or economic, or anything else. Not only universities and colleges maintain sports teams, but so do a great many economic institutions. Many kinds of institutions employ professional or quasi-professional athletes as a means not of resolving value incoherence but of suppressing it, so far as is possible. The team wins a game and thus displays a high competence. Value is then ascribed to the members of the team as a team. Since they are also members of the institution, the value ascribed to the team is thus subsumed by the institution by response transfer. The nonteam members of the institution now ascribe that value, defined as an attribute of the institution, to themselves. Moreover, even if the team should usually lose, mere membership serves as a means for maintaining value. This is known as loyalty. (In all this it must be remembered that the institution is a word and that this way of subduing value incoherence is entirely verbal, or under verbal control, as is the game itself.)

The next point to be drawn from the imaginary example of the toaster company is the instability of institutions, which are continuously threatened with both undermining and redundancy conflicts. This is the result of the fact that institutional verbal behavior not only maintains redundancy systems but is itself composed of segments of redundancy systems; hence, the institution is subject to the instability to which all redundancy systems are subject. Suppose, for example, that the recession of the mid-1970s should be the beginning of a cycle of recessions, the cumulative effect of which will be a gradual impoverishment of the population of the United States, compared at least with its current wealth. What will be the effect on the pet-food industry? That industry, which since World War II has become unbelievably successful, exists by maintaining the redundancy that families with children and people without children—and especially people living alone—should have pets. (One could well add plants.) We have seen that pet keeping is part of the larger redundancy system of agape. Since part of this redundancy system must necessarily be that pets should be taken good care of, the pet food industry hardly needed to work very hard in order to control people towards increasingly elaborate and expensive care of their pets. If the recessionary impoverishment does take place, the discretionary income available for expensive feeding and care of pets will disappear. Already a certain amount of this is taking place. In some families, pets are once again fed from table scraps or with cheap pet food; and in others no doubt pets have been disposed of (or irresponsibly abandoned), or the decision not to acquire a pet has been made. From the point of view of the pet food manufacturing and distributing institutions, the feeding behavior of pet owners is becoming random and in all probability will continue to become more so. It will become increasingly difficult for such institutions to subsume and to control pet-feeding behavior. One can predict, then, that in all probability a number of such institutions either will go into bankruptcy or will switch their manufacturing behavior to some other product, just as cigarette companies, seemingly threatened by the statistical connection between cigarette smoking and cancer, are already diversifying the products they manufacture and distribute.

This consideration makes it possible to determine the behavioral boundary of an institution. The purchasers of pet food cannot be controlled by sanctions emanating from pet food–producing institutions. The control must be seduction instead. Thus, an institution may be understood as an explanatory system, the performers of which can be controlled by the application of ultimate sanctions. For economic institutions in our society the only ultimate sanction available is economic deprivation, or dismissal (picturesquely and significantly known as getting the axe, a recognition that it falls into the same category as control by killing). In other societies, however, the more stringent ultimate sanctions of imprisonment and torture were, and are, available, as in the old American slave society and today in Uganda and other ex-colonial nations. In ancient Roman slave institutions, killing was also available. In this sense an institution controls not merely behaviors but also individuals; yet it is to be recognized that the individual is the recipient of an ultimate sanction because a segment of his behavior judged necessary for the institution cannot be subsumed at any level of the explanatory system which is the institution. The emphasis here is to be placed upon "judgment," for the sanction may be applied because of behavior or even suspected behavior which has nothing to do with the redundancy system maintained by that particular institution. Thus, a homosexual may be dismissed from a pet-food company, not because his behavior is ineffective in manipulating that redundancy system, but only because he is homosexual (even if he has never made improper advances to any individual in the organization).

Two instructive points may be derived from the preceding. *The first is that it sharply reveals the verbal character of institutional behavior.* Making pet food is "good," or working in an economic institution is "good," but preferring sexual interaction with someone of one's own sex is "bad." Therefore, the individual who does both is incoherent, for the redundancy system that controls his sexual behavior is incoherent with the redundancy system that controls his economic institutional behavior. Procedural overdetermination being the character of all explanatory systems, such an incoherence within that system is not to be tolerated. *The second point is that the boundary of the redundancy system which an institution maintains is not definable.* The reason for this is that since there is no immanent connection between the various levels of an explanatory system, the relationships between any two levels is open to randomness of response, or randomness of subsumption. But there is a further reason. In modern societies virtually all members of an institution have emerged from families and schools—which are teaching-learning institutions, the task of which is to initiate and stabilize performance patterns to be used in other institutions, particularly economic ones. Consequently, at any given level of an institution the sanction-controlling individuals at that level are engaged in the continuation of that stabilization and on occasion are engaged in initiatory behavior towards individuals in a lower hierarchical level. They continue the general behavioral control which lower members have learned, from families and schools, to apply to themselves. But since behavioral *signs* (and not individuals) are controlled, controlling personnel apply sanctions to all behavior initiated in families and schools. The point is that behaviors are controlled, not individuals. However, the individual plays an extremely important part in this system, because it is through the individual that randomness is introduced. For the moment the full explanation of this must be postponed until Chapter IV; here it is sufficient to point out that the individual, as individual, is itself a randomly assembled package of behaviors. Thus, what the sanction-controlling individual applies his sanction to is determined on the one hand by the redundancy the institution is engaged in maintaining and on the other hand by what random redundancy that individual judges he ought to maintain. It is interesting for these considerations to remember that the term "family" is constantly used for nonfamilial and nonschooling institutions, such as business institutions, and that such institutions ordinarily engage in ritual celebrations, such as the office Christmas party, which have a familial origin—but examples are almost endless.

The lower boundary, then, of an institution is determined by the frontier beyond which the controlling personnel of that institution are unable to apply ultimate sanctions or the threat of such sanctions, and likewise the upward boundary is determined by the stringency of sanctions they can apply. To use again the example of the dismissed homosexual, the explanatory justification for that dismissal might well be that homosexuality is illegal in this country, except for a tiny number of states, and that no economic institution has a right to condone behavior which is illegal, let alone to reward the individual who engages in it. This is tantamount to saying, "The explanatory-validational behavior of this institution is controlled by the explanatory-validational behavior of an institution which is hierarchically superior to it, namely, the government."

SOCIAL INSTITUTIONS: 4. GOVERNMENTAL

We thus arrive at a fourth kind of institution and, perforce, must attempt to deal with that thorniest of all subjects, politics. One clue to the character of governmental institutions is their gradual divestment from other institutions of the power to wield the ultimate sanctions. In the present century, this divestment has extended increasingly to economic deprivation, or institutional dismissal. Institutions maintain redundancy systems, but it is impossible to know if an institution has been successful in doing so. Consequently, every institution tends to demand of its personnel as much energy output as it can possibly get. From this point of view, every institution is a bottomless pit, an abyss which can never be filled up, a hungry maw which can never be satisfied. This applies even to the self-employed individual as an institution, who in modern society is much more likely to overwork himself than the individual employed by a multi-individual institution.

For the same reason every institution tends to reward its personnel as little as possible. Since the internal explanatory structure (and, therefore, the hierarchical organization) of an institution is not immanent, it is, as we have seen, always threatened with incoherence, negation, and randomization. Consequently, the higher in the organization an individual performs, the more likely he is to suffer from what has been aptly called the "siege mentality." His verbal behavior subsumes all the verbal behavior within the institution, but it gives him no directions in how to perceive the behavior at the lowest levels, let alone respond to it. He knows the structure of the institution better than anyone, but he knows less than anyone about the fine grain of verbal and nonverbal behavior at even several grades lower than his level, an ignorance that increases as the hierarchy moves downward. For both reasons he is aware of the institution's instability. At the highest hierarchical level (and indeed at all of the higher ones) the response to this judgment of constant threat is the husbanding of economic resources. He will thus overwork and underpay as much as he possibly can, always in the interests of the survival of the institution.

The difficulty arises that overworked and underpaid personnel are thus left with insufficient energy and economic resources to respond to the power and seduction rhetoric of the other institutions which control their lives outside of that institution which protects them from total or nearly total economic deprivation, for their wages make their control by other institutions possible. The result can be the disintegration of redundancy systems. That is precisely what happened during the course of the nineteenth century, during which there was an enormous multiplication of complex and inexhaustibly demanding economic institutions. The founder of modern anthropology, Edward Tylor, thus was able to say that the justification for the study of primitive tribes was that they had a far richer culture than did the proletariat of modern Europe. He saw, as did many others at the time, a deterioriation of lower-class culture as a result of the industrial revolution. Even before Tylor's time, however, the English government responded to the fact that the industrial revolution required a novel degree of coordination of behavior by placing extremely heavy taxes on spirits, hitherto the principal source of that drug which in Western society maintains social stability, and thus turned the proletariat from a class of spirit drinkers into a class of beer and ale drinkers. This was followed in the course of the next century by a gradual reduction of the alcoholic content of beer and ale. Andy Capp, the proletarian hero of an English comic strip widely printed in the United States, a character who has even been celebrated in *Time,* never drinks spirits and thus has to spend an inordinate amount of time in order to get thoroughly drunk. Indeed, he does very little else, except to sleep or watch television when the pubs are closed. His wife, a charlady, supports him. He is a proletarian hero because he never works; but nevertheless he profits from economic institutions. He is thus a perfectly symmetrical antithesis to an economic institution.

This policy of the English government is an example of a modification of an institutionalized redundancy system, getting drunk as thoroughly and as often as you can, and in public houses—cheap spirits being the governmental device for maintaining social stability among the underemployed urban population of the eighteenth century. That system became incoherent with an historically emergent redundancy system, the necessity for sufficient sobriety to maintain the complex coordination of behavior required by the emergent industrial processes. The judgment of Tylor and others, however, had even profounder effects, for it was translated by hundreds of intellectuals throughout Europe and the United States into a rhetoric (the central term of which was "exploitation"). This innovative rhetoric set on fire an inflammable material—the necessary incoherence between the claims of economic institutions and the claims of other institutions. The role of the ideological intellectuals—a class to which we shall have to return—in introducing a new redundancy system into the culture led in short order to the organization of workers' institutions, or unions, and to the employment against economic institutions of an ultimate sanction, economic deprivation—the strike. By outlawing unions and strikes, the governmental institutions initially attempted to resolve this conflict and to rid society of a new kind of institution with a power to wield an ultimate sanction. That device necessarily failed, for it could not be accomplished without extirpating the redundancy systems which supported union and strike behavior—justice and various Christian-Enlightenment values (the agape system). Since this extirpation was quite beyond its power, as it discovered early in the century, it stepped in to regulate the even now unresolved incoherence between union economic institutions (more pay and less work) and production and service economic institutions (less pay and more work).

The important consideration in all this is the fact that a governmental institution confines itself entirely to verbal behavior, with one exception, the restriction to itself of the more stringent ultimate sanctions, imprisonment, torture, and execution, and the universalization of the remaining sanction, economic deprivation through taxation. Taxation is a redundancy system which, besides supporting the government economically, maintains the redundancy of its control of ultimate sanctions. This proposition can be exemplified by observing the fact that countergovernments—extreme political action groups, guerrilla groups, and criminal groups—attempt to establish themselves by an indiscriminate and preferably random use of the most stringent ultimate sanctions, killing. Moreover, the fact that behavior in governmental institutions is more completely verbal than in any other kind is illustrated by these same groups, for what they are attempting to sanction—and sometimes succeeding—by their terrorism of killing, are ideologies (sequences of verbal utterances). Their claim to be governmental institutions—they are quite correct—is exemplified in the practice of dignifying their random killings by the name of "execution." Further, their use of that word and their ideological utterances are invariably sanctioned by the highest level of the rhetoric of seduction. That is, they build their statements around such words as "justice," "reason," "nature," "freedom," "brotherhood," "human rights," "humanization," "love," "truth," and so on. The instructive redundancy is that established governments use the same sanctioning rhetoric of seduction (the effectiveness of which is made possible, of course, by the instability of value ascription).

With these exceptions, even more than in economic institutions, but in common with the higher hierarchical levels of such institutions, the pervasive and dominating behavior of governmental institutions is verbal. An obvious example is legal institutions, those governmental institutions which, in the name of dispensing justice, are concerned with resolving redundancy conflicts which can be subsumed by conflict-resolving categories which are well established: precedents. Such behavior is an instance of response transfer. On a small scale, legal institutions exhibit very well the ideological task of governments, for actual legal behavior is frequently concerned with modifying the attributes of a category so that it can subsume a case which, by the accumulation of previous interpretations of that category, cannot be immediately subsumed. *Manipulative* interpretation is indeed one of the most interesting as well as one of the most obvious and richest examples of the general proposition that meaning is not immanent. Such interpretative modification of the verbal utterances sanctioned by governmental force (and called laws) goes hand in glove with legal institutions' other task of applying the ultimate sanctions, thereby exercising the force which is the ultimate sanction of government. The task of the law is to prevent a simple redundancy conflict or an explanatory conflict, such as that between institutions, from moving upward in an explanatory regress to levels of government itself. If it does, then an ideological crisis, major or minor, invariably breaks out.

An effort to prevent such a crisis from rising to a higher governmental level was the famous Supreme Court decision forbidding segregated school systems and giving verbal directions to all such systems that they must proceed at once toward total desegregation. First of all, it is to be observed that what the Supreme Court ordered was a decategorization, an interesting and instructive example of the attempt to destroy an explanatory regress by pressure from above rather than by undermining it. The validational-explanatory justification for the existing system was that the two races, white and black, ought to be separated for schooling purposes. The regressive justifications and explanations for this proposition were many, and everyone knows them. What the Court did was to attempt to sweep aside—to destroy from above—such validations, and in doing so it imposed an innovating validational regress, sustained by governmental force. That explanatory system (regressive from the schools—one of many such) had not hitherto existed. The necessary result was an enormous resentment, for in any hierarchical system, the ordinary regulatory mode of response directed upward is that of resentment (since hierarchy requires control and, frequently, suppression of aggression at the lower levels, except for situations in which the upper levels demand aggression, as in war). The corresponding regulatory mode of response directed downward is that of contempt for individuals who allow their aggression to be controlled and suppressed. (We shall return to this later, for both attitudes are to a considerable extent justified or at least easily justifiable.) This resentment, with considerable accuracy, interpreted the decision as an expression by the Court of contempt towards a way of life (by no means confined to the South, as events revealed) sustained by extremely widespread and powerful redundancy systems, a pervasiveness indicated by the rapidity with which attacks upon other modes of segregation spread out through the culture. Obviously, to attempt to modify only a few of the many institutions which maintain that redundancy system without attempting to modify the entire redundancy system—a task which, if possible at all, will take generations—was as absurd as attempting to reform one prisoner by placing him in a situation in which his deviant behavior is sustained by the redundancies continuously reiterated by the other prisoners. Typically, a few small institutions were modified, such as segregated public places, beginning with buses. But the redundancy system which sustains racism has scarcely been affected.

The decision was an effort to resolve an explanatory incoherence at the governmental level, but in that branch of the government—the courts—the task of which is to *prevent* ideological crises from breaking out. The Supreme Court attempted a resolution of an ideological incoherence, which had been verbally resolved by an amendment to the Constitution but which had never been used to control racial behavior, since it was so profoundly incoherent with the existent redundancy system. But this attempt revealed incoherencies within the government. In the system of governmental institutions currently in verbal existence in the United States, the explanatory-justificatory-validational task (the Congress), the sustaining task (the executive), and the sanctioning task (the Supreme Court) are said to be of equal importance. The difficulty involved here appears in the fact that the executive can overrule the sanctioning power of the legal branch, in this case dilatory and unpredictable tactics in enforcing the Supreme Court's decision. The result has been a constant behavioral moving back and forth of the ultimate hierarchical position among the three powers. If this is not a defect, the explanation is that this government is not controlled by a single ideology but by numerous ideologies and that it is flexible in modifying its own ideologies. (But this problem must be postponed for the moment.)

The existent redundancy systems of this nation, therefore, need a glance or two. The explanatory incoherence which the Court tried to resolve and which led to an ideological crisis not yet resolved by the government, either verbally or behaviorally, was the incoherence between the explanatory and seductive sanctions of "racism" and "equality" (a term the interpretational responses to which are riddled with such incoherence that how to respond to the term "equality" either verbally or behaviorally is a continuous problem for citizens of this country). This in itself indicates that it is an explanatory term at the farthest possible distance from nonverbal behavior, a fact further indicated by the enormous amount of killing, torture, imprisonment, and economic deprivation which the response to "equality" has always produced. Like "brotherhood" and "liberty" and other such remote explanatory terms, the only sanction for it is the sanction of force. The attempt to subsume such terms by words like "God" and "Nature" accomplished little, for, since they are ultimate sanctions of the rhetoric of seduction, response to them has been equally bloody. In this case, the problem is compounded by the fact that "racism" also makes its ultimate appeal to God and Nature.

The incoherence that "equality" is designed to resolve is reasonably apparent; it is the incoherence between resentment and contempt, both sustained by redundancy, in every institution, the ultimate source of that resentment being any hierarchical and institutional hindrance to aggressive behavior. From what has been proposed so far, the incoherence racism attempts to resolve is not too difficult to understand. Among the redundancies which institutions maintain is that of the value of the individual. However, since an individual is controlled by a great number and variety of institutions, he is rarely if ever ascribed the same degree (and *assured* the same degree) of value stability in each. This incoherence is handsomely exemplified (if negatively) in eighteenth- and nineteenth-century tombstones, on which it is asserted that the individual buried there was of the greatest possible value in every institution—church, business, government, home, charity, and so on. Who has ever believed them? What these tombstone inscriptions exemplify is simply the value-ascribing power of the church, a value institution. Our institutions maintain a hierarchical superiority of white to black which runs through all institutions. That pervasive redundancy is sustained by all verbal and nonverbal instances of any difference between any two or more members of the two races, and it is of inexhaustible service to the individual, for it stabilizes for the white individual (some 85 percent of the population) a minimal ascription of value below which the value ascription cannot descend. That this hierarchical institution of white above black creates among blacks an equally inexhaustible reserve of hierarchical hatred and resentment is something that shocked even liberal, egalitarian whites when it appeared in literary form in Ethel Waters' remarkable autobiography, *His Eye Is on the Sparrow*. That response indicates both the pervasiveness of the redundancy and its enormous advantages for whites; thus, liberal intellectuals scolded her and even had the gall to call her neurotic. (Above all they were puzzled.) That there are many and elaborate explanatory validations for racism hardly needs saying, nor that there are countergovernmental institutions to sustain it, such as the Ku Klux Klan, the countergovernmental status of which is indicated by its certain employment of the sanctions of economic deprivation, imprisonment, and torture—and at least in the past (and possibly in the present) of killing. The rhetoric of black liberation was obviously a value-ascribing rhetoric, a counter-rhetoric to the white denigration of black. Thus "Black is Beautiful" became an important verbal factor in the black redundancy system around 1965. Similarly, there was the assertion that only blacks have "soul." No one has ever discovered what was meant by "soul," and in fact it subsumes no attributes but merely asserts that the value of being black is greater than that of being white. It was a milder form of the less common black redundancy that all whites are devils—literally.

To return to the decision of the Supreme Court on school segregation, it was an ideological decision: the word "ideology" directs our attention to those redundant utterances which together form the ultimate explanatory rhetoric of a society. The personnel of a governmental institution, however, may or may not be interested in the entire ideological range of a society. Yet the experience of the last few hundred years in Western societies, and in those societies which are modeling themselves on the West, suggests that as societies become more complex, governmental institutions tend to be interested in extending the government's interests over the ideological range of the geographical area in which they can successfully apply the ultimate sanctions—that is, a country. The reason we have already seen. Modern societies become increasingly complex, with greater subcategories of institution; and the result is a steady quantitative increase in the society's total incoherence, with a consequent increase of random or unpredictable behavior. The resolution of incoherence being the explanatory task of governmental institutions, it follows that they must unavoidably be concerned with kinds of incoherence they did not previously attempt to resolve—such as Women's Liberation. The resolution of such incoherences means a further explanatory regress, and the effort is constantly made to resolve these incoherences by the ideology which sanctions the behavior of the personnel of government institutions. This can be done, of course, only by a process of continuously reinterpreting the ideological documents. One result in this country has been the emergence of different ideologies about the powers of the Supreme Court. Should the Constitution be strictly interpreted? Or should it be reinterpreted to meet the demands of a changing cultural and social situation? This itself is an ideological crisis (confused by the fact that a strict interpretation is itself necessarily a reinterpretation).

There is an additional factor as well, for new terminal ideologies and "families of ideologies"—as we speak of the "family of socialist ideologies"—emerge; and these are frequently sufficiently different from the ideology of the government in power to lead to the emergence of countergovernments and to the attempted removal (at times successful) of the current governmental personnel and its sanctioning ideology. What governmental institutions tend to do is to resolve such ideological incoherence by incorporating significant sections of the challenging ideology into the ideology which the government uses to control behavior and for its rhetoric of seduction and denigration, its sanction, of course, being naked force.

This brings out several tasks of governmental institutions. Like economic institutions, they are concerned first of all with maintaining redundancies; but unlike economic institutions their task is to sustain those ideological redundancies which form the armory of verbal behavior used to resolve incoherences at a lower explanatory level. Not infrequently, it is necessary to construct an explanatory regress from such a lower incoherence to the ultimate ideological utterances. That is what happened, for example, during the Great Depression of the 1930s, when the government forged an explanatory regress from the mass of the unemployed to the controlling ideology in order to justify governmental responsibility for the economic survival of great masses of individuals. To do this, it was necessary to reinterpret the ideological documents, and some of these interpretations were found to be unconstitutional, but not until the worst of the crisis was over. But all that was found unconstitutional were certain laws. There remained intact the explanatory regress of the responsibility of governmental institutions for the economic welfare of the geographical area in which the government can successfully apply the ultimate sanctions. Thus, governmental institutions not only *sustain* ideologies; but they also *modify* ideologies; and they *resolve ideological incoherence*. But in order to do so, they must retain control of the ultimate sanctions and explanatory regresses.

In summary then, a governmental institution is like all other institutions; it is constantly threatened with instability, particularly with ideological instability. Like the higher hierarchical personnel of all institutions, the higher personnel of governmental institutions are marked by a siege mentality. As in other institutions, this attitude is responded to by the effort to "rationalize" the institution—that is, to make a single ideology pervasive not only through all the *governmental* institutions but through *all* institutions, as government institutions currently are endeavoring to eliminate "racism" and "sexism" from all institutions. However, such an effort at stabilization, carried out in the rhetoric of "justice," comes in conflict with the socioculturally pervasive redundancies of the superiority of white to black and men to women. There are some indications that the resultant destabilization may be too great for the governmental institutions to tolerate. Moreover, since their concern is with ideological incoherence, governmental personnel are particularly sensitive to the nonimmanence of ideological incoherence. (This is the problem one of America's great jurists was responding to when he said that hard cases make bad law. Hard cases are those which reveal all too sharply the fact that the coherence of an ideology can always be judged by someone to be incoherence.) Siege mentality is particularly powerful in modern countries in which the upper levels of the personnel of government institutions are elected. In campaigning for election, the only possible strategy is one which sustains the ideology currently in use, or some aspect of it. The candidate's verbal behavior is at the level of a high explanatory regress. As we have seen, the higher the explanatory regress, the more exemplifications it can subsume, but the less precise directions it gives to respond to those exemplifications (and of course the directions are less precise when the signs it subsumes are nonverbal). Since there are many levels between the ideological rhetoric of the elected official and the exemplifications he has to make on taking office (and since, of course, that connection between the two is not immanent), the possibilities for random response to the behavioral (verbal and nonverbal) application of his rhetoric are indefinably large in number and generally cover the entire spectrum of related but incoherent redundancies. Thus, it is impossible to be an elected governmental official without having someone call you dishonest or accuse you of having betrayed your election promises.

Because governmental institutions are primarily concerned with manipulating that mode of verbal behavior known as an ideology, they are particularly threatened by incoherence, random response, and negation.

POLITICS

At this point it is useful to remember that "institution" is an explanatory term which subsumes a category of verbal and nonverbal behavior, the former controlling the latter. Since an institution maintains redundancies, the redundancies are maintained by a stabilization of the verbal behavior. This is, of course, a problem for all institutions; but since governmental institutions are particularly threatened by and subject to incoherence and disintegration of verbal behavior because of their ideological tasks, they are particularly subject to destabilization.

From this situation arises, first, the great amount of redundancy in the verbal behavior of governmental institutions, both that directed outward from the institution and that directed into and down through it.

Second, there arises the demand for supportive redundancy. At this point, the individual in a governmental institution becomes a politician. To put it somewhat differently, in order to predict the continuance of the performance of maintaining and modifying ideologies, including applying the ultimate sanctions, the governmental institution must acquire strategies for maintaining itself other than those provided by the supportive redundancies of the culture. Politics, then, can be understood as that category of behavior of personnel of governmental institutions which is *not* engaged in manipulating and applying ideologies, but which *is* engaged in maintaining the continuity and stability of the institution, or the negation of such activity, or the removal of personnel from office, or the removal of the entire institution from existence and the substitution for it of a set of governmental institutions validated by, and applying, an ideology which is judged to be antithetical.

For example, let us suppose that documents and tapes were made public which revealed that the Supreme Court decision on segregation was not controlled by the effort to resolve the ideological incoherence which was the issue in that case but was rather the result of the insistence by the president that the only way to avoid an armed black rebellion in the South was to rule that segregated school systems must be done away with. Such evidence causes the decision to be revealed as a political rather than an ideological decision, for such a rebellion would have threatened the stability of the governmental institutions. On the other hand, because of that decision and others of the same ideological character, there was a movement to impeach the Chief

Justice of the Supreme Court. That was political effort, since it was hoped that success would have made it possible to reverse a great many of the resolutions of ideological incoherence for which he was held to be responsible. It would have been a political act of governmental destabilization, preventing the continuance of that mode of ideological manipulation.

Another example of a political decision is to be found in the federal government's decisions about economic sanctions to publicly and privately owned schools, colleges, and universities. In the 1930s at the insistence of union leaders the school leaving age was legally raised by several years. This was done at the insistence of union leaders, who at a time of massive unemployment wished to remove some of the adolescent population from the labor market. For two political reasons the government was willing to oblige. The first was that the unions had become sufficiently powerful to play both a threatening and a supporting role in relation to the stability of the government. Second, the experience of modern industrial nations had shown that a large class of youthful unemployed had two clearly predictable consequences: a randomization of behavior and an emergence of support for rival ideologies. (Recent events in Europe had shown these two results only too clearly.) The ideological redundancies drawn upon for the application of this policy were "humanitarianism" and "egalitarianism," providing the children of the poor with a chance for a better education. (Use was also made of the recently established explanatory regress of governmental responsibility for the economic welfare of all members of the population.) Thus it was asserted that raising the school-leaving age would raise the general skill and competence of adolescents and, therefore, improve their employability and their ability to contribute to the country's economic resources. This was propaganda (which may be understood as the wide-scale dissemination of an ideological redundancy in order to justify a political act). The result was what a great many clear-eyed educators predicted—the deterioration of the quality of teaching in the high schools, except in self-governing enclaves of the upper middle and wealthy classes. There is no mystery about this. The ability to learn in school depends first of all upon the ability to sit still in one place for considerable stretches of time and to do what you are told to do. (The principal task of secondary education is to provide the replacement and growth personnel of lower-level bureaucracies of

economic and governmental institutions.) However, a great many adolescents find such behavior beyond the limits of their control of
aggressiveness—i.e., behavior. This does not mean they are socially
useless; quite the contrary. It means simply that they are not suitable
for the kind of economic and governmental institution in which such
behavior is the first requirement.

In the 1960s and 1970s the federal government, faced with a similar
problem took similar action; but this time, apparently, pressure from
the unions was not necessary. This destabilizing problem was that of a
more rapid population growth than could be successfully absorbed in
the economic institutions of the country, coupled with technological
development which threatened massive unemployment. This phenomenon was supported by the practice of economic institutions' converting their operations from labor-intensive to capital-intensive modes at
times of business depression. (This device reduces randomness and
behavioral incoherence and also is a defense against incoherent economic institutions, unions.) Money was poured into colleges and universities, with the result that the number of high-school graduates
going on to college rose from 25 percent in 1945 to more than 60
percent now. The propaganda was again an appeal to egalitarianism
and economic upgrading—even more boldly, for the federal government engaged in the wide dissemination of the instruction that a college education produced in subsequent life a much larger income. Yet
it is obvious that the more people who go to college, the less true this
will be, a simple statistical phenomenon which the propagandists did
not trouble to point out. (A journal devoted to the problems of higher
education has now demonstrated that this necessary consequence has
already taken effect and that a college education no longer assures an
economic advantage and in some areas of employment actually entails
a disadvantage.) Part of the propaganda was that the growth in college
and university population was a result of what was called the baby
boom. But if that were true, only 25 percent of high-school graduates
would now be going on to college. The effect on the colleges and the
universities has been what might have been expected: their educational
deterioration. The explanation is that because of the randomization in
the population of intelligence and personality, the number of adolescents is limited who can effectively learn the kinds of behavior which
are initiated and stabilized in higher education. Bluntly, the institutions

of higher education have for the most part been turned into custodial institutions, a mode of social management which is a mild form of economic deprivation and imprisonment.

This analysis of society can be summed up, then, in the following manner: culture consists of semiotic directions for performance; redundancies maintain culture; institutions maintain redundancies; and politics maintains institutions—when force does not do so or cannot do so. Politics is not government, but it sustains government. The difference between the two can be seen particularly in law but with less clarity in all governmental resolutions of incoherence. Governmental verbal behavior is marked by procedural overdetermination; but the verbal behavior of politics is the rhetoric of seduction, which is a matter of providing (or promising) the negations of the ultimate sanctions—economic improvement; increased freedom from institutional control so the redundancy incoherence is reduced or made less severe; increased pleasure; and the increased ascription of value, which politicians and others call human dignity. Further, the necessity for politics we have already seen. Governmental institutions are ultimately supported by the ultimate sanction—force; but if force fails, then there is no other possibility for governmental institutions than to submit to control by a governmental institution with greater force or to go out of existence. The fact that force often does fail is shown only too clearly by the history of the external politics of nations in the application of the ultimate sanction: that is, war. The necessity, therefore, for politics is clear enough. Its task is to forestall the use of ultimate sanctions. The creation of the United Nations was a political act, designed (as has often been said) to keep them talking, for the mere maintenance of verbal behavior is often sufficient to forestall the application of force. Diplomacy is external politics.

From the example of the United Nations and similar deliberative institutions (when they are behaving politically rather than ideologically) emerges a most interesting modification of the rhetoric of seduction. The rhetoric of abuse uses the ascription of negative value—denigration—a substitute for the most stringent ultimate sanction, as is tellingly indicated by the old statement that words can kill. Abuse is a negative redundancy. By revoking the ascription of value, it attempts to reduce (not so much for the individual attacked as for others in the redundancy system) the effectiveness of the redundancies emanating from the individual or the institution attacked. "Since this individual is bad, his behavior, particularly his verbal behavior, is bad.'' Nothing more illogical can be imagined, but such is the nature of logic, as we have seen. Both the seductional rhetoric of the ascription of value and the revocation of value use the rhetoric of procedural overdetermination for political purposes.

It is obvious from all this that politics is and must be an attribute of all institutions, since all institutions must have as their basic concern the maintenance of a nonimmanent explanatory coherence. In this sense also, the explanation within even the simplest institution is ideological, but the term here is best reserved for high-level explanatory terminational levels, in particular the ideological incoherence which it is the task of governmental institutions to resolve. From this a general principle may be derived. The higher the explanatory regress an institution maintains, the farther it is from the exemplificatory frontier, the more unstable it is, and the more it depends on ultimate sanctions, and therefore the more it must depend on politics for survival. The explanation is obvious. Such an explanatory statement as ''Things are as they are because the world is controlled by a divine being'' is far more easily undermined than such a statement as ''When you stand in the rain without an umbrella, you get wet, because rain is water and water is wet.'' As Kierkegaard realized, the moment you accept the former statement and then ascribe attributes to that divine being, you create the possibilities of subsumptional incoherence. (''God is good, therefore everything is good, but nevertheless there is evil.'') Once again, why this should be so we have already seen: the higher the explanatory level, the more verbal exemplifications and nonverbal instances or cases it categorizes, but the less precise and controlling the verbal directions for responding to any *particular* example or instance. (Statistical statements, for example, are very high-level explanations, for they can give information about the total population of anything, but they can give no information whatsoever about any individual member within that population.)

SOCIAL INSTITUTIONS: 5. IDEOLOGICAL

From this analysis of political institutions, an obvious problem emerges which has not yet been examined, though it has been mentioned more than once. Governmental institutions have as their task the resolution of ideological incoherence and the rejection or absorption of ideological rivals. But where does the judgment of incoherence and the innovation of rivalries come from? It cannot come from governmental institutions, for governmental stability depends upon preventing ideological crises from arising. Indeed, one of the most important uses of the political rhetoric of seduction is to conceal the fact that the governmental personnel recognize that an ideological crisis is present or emerging. This problem makes it possible to recognize a fifth kind of social institution, which I am here calling "ideological institutions." These are institutions from which emerge those semiotic products we call the physical and behavioral sciences, philosophy, theology, and the arts, including the decorative arts. The last is important for maintaining the redundancy of regulatory signs. The simplest task of an ideological institution is to maintain ideological redundancies— both those in which the government is interested and those in which it is not (but *can* be, because of their high-level explanatory regression). This is done in several modes of verbal behavior. One is the reiteration of the ideology, which most frequently takes the verbal form of redundancy by means of verbal modification. This is possible because, since meaning is not immanent, verbal response behavior can be transferred from one sentence to another. For this reason the term "proposition" cannot be dispensed with, although various modern philosophers have attempted to do so. The term "proposition" subsumes those different sentences which elicit the same verbal and nonverbal behavior. Thus, ideological institutions maintain ideologies by propositional redundancy, often dignified by some terms which develop or elaborate the foundations of an intellectual discipline or by the kind of theoretical development which elaborates but does not innovate. This is one of the modes of ideological seductive rhetoric, for it persuades that something new has been said when no significant innovation has in fact taken place.

The second task of ideological institutions is exemplification. Modern ideological institutions are often large organizations, such as the Modern Language Association of America, which have annual meetings and publish journals. Chemical associations and bankers' associations do much the same thing. A Chamber of Commerce, with its weekly luncheon meetings combined with an address on some matter of business interest, is not different and is an ideological institution in the sense used here. The enormous bulk of the verbal behavior of any such institution consists of papers, reports, addresses, essays which *exemplify* the ultimate ideology of the mode of explanatory

verbal behavior—the "discipline"—of the institution in which the
material is presented.

This exemplificatory task is particularly true of the arts, above all
the nonverbal ones. Among the arts only literature, the art of language,
has an explanatory dimension. The arts present a particularly interesting case among ideological institutions because of the present condition of avant-garde art. An art exemplifies not only the ideology of a
particular art—the standards of technique, for example, or its more
ultimate explanatory justification—but also exemplifies *any* ideology,
any explanatory proposition. If we confine our attention to the arts of
the high cultural level—those which exemplify the ultimate explanatory fictive and normative verbal constructs of a culture which are
the ultimate seductive sanctions of performance—it can be observed
without difficulty that the arts traditionally have been engaged in
exemplifying the ideologies with which governmental institutions happen to be particularly concerned. That was the situation in the European culture area until the nineteenth-century and to a decreasing extent since; and it still is the situation in Russia and China and other
countries in which the governmental institutions are committed to
maintaining a Marxist ideology or some other ideology alleged to be
immanently and internally coherent and true. For complex reasons
explainable only by cultural history, the situation today in the West
(and in countries which have adopted Western culture, such as Japan),
avant-garde art—art at the highest cultural level, that which
exemplifies the most recently emergent and innovating ideology—has
been reduced to exemplifying the self. To anticipate the argument of
the next chapter, what the term "self" subsumes in this cultural situation has increasingly been decontrolled aggression in artistic semiotic
transformation, especially in those arts particularly dependent upon the
presentation of regulatory signs. The explanation for this is that regulatory signs in the course of the nineteenth century became identified with
"self-expression," since they were understood as emotional expression.
This ideology has been fused with an ideology of "creativity," or
innovation, to the point at which *any* innovation is validated as "creative." Since these ideologies emerged as a consequence of the collapse
of traditional European ultimate explanatory systems, they have been
otherwise anti-ideological. The result has been a randomization of art,
a remarkable delta effect which to conservatives is so deviant as to
involve the destruction of art. The resulting impoverishment of artistic

semiosis can easily be seen in current confessional poetry, the poetry of "self-expression," which makes it evident what an extraordinarily narrow range of behavior constitutes the self as thus conceived. It amounts to little more than cries of joy, alarm, and despair over the release of aggression or its impedance. It certainly exemplifies an ideology, but it is equally certainly an ideology which offers little possibility of variation.

A third task of ideological institutions is criticism, but this term subsumes two quite different modes of verbal behavior (and nonverbal behavior under the former's control). *Evaluative criticism* judges an example or instance of one of the scientific, intellectual, or artistic disciplines as being an appropriate or inappropriate exemplification of some attribute of the ideology of that discipline or (in the case of the arts) some other ideology or redundancy. It is thus no different from any normative judgment. A second kind of criticism is quite different and is better referred to as *critique*, in order to distinguish it from evaluative criticism. A critique is an analysis of ideology itself, as well as a judgment of the coherence and appropriateness of its explanatory character. (It is also sometimes called theoretical criticism.) Philosophy has a special task here, for it is concerned with critiques of the ideologies of the other disciplines and of the adequacy of their procedural overdeterminations (and its own), as well as with critiques of all ideologies.

Critiques, however, rarely and perhaps never appear in the behavior of ideological institutions unless there has been some effect from the most interesting task of those institutions, the undermining of the very ideologies they exemplify. In this, the arts are of particular importance. The nonverbal arts at the simplest level (the categorization of a configuration as a member or sign of a configurational category) proceed by violating or frustrating the configurational expectancy aroused by that act of perceptual categorization. In a previous work, *Man's Rage for Chaos*, I have explored this attribute of the nonverbal arts in some detail, calling it the formal aspect of art. (To give a simple but sufficiently lucid example, Malevich's "White on White," now in the New York Museum of Modern Art, presents in a square frame a configuration which implies a perfect square, but which is not. Most people initially perceptually categorize this configuration as a square, and some continue to do so. It is, however, the perceptual disorientation that results from the effort to perceive it as a square, apparently confirmed by the frame, that places it in the general field of art.) In the nonverbal arts at the configurational level, one cannot appropriately escape an incoherence between the actual configuration and the configurational category which appears to subsume it. The actual configuration simultaneously offers and withholds an occasion for response transfer. This same effect is to be found in traditional poetry. In prose fiction, the same effect is to be found, for example, in the presentation of an attribute of a proper name, followed by a sentence which exemplifies a categorial attribute incoherent with the attributes already ascribed to that name. Or it presents a problem, that is, an incoherence between two sentences: "The room was locked"; "During the time it was locked, a man alone in the room was murdered." Or it establishes a rhetorical mode and then violates it, as Shakespeare establishes a blank-verse mode and then suddenly shifts to prose. Thus, the arts offer rehearsal in the perception of and toleration of categorial incoherence, a training in sustained problem exposure—behavior necessary as preliminary to the resolution of categorial incoherence. A work of art may or may not offer that resolution. The arts, therefore, are analogous to the scientific laboratory in that the presentation of this categorial incoherence facilitates the presentation of randomness of other semiotic information, though a work of art need not do so, just as a scientific experiment need not produce randomness. However, art often does produce that randomness by spreading its categorial incoherence upwards from the simplest levels. Thus, the arts are particularly adept in undermining ideologies by presenting signs which current ideologies cannot subsume, even an ideology which the work is otherwise exemplifying. This is borne out by the fact that the higher the cultural level at which the art is produced—that is, the nearer it is to the ultimate explanatory modes of a culture—the greater the categorial discontinuity the work is likely to offer.

As we have seen, randomization is the necessary precondition of innovation. Consequently, the major ideological disciplines have as one of their tasks the search for semiotic material which cannot be subsumed by the current ideologies, and this is true of scholarship, philosophy, the sciences, and the arts. It is a behavioral mode generically known as research; and although in the past that word has been rarely applied to the arts, the word "creativity" is the analogous equivalent. In fact, the application of "research" to the arts is becoming more and more frequent, as the scientific ideology becomes increasingly dominant in the culture. It is the final task of the ideological disciplines, and the apparent paradox of ideological behavior, that ideological institutions are engaged in undermining the very ideologies which they are also engaged in maintaining and exemplifying. History, which on the whole has very weak explanatory regresses, is a particularly good discipline in which to observe this process. Even better are the academic disciplines known as the humanities and their scholarship, as well as philosophy to a considerable extent, but above all the arts, especially the art of literature. Humanistic scholarship maintains and exemplifies the ideologies of a culture, as well as of a discipline, through research which is used to justify interpretations coherent with those ideologies. Hermeneutics, or the art of interpretation, is an explanatory response to utterances judged to be exemplificatory. Hermeneutics has three possibilities: first, to determine, by means of research, those documents of the past which the researcher judges to provide the appropriate explanatory regress of a work of literature roughly contemporaneous with those documents; second, to participate in the culture's redundancy system of the ascription of value to literary documents, thus maintaining the agape redundancy system, and to justify a current ideology of some literary work; and third, to reinterpret the work of literature by employing an innovative ideology, one which is incoherent with or a rival to disciplinary ideologies or more general cultural ideologies, particularly those in which government institutions are interested. (In this country a Marxist interpretation of *Romeo and Juliet* would be an example, or a Freudian interpretation seventy years ago when Freudianism had not itself become one of the redundancy systems of the culture—with an explanatory regress in which governmental institutions now show considerable interest.)

In the task of undermining ideologies, the arts are fundamentally important, for they offer the occasion for rehearsing in protected situations (and frequently with trivial semiotic content) the fundamental behavioral mode which is preliminary to innovation. From such randomization, which is the first step in innovative research of any kind, critiques arise. It is not at all surprising, therefore, that ideological institutions and their products should be looked upon with suspicion by governmental institutions and by individuals who are easily disturbed by a violation of any of the redundancies which control their behavior. Whenever a revolutionary government seizes power, one of the very first things it does is to seize control of the ideological institutions and apply to them the ultimate sanctions. The object is to insure that they exemplify only the ideology which sanctions the new government and that they engage in research limited to such exemplification. In such circumstances, evaluative criticism—which always uses the rhetoric of abuse—becomes intensely abusive and denigrating. A government committed to an ideology invariably discourages the randomization of behavior within ideological disciplines, for it must prevent the emergence of ideological innovations and critiques.

This creates a severe difficulty for the ability of such a government to modify its ideology and to incorporate within itself the attributes of rival ideologies. The political possibilities of such a government are also severely limited, for the political rhetoric of seduction must itself be under the control of the ideology to which the government is committed. Consequently, for both ideological and political reasons, such governments must arm themselves to the teeth and be ready to defend themselves against both external and internal recourses to the ultimate sanctions of war and rebellion. Committed to an ideology, they are particularly sensitive to any challenge to that ideology's coherence and the modes of its procedural determination. All other redundancy systems, therefore, are increasingly brought under ideological control. The basic reason for this is that an ideology consists of sentences. It is verbal behavior, and it is therefore both fictive and normative. Furthermore, since it is at a high level of explanatory regress, it is peculiarly unstable. The effort to repel all awareness of ideological incoherence and ideological rivalry necessarily requires an increasing appeal to (and application of) the ultimate sanction of force in its various modes of stringency. The Solzhenitsyn case is a classic example of the principle, for exile itself is a form of imprisonment, since the affected individual is excluded from the social interaction he is interested in participating in.

Modern governments lie along a continuum extending from those committed to a single and highly coherent ideology to those sanctioned by a number of ideologies, incoherent with each other and easily accessible to the critiques of ideological institutions. Such governments have complete access to all the possibilities of ideological modification, ideological incorporation, and political rhetoric. They are like the most advanced modern science, which exploits the instability of explanatory regression. Under such conditions, ideological institutions are not subsumed by government institutions but enter into a symbiotic relation with them. Ideological institutions at a high cultural level are not economically self-sustaining, for their products do not command a market large enough to provide an income sufficient to support them, their premises, their material requirements, and their personnel. About the only current exceptions are some painters and a few musical performers, together (in this country) with two or three writers. Consequently, such institutions must be supported either by governments—that is, taxes—or by wealth derived from economic institutions. In the latter case, the cultural redundancies must include affirmations or ascriptions of the value of ideological institutions. Thus, the political rhetoric of ideological institutions is devoted to such redundancies; and so long as it is effective, it makes little difference what the semantic content of that rhetoric might be. In this country, however, the redundancy of the value of ideological institutions is incoherent with the redundancy that profit making (or that which contributes indirectly to profit making) is the justification for the ascription of value to an institution which produces salable products. This profit redundancy system has its own highly developed ideology and is an ideology to which the governmental institutions are committed— and which indeed subsumes governmental institutions in many areas of behavior. Some ideological institutions, then, are subsumed under the ideology of capitalism, or profit making. Which ones are thus subsumed and which ones are not appears very much to be the product of that randomness which is inevitably the consequence of ideological and redundancy incoherence. Government institutions have taken some measures to resolve this incoherence, but thus far they are few and rather timid. That the ideological institutions at a high cultural level are still in great measure economically dependent upon both government institutions and economic institutions indicates that they have not yet entered into a complete symbiotic relationship with governmental institutions. Our government, for example, has made it possible for economic institutions to provide support for ideological institutions by granting funds so provided a tax-free status, but the economic institutions have by no means taken full advantage of this provision. On the other hand, individuals of wealth derived from economic institutions do support ideological institutions. No doubt one explanation is that such individuals have the opportunity to develop an interest in high culture and its products, but the principal reason is that such individuals assign high culture a quasi-governmental status. Only during the Great Depression of the 1930s did the government attempt a more complete symbiotic condition. Clearly, the political rhetoric of ideological institutions needs to be improved, especially if the incoherence of dual support is not to be resolved. At the present time, that rhetoric consists principally of redundancies of the great value and importance of high culture, unaccompanied by anything but feeble explanatory and validational regresses. Governments at the opposite end of the continuum, governments committed to a single and coherent ideology, provide extensive economic support for academic institutions, but such support is used as a means of creating a dependency which facilitates the application of the ultimate sanctions. In return for such support the verbal and nonverbal behavior of ideological institutions must be subsumed by the government's ideology. Any deviation is immediately the justification to the government for economic deprivation and the more stringent ultimate sanctions. Thus, it is not a symbiotic relationship but is one of hierarchical explanatory subsumption.

CULTURAL LEVELS

This consideration of the economic dependence of ideological institutions at a high cultural level upon other institutions, governmental, economic, value, and schooling—in the incorporation of many ideological institutions into universities—requires a fuller examination of the question of cultural levels, for it must not be imagined that ideological behavior is found only at the highest cultural levels. It is only, for example, the identification of high culture with "culture" that has led to the untenable distinction between art and entertainment, between high (or serious) art and kitsch, between history based upon wide-ranging original research and anecdotal history to be found in popular magazines, or such series of books as *Memoirs of Famous Courtesans*, or between the philosophy of Kant and that of Norman Vincent Peale. Ideological behavior and ideological institutions can be found at an even lower cultural level than this. A group of working men, none of whom has gone beyond high school, or even grade school, and who meet nightly in a neighborhood bar and argue and heatedly discuss why things are as they are, conversations in which one often hears scraps of utterances derived ultimately from very high-level culture, is as much an ideological institution as was Plato's academy.

High ideological explanation is marked by articulation of discourse governed by severe procedural overdetermination; but the lower one goes in cultural levels, the more the intuitive character of connections between sentences emerges. Moreover, as one moves down through the various cultural levels, what is observable is a gradual disappearance of the upper levels of explanation, all that survives being merely key words divested of complex ideological support—words such as "truth," "logic," "natural," and so on. That is, the response to key words becomes increasingly simplified as one moves downward. At the lowest level, explanation entirely disappears, and one is left with a kind of discourse best categorized as gossip, a rhetorical mode in which virtually all explanatory and subsumptional connectives have disappeared except the copulative, "and," the foundation of all other connectives. For the amateur gardener at a low cultural level, botany becomes a random experimentation with plants, and biology a cross-breading of pigeons. Yet working men's pigeon breeding provided material of great value for Darwin, a fact that demonstrates on the one hand the notion that the lower the cultural level, the less the ideological behavior is under the control of ideological explanation, and, on the other, that a high explanatory regress from the results of such low-level research can be developed by behavior under the control of procedural overdetermination, a possibility particularly valuable if the individual who does it is interested in innovative explanation. In the early sixteenth-century Paracelsus began the foundation of modern chemistry by undermining traditional alchemy, and he did so by observing and questioning workmen, particularly miners. They were performing under the control of the simplest and most traditional redundancy system, one with low explanatory regress; and their techniques were marked by an environmental control gradually organized through years of more or less random experimentation.

Thus it can be said that high-level ideological behavior is not a kind of behavior different from research behavior at the lowest level—such as an inquiry by a boy as to the character of his grandfather (clearly historical research). Rather, by means of explanatory regression, the organization and hierarchical institutionalization of basic philosophical, historical, scientific, scholarly, and artistic behavior is a development of ideological behavior from its simplest and most purely exemplificatory modes. The ancestor of modern literary research was the purely intuitive reinterpretation of the Bible in response to changing cultural, social, and environmental circumstances. Further, at the lowest cultural level multi-individual ideological institutions barely exist and are frequently of brief duration. For the most part, they consist of the individual as institution, though he is frequently maintained by the redundancies of a well-established tradition, often enough learned from a single predecessor. The importance of tradition in low-level culture brings out another of its attributes, its extraordinary stability, when compared with the instability of high-level culture. Until very recently, folk art in Europe showed very little change compared with the rapid stylistic change going on simultaneously in the high-level arts. The same attribute is observable in traditional herbal medicine, which in the rural areas of South Carolina appears to be almost exactly what it was several hundred years ago. This stability is yet another instance of what we have already observed in a variety of situations—the instability of high explanatory regress.

A further differentiation to be found as one moves down through the levels of culture is the difference in economic support for ideological institutions. The lower the cultural level, the more widespread the support; although the high cultural level is, with rare exceptions, not economically self-supporting, when we arrive at the middle and lower cultural levels, ideological institutions are not merely self-supporting; they are frequently highly profitable. The lower the cultural level, the more extensive is the potential market for ideological products. The explanation is simple enough. The higher any level of explanatory regress, the greater the amount of time and energy it takes to learn to respond appropriately to the utterances and nonverbal exemplifications at that level and to place onself under the control of the redundancies particular to that level of institution or institutional hierarchy. Furthermore, since the bulk of the population necessarily places itself under the control of economic institutions (and secondarily of governmental institutions), the proportion of the population remaining for high-level ideological institutions must necessarily be small. In addition, for those in other than ideological institutions, the disposable time and energy—that left over from their control by economic institutions—available for response to ideological products, must be limited. One occasionally meets a member of the middle or working classes who is highly adept in high-level ideological response and even performance and production, but such encounters are rare. One usually discovers that such an individual devotes virtually all of his discretionary time and energy to his ideological interest. Such individuals are probably more common in the total population than the personnel of high-level cultural institutions tend to imagine, even though there are not enough of them to provide a market large enough to support high-level ideological institutions. On the other hand, since an interest in ideological products of some kind is universal, there is a sufficiently large market for all but the highest level of cultural products to sustain the institutions which produce them.

In short, as an ideological activity moves down the cultural scale, or as a product of the high level is imitated at a lower one, everything becomes simplified: explanation weakens and tends to disappear; exemplification proportionately increases; innovation, whether explanatory or stylistic, is less frequent; redundancy incoherence is softened and more facilely resolved; procedural overdetermination gradually vanishes and, obviously, intuitive connections replace it; ideological products become increasingly alike; and semiotic randomization within the boundaries of a product or an institution is gradually minimized.

All this may be summed up by the proposition that *the higher the cultural level, the greater the exploitation of behavioral instability, and the lower the cultural level the greater the behavioral stabilization*. It is for this reason that governmental institutions tend to be interested in ideological institutions and products at all cultural levels. This emerges clearly if we refer to the continuum between (1) *governments committed to a single ideology in which no incoherence is perceived and* (2) *governments whose behavior is sanctioned by a variety of ideologies and which are open to the judgment of ideological incoherence (and to ideological modification, innovation, and absorption)*. In the former, the attributes of low-level culture spread upward to high-level culture, while in the latter the opposite takes place. In the 1960s, for example, the sudden demand for films and literature with a sexually explicit semiotic content was ultimately met by a Supreme Court decision which prevented an ideological crisis, which permitted in a hopelessly confusing way control at the lowest governmental level (the ill-defined notion of community), and which thus permitted the public presentation of the sharp incoherence between two incoherent redundancies controlling sexual behavior in the society: one should be sexually puritanical, and one should be licentious. The incorporation of sexual explicitness in ideological products was a move upward on the cultural scale because it was innovative and because it sharpened an incoherence, though to be sure the upward move was not very much higher. In contrast, the wave of pornography that rolled through the West and is only now, after more than a decade, beginning to subside shattered helplessly against the wall of the Iron Curtain, precisely because it was innovative and because it pointedly presented a redundancy incoherence.

Before arriving at the conclusion to the explanations offered in this chapter, it is useful to point out that the five kinds of institutions I have identified—schooling, value, economic, governmental, and ideological—are to a considerable degree abstractions, fairly high-level explanatory categories. Institutions have their primary performance in these five kinds of social management, but that does not prevent every institution from having as its secondary performance or performances those of any or all of the other institutional categories. A business concern ordinarily engages at the higher levels in activities which lead the members of that institution, primarily at the lower levels, to the self-ascription of value by virtue of being members of that institution. And it is also a schooling institution, insofar as it trains recruits in the tasks peculiar to it. Its tendency is also to be a governmental institution, insofar as it seeks to control the lives of its members when they are not engaged in the activities of the institution. And it is an ideological institution to the extent that it engages in verbal behavior which maintains or modifies the ideology of capitalism—or of socialism in those contemporary nations in which the government employs a socialist ideology in its behavioral control. In the same way churches, clubs, and sports can be profit-making institutions, while a university, though it runs at a loss, is in every other way a business or economic enterprise in using capital to produce individuals with certain competencies. Awareness of a family history and family pride can bring out the secondary institution characteristic of that kind of schooling institution. At all but the highest cultural levels, ideological institutions which produce the arts are not only business enterprises but even highly profitable ones—such as movies and television. Governmental institutions are secondarily value institutions, insofar as they seek to maintain self-ascription of value—and thus loyalty—by redundant assertions and exemplifications of the glories of that particular nation, establishing a connection, for example, between the nationality of a great scientist or artist and his scientific or artistic achievements.

CONCLUSION

The anthropologist George Buelow has suggested to me that if bees
and ants are properly categorized as social animals, then human beings
are not. This proposition makes very good sense. It explains the
uniqueness of individual semiotic interpretational response to the
world and, hence, the necessity for controlling and channeling those
unique responses if interaction is to be carried on—as it must be, for
economic maintenance. It provides an explanatory termination for the
proposition that verbalization has made men free: each individual is
uniquely responsible for his own economic maintenance, that uniqueness appearing in the aggression of all behavior. One of the most
common of all redundancies is that man is a social animal; but if he
were, that redundancy would scarcely be necessary or even exist. Nor
would there exist the almost universal conviction that social trauma
threatens the disintegration of sociality. "Man is a social animal" is
quite obviously an agape redundancy, one, moreover, that explains
and justifies and validates all agape systems. "Man is an asocial animal," however, resolves a most perplexing puzzle—deviant behavior,
particularly asocial criminality. All the available explanations for such
behavior are derived from the notion that man is "naturally social,"
and all of them have failed. But if we accept the proposition that man is
asocial, then criminal behavior can be understood as a failure to learn
the central agape systems; no one can learn anything perfectly, and the
continuum of imperfection reaches all the way to a total failure of
learning. Criminal—or sociopathic—behavior falls in the same category
of learning failure as the failure to learn table manners. That man is
asocial also explains with great precision the behavioral phenomenon
to be examined in the next chapter: significant innovation and cultural
transcendence depend upon social withdrawal and sustained isolation.
Finally, that man is asocial explains why behavior is—and must be—
controlled; that control begins, as we have seen, with seduction and
force. Those who never learn the judicious application of force in
bringing up children become child-batterers.

From the argument of this book as it has so far developed, one
arrives at rather melancholy conclusions. Culture controls behavior;
culture consists of performatory and regulatory semiotic redundancy
systems; words control redundancy systems; the defining attribute of
verbal behavior is explanation; explanation is hierarchical; behavioral
control is thus hierarchical, and all institutions are hierarchically or-

ganized; behavioral control is a matter of learning socially validated performances; performances consist of responses appropriate to the presentation of particular signs; behavioral control depends upon the meaning of those signs; smooth behavioral interaction of any kind depends upon the illusion that meaning is immanent; but since meaning is not immanent, appropriate response can ultimately be maintained only by the application of force in the form of economic deprivation, imprisonment, torture, and execution.

It is vain to hope for a society in which the institutions are not hierarchically structured or for a society in which the ultimate sanctions have vanished, or for a society which is not run by an elite which is competent in explanation and especially in that high level of explanation, ideology. It is equally vain to hope for a society in which there is no incoherence between public and private interests, no rivalry between institutions, and no institutional incoherence, no incoherence in the ascription of individual value, and no politics.

There is one brighter spot in this vision, and that is the possibility that governmental institutions may learn that the best model for all levels of behavioral control is science—not the commitment to an ideology but the exploitation of ideological instability. Cultural history is a very perilous field, but it does not seem to be accidental that Western culture, which exploited the incoherence of its ultimate explanatory systems by creating modern science, is also the geographical area in which there is to be found the greatest incidence or at least a modest exploitation of ideological incoherence and instability, nor that in the culture area of the West is to be found the greatest proportion of the population which experiences the life enhancement of the negative inversions of the ultimate sanctions: economic ease, the privileges of freedom, pleasures, and the enhancement of the individual's own value (i.e., human dignity).

However, there is a difficulty here. "We live in an oppressive society," a young radical said to me. "True," I replied, "but it is not because we live in *this* society; it is because we live in *a* society." But there is no such entity as society. There are only individual organisms, behaving semiotically. The oppressor of any individual is that individual himself. The individual is the catch-22 of human life, and to that individual I shall now turn.

THE INDIVIDUAL

PERSONA

By "individual" I mean the individual organism as mere observable configuration—a mere sign—separable from its ground. There is no difficulty in the notion that the individual as an observable physiological organism is an entity. All the physiological processes subsumed by the category "individual organism" have at least one attribute in common; they all cease when the heart ceases to beat. (This does not mean, of course, chemical processes, but only those processes by which the individual organism is self-propelling.) An "entity," then, is no more than such a conjunctive category, one which subsumes a set all members of which are interpreted to have some attribute or a set of attributes in common. But is the *behavioral* individual an entity?

Culture has metamorphosed the individual organism into a category of higher value called various things like "self," or "soul," or "ego"—a more modern but equally delusive term. Currently, the most common word seems to be "personality," the root of which is "persona," a word that originally meant "mask." Masks are of three sorts: one presents conventionalized signs of behavioral attributes of the individual wearing the mask; a second presents conventionalized signs of behavioral attributes which the masker never otherwise exhibits; a third presents both kinds of signs. (A possible fourth kind, that which conceals the facial signs of the masker, is best subsumed under the second.) The attribute of "mask" to be useful here is that a mask is a selection of signs of behavioral attributes or, more precisely, physical configurations which cultural convention interprets as signs of behavioral attributes. Moreover, the selected signs are conventionally coherent. (The coherence may be polarized, as in a mask which presents on one side signs of "goodness," and the other signs of "evil.") "Personality," then, is a metaphor which ascribes to the behavioral

individual a structural coherence and asserts that the behavioral individual is an entity. What has happened is that the physical organism, a
conjunctive category, has been interpreted as a sign of the behavioral
individual, a disjunctive category; and the conjunctivity of the one has
masked the disjunctivity of the other. Thus, "personality" asserts that
all of the behavioral patterns of the behavioral individual have attributes in common, if only participation in the alleged structural coherence of the personality. Nevertheless, an analysis of the metaphor also
shows that the interpretation of the behavioral individual as an entity is
selective and that the ascription of coherence can be maintained only
by ignoring behavioral attributes which cannot be subsumed by that
coherence.

In actual fact the behavioral individual, no matter what term identifies him, performs a set of behaviors the members of which have
nothing in common except that they are performances, each of which is
under the control of a different cultural redundancy. The members of
the set are properly subsumed by the categories of those redundancies,
not by the category of "personality." The soul, or self, or spirit, or
personality, or ego, then, is not a conjunctive but a disjunctive category, one which is created by culturally conventionalized interpretation. "Personality" is a creation of verbal behavior at a fairly high
level of explanatory regress. Yet the word is so powerful a conjunctive
redundancy, no matter how misleading, that it is virtually unusable.
Instead, I shall use "persona"; and I define it thus: *the persona is the
selective, deceptive, and coherent semiotic interpretation of the behavioral individual, either by the individual himself or by someone else.*

The persona, then, is a semiotic construct. To be more precise, it is a
semiotic transformation of the perceptual data of an individual human
organism, analogically organized into behavioral patterns. This definition gives us a hint as to why it emerges, both from the encounter of the
individual with himself and from his encounters with others. As we
have seen, all interpretation is at least two leveled. As a form of
explanation, interpretation is hierarchically structured, the upper level
(a series of semiotic matrices) controlling the interpretation of the
lower level (recurrent semiotic patterns). From this, two incoherent
functions of the persona emerge. First, it stabilizes behavior. But in
this it is no different from any interpretation. That is, the problem, so
mysterious, of how it is that an individual "thinks" of "himself" as
continuing through a series of unrelated situations, is precisely the

same problem as that of recognizing a chair every time one sees it, namely, the analogical determination of a semiotic configuration as one of a series of semiotic matrices. The problem of "identity" is merely a matter of continuous interpretational control over the interpretation of one's behavior. It is just as sensible (and almost as common) to talk about the persona of an object as it is to talk about the identity of an individual.

But second, an interpretation-controlling persona works like any explanatory regress. It is subject to modification from feedback. It is by no means an uncommon, though ordinarily brief, experience for the persona to be so undermined by hitherto unencountered or ignored behavioral data that the individual has the disorienting experience of not knowing who he is—at least for a moment. Like any explanatory construct, then, the persona is inherently unstable. If its stability is too seriously disturbed for too long a time, psychosis can be the temporary or permanent consequence. Moreover, as with any explanatory construct or regress, the persona is kept flexible and responsive by that very feedback modification. The conflict between the two functions of the persona emerges from the fact that both the stability and the instability are to the advantage and the disadvantage of the adaptive behavior of the individual. Or, to put it differently, it is useful for the individual to judge his persona, at various times, to be both a disjunctive and a conjunctive category.

Nevertheless, the acceptance of disjunctiveness and inherent persona instability is universally masked by persona conjunctivity. Modification of the persona by feedback is interpreted as "insight" as to what "one really is." The explanation for this lies in the fact that to the individual the persona is a value-ascribing sign, the justification for the value ascription having been derived from value institutions and the value-granting functions of all institutions which subsume him, and maintained by the agape systems. Hence, the universal assumption of the persona as a conjunctive category hypostatized into an entity or "id-entity." A few examples of the consequences are worth considering.

At the present time, one of the most common cultural redundancies is the demand that the individual be recognized as a "person," as an "individual," as a "self." For example, it is a complaint of the women's liberation movement that women are not recognized by men as persons, but only as sex objects or household drudges. This is other than the complaint that one is not ascribed the value that one feels ought to be ascribed. It is a complaint that the relationship between a man and a woman is not the relationship that Martin Buber calls the I-thou relationship, the recognition that the individual is a person and not an object, that to the individual should be ascribed value on the ground that he (or in this case, she) is an entity, not a nonhuman object. *As an object the individual is ascribed value because of his performances; as an individual, a "thou," he is ascribed value merely because he performs.* This separation between competence and value reveals quite clearly what is going in the "thou" relationship. It obviously is a factor in the agape redundancy system. In Christian theology this distinction between value and competencies is known as the forgiveness of sin. The Buberian notion is that the individual ought to be ascribed value, no matter whether or not he is under the control of cultural redundancies and of institutions, even if his behavior is incompetent or negational or random. It is thus another instance of the rhetoric of seduction, without which social interaction cannot take place. The ascription of "selfhood" or "personality" or "identity" is thus another verbal mode of the ascription of value.

This same process can be seen in the phenomenon of proper names for individuals. It may be that at one time individuals were distinguished by proper names for the same reason that proper names are still given to places and objects. A proper name is a recognition that all members of a category are interchangeable for some purposes but not for others—that each member of a category can be and should be ascribed attributes which are shared by no other members of that category. Proper names are thus a normative device for selecting out and giving initial directions to locate a member of a category as properly distinguishable, for whatever reason, from all other members of that category. The Romans were sensible; they numbered their children. However, a mountain does not appear to be particularly upset if you get its name wrong, or misspell it, whereas human beings almost always are, though some learn not to act upon it. Such an error tends to be interpreted as an ascription of negative value, as a denigration. Somebody did not think you were worth the trouble it takes to get your name right. For us, one's name has come to be an ascription of individuality, of selfhood, of personality, of being an ego. This is not difficult to understand in the light of what has already been proposed, in addition to its negation of agape. All categories are unstable in that no two members of a category have absolutely the same attributes. Categories are semiotic fictive and normative constructs. But smooth interactional behavior depends upon categorial stability, upon successful prediction that the response to a configuration (that is, to a categorial sign) will be appropriate, and that in behavioral interaction the individual organism, the sign, will respond in a way that you will judge to be appropriate. The worst thing one can say about anybody is that he is unpredictable, and it is even worse if you are in a position of saying it about yourself. However, all behavior is to a certain extent unpredictable; it is judged to be predictable only by omitting from the judgment certain behavioral attributes or signs. Further, since the persona is a disjunctive category, the instability of all categories is intensified in human performance. Interaction is always threatened with unpredictability, with dissolution of appropriate behavior, with what appears (at the time, certainly) to be random behavior. A proper name stabilizes the persona as a category. The persona is always threatened with the kind of experience of the old lady in the nursery rhyme. On her way home from market she fell asleep by the roadside. Along came a thief and cut off her skirt. When she awoke and looked at herself, "Lord 'a mercy on us," she said, "this is none of I!" People in states so confused that they are bewildered by possible alternatives and are unable to act frequently stabilize their behavior by reminding themselves of who they really are, by repeating to themselves overtly or covertly their proper names. The disappearance from behavior of any attribute, prized or not, entails the judgment that the persona is no longer the same—that one is, for better or worse, a new person. Hence, a mistake in a proper name is responded to as a divestment of identifying attributes, a threat of the categorial dissolution of persona or, to use a comic term, of the loss of the "integrity" of the personality. Thus we cannot speak of identity but only of the judgment of identity, of identity as a construct, and of a proper name as a normative and fictive sign which stabilizes a disjunctive category.

Another consequence arises from the peculiar status of explanatory regressions from the disjunctive behavior of the behavioral individual. Such explanations are called "psychology," rather amusingly, for the notion of the "psyche" merely subsumes proper names and thus ascribes categorial conjunctivity, or entity, to the individual's behavior. For centuries all cultural levels have attempted to construct explanatory theories of personality, and the twentieth century (in part as a result of secularization, in part as a result of the triumph of science) has been particularly rich in such efforts. Yet Karl Menninger, after a lifetime of working with available theories of personality and categorizations of personality types, rejected them all in *The Vital Balance*. It is evident that a personality explanation is constructed to account causally for the degree to which an individual is under the control of the redundancies of some institution or set of institutions. Since the basic unit of human behavior is learned sign response, it is obvious that no explanation of a personality can be regressive from all of his sign behavior. Furthermore, any sign response can be subsumed by an indefinably large number of categorizations. A personality explanation must necessarily be, first, selective of sign response; and, second, that selection must be under the control of cultural redundancies and institutions. As Menninger discovered, though he did not put it quite this way, if the signs controlling an incurable psychotic patient who had spent years in a mental hospital were changed to signs well established in the hospital redundancy system as signs used to control curable patients (by moving him from the back wards to the front wards, say), the incurable patient not infrequently improved, even to the point of leaving the hospital and resuming a normal life.

Psychiatry is an economic institution, the task of which is to produce the service of modifying the individuals' behavior which has been judged by themselves or others to be inappropriate in particular situations or categories of situations. The psychiatrist has the delicate task of simultaneously ascribing value to the persona while ascribing negative value to bits of the individual's total behavior. The usual technique of verbal psychiatry and psychoanalysis is to seduce the patient into constructing a causal explanation such that the persona is no longer judged to be the cause of the individual's undesirable behavior. Since causality is a fictive subsumption, it is not surprising that psychiatric and psychoanalytic explanatory regresses evince an extraordinary instability. In successful therapy the individual, having freed the personality from its negative value ascription, can proceed to derive instructions to himself from the causally constructed explanation. The great problem is that the individual-as-an-institution maintains its behavior by self-generated redundancies and redundancy systems. The simplest form of a self-redundancy is the categorization of the persona. "I am *this* kind of person." The attributes of that category thereupon become directions for performance. (This is certainly one of the reasons for the high rate of criminal recidivism. If you place a member of a criminal economic or countergovernmental institution in a prison, you merely provide redundancies which sustain his self-categorization, and thus you confirm it. It is not at all surprising that when he is let out, he should continue to be a criminal, though a more successful one.) In psychiatric practice the rate of actual behavioral modification seems to be low, but the rate of recategorization of the patient's persona from "bad" to "good" is certainly much higher. This is the first step, one which accomplishes little or no modification of behavior but which enables the individual to be more competent in areas of behavior other than that of his "neurosis," the behavior designated as "bad," that is, judged incompetent, as, for example, sexual impotency. This is known as learning to live with your neurosis. Behavioral modification can be more successful, however, if the individual generates self-directing signs which are semiotic factors in a redundancy system which elicits behavior alternative to that judged inappropriate and if this generation is maintained by semiotically rich situations appropriate for such behavior. For example, the alcoholic is rarely successful in modifying his interest in alcohol if he merely tries to avoid drinking or occasions for drinking. What he has to do is to instruct himself to search for and find sources of pleasure and amusement and interest and then to spend his disposable time in situations in which the signs of what to him are "pleasant" and "amusing" and "interesting" are richly and continuously presented over considerable periods of time. Nevertheless, the first step is the essential step, the ascription of value to the persona and the confirmation of that ascription.

This brings us to the fundamental reason for those redundancy systems which stabilize the personality by ascribing to the individual personal identity, or categorial conjunctivity. The fact that an individual is constantly moving from one situation to another (each of which maintains a different set of redundancies and therefore elicits different performances) creates, as we have seen, value incoherence. But it also creates personality incoherence. Who has not heard someone say or heard himself say, "It was such a different situation for me that I hardly knew myself," or, "When I saw him for the first time in his family situation, I scarcely recognized him." As the individual moves from one situation to another, he observes himself generating different kinds of behavior. Faced with a totally new situation, he is at a loss in predicting his behavior, for the addition of a new kind of behavior to the range of his behavior can be as threatening to the categorial stability of the persona as the deprivation of a mode of behavior. Stage fright, from which some actors always suffer, is, from this point of view, the self-judgment of threatened dissolution of the personal category into disjunctive categories. Whether a category of behavior is added or subtracted, the individual is required in both cases to modify the attributes of the persona as categorial sign. When he is threatened with behavioral dissolution, the individual's obvious strategy is to use some other strategy to stabilize the persona. The obvious strategy is to maintain some attribute of behavior in all situations and, insofar as is possible, to control his own behavior in any situation according to the demands of that strategy. The first step is to reify the persona, then to support the reification with a proper name (possibly by identifying the persona as an exemplification of a constructed category of personality), then to maintain certain behavioral traits in all situations (rigidity of stance, for example), and then to stabilize other signs of costume. A confidence man is an excellent example of this. He presents highly redundant signs, redundant both in the presentation and in the culture, of a highly trustworthy persona. Thus he controls the behavior of his victims. The strategies for stabilizing the persona are con-games or tricks on ourselves, by which we stave off behavioral dissolution and maintain certain behaviors through all situations, even though they are inappropriate.

The truly clever and successful confidence man, however, knows that too coherent and redundant a presentation of trustworthy persona signs may very well trip him up, for such coherence is not the norm of behavior. It is instructive that in theatrical comedy, persona signs show a high degree of consistency (and almost total consistency in farce), while exactly the opposite is the case in tragedy. Off the stage the individual who always presents highly redundant signs of his strategy is likewise a comic or absurd or grotesque or eccentric figure. The individual who is always excessively well dressed and excessively well groomed, no matter what the situation, becomes in time a source of amusement—or, like the confidence man, a source of suspicion. Individuals who do not arouse amusement are not individuals who have no such strategies but instead are people who have a variety of strategies, each of which can be judged more or less appropriate to the situation in which he finds himself or at least sufficiently appropriate so that random response is not elicited from the individual with whom he is interacting. The same principle is appropriately judged to be exemplified in certain kinds of bizarre behavior. Costume is a particularly good example. When the hippie costume of ragged jeans and other accoutrements became popular among a certain segment of the young, its justification was "self-expression." This statement was frequently misunderstood to mean that the costume signs themselves were indicators of a unique personality configuration; and it was obvious that since all the costumes were alike, this could not be the case. If, however, it is recognized as a strategy for maintaining persona stability in the face of rejection of socially validated redundancies, the problem immediately clears up. The statement by a bank vice-president that bankers must have gray hair is a recognition of the same strategy. That is, the strategies for maintaining persona stability to others or to oneself are identical, for the individual is a social dyad.

INTERESTS

These considerations make it possible to answer the troublesome and baffling question, Why is anybody interested in anything? An interest is a strategy that maintains persona stability. Moreover, such strategies or interests are less varied and less numerous than the situations or institutions in which an individual actually performs. (Otherwise, the strategy would be ineffective.) Moreover, the individual in responding to himself does not have the same problem in achieving predictability and maintaining persona stability that he has when he responds to others. First, any individual observes himself in more kinds of situations (and in a greater variety of kinds) than anybody he is likely to observe, for we encounter others in a very limited number of situations but ourselves in an almost unlimited number in the course of a lifetime. Second, the individual is himself an institution in hierarchical relation to his own responses. As we have seen, his response to his own response may be mediating, or on the other hand his response to self-generated instructions may not be the anticipated response. In that case he may very well place his subsequent behavior under the control of such unanticipated response. The hierarchy of mediated and immediate response may be reversed. Thus the individual-as-institution is in fact a series of institutions, each with its particular redundancies. The problem of constructing the persona of another is thus much easier than that of constructing a persona of oneself, and this condition increases the instability of the personality category (and explains, too, why any individual is more interested in himself than in anyone else). His strategies in relation to himself can be resolved only by limiting the range of his behavior, by countering the randomness with a limitation of randomness. Thus, an interest may be further defined as a strategy that limits the range of behavior.

This strategy can be seen very well in the behavioral phenomenon of collecting. A discretionary income presents a problem because it increases the possibilities of extending the range of kinds of behavior. It is to the point to observe that the behavioral range of the very rich is ordinarily much narrower than that of the ghetto dweller, for the latter has to develop a fairly wide range in order to survive. And it is also to the point to observe that collection of valuable objects by the rich has a tradition extending back beyond the beginnings of recorded history. It is not surprising therefore that as this country became increasingly affluent during the 1950s and the 1960s and as that affluence spread to more and more individuals, collecting became increasingly popular. Moreover, this increasing affluence was accompanied by an increasing amount of leisure time as the work week was reduced for the majority of the working population. Twenty-five years ago bus stations were at the busiest after Saturday noon, but now it is early Friday evening.

Disposable time presents exactly the same problem as discretionary income. What should one do with it? Collecting sops up both disposable time and discretionary income. By 1970 almost anything was being collected—rocks, at first in the field and then increasingly in rock shops, old streetcar transfers, and at the moment of writing anything at all nostalgic (e.g., comic books, playing cards, Coca-Cola trays). One collects items which have a fairly stable market value and which are more expensive than one can quite afford. Coin collection became increasingly popular and finally burgeoned into the manufacture of silver bars engraved with facsimiles of dollar bills and their multiples. It was as fascinating as it was instructive to observe in the 1960s the emergence of those business enterprises which began to produce objects solely to be collected. Collecting is one of the most splendid of strategies for limiting the range of behavior and, thus, circumventing that threat of behavioral dissolution and destabilization of the persona which is the unavoidable consequence of extending the range of behavior. Another example may be found in the strange phenomenon of the frequency with which one encounters boats being towed along the highways in that enormous part of the United States which is in fact desert. They are being towed, one learns, to the large artificial lakes in the area. To buy an expensive boat, to tow it for hours to an artificial lake, to launch it, to be pushed around the lake for a couple of hours by an outboard motor, to reload it from the launching ramp onto its carrier, to drive for hours home again—all this is an incomparable strategy for sopping up disposable time and money. An interest is, then, a self-generated redundancy system which limits the range of behavior and thus stabilizes the persona as a pseudo conjunctive category, although it is actually a disjunctive category which subsumes a random assemblage of behavior patterns controlled by a wide variety of unrelated institutions. In the relation of the individual to himself, an interest is the equivalent of an institution for the purposes of inter-individual relations. An interest enables the individual to define himself as a persona with a particular interest or interests, and this mode of persona definition can be used in identifying others, that is, in limiting the categories of behavior to which one responds.

Interests are the repressive oppressor of the individual upon himself, no matter what a given interest might be. For example, the available explanations for alcoholic or other drug addictions currently available are theoretically unsatisfactory, though to be sure any explanation can be successfully used to modify the behavior of some addicts. Since drugs are chemical means for limiting the range of behavior, it is readily understandable that virtually all cultures depend in part on drugs for social stability and that one of the redundancy systems in almost any culture for stabilizing the persona is the use of drugs. Given that fact, it is equally understandable that in any given population group in which drug use is a redundancy, some individuals will select drugs as their dominating interest. Addiction to a drug is thus a phenomenon to be understood statistically; causal explanations must necessarily be unsatisfactory. But the shoe goes on the other foot as well, for any interest can be easily understood as an addiction, a point which William Burroughs has made, though he has not provided a very satisfactory explanation for it (a point which once, I admit, I could not accept). Making money or writing poetry are, from this point of view, as much addictions as using cocaine. The obvious answer to this is that an addiction is harmful to the individual or to his society (that is, to the individuals with whom he interacts or, at any rate, to some of them). But this makes transparently clear how normative a term "addiction" is. If a behavior is harmful, it is harmful in someone's judgment, and if it does not seem harmful to the addicted person, then the judgment of addiction asserts that he ought to judge it to be harmful, and the usual steps of applying the ultimate sanctions are brought to bear upon him, so that he will change his mind. The most truly harmful addictions are probably addictions to words structured into belief systems, i.e., ideologies asserted to be "true."

EROS AND REDEMPTION

There is one resolution to the problem of sustaining the (attributionally incoherent) persona which is quite the opposite of those we have considered, though it too can easily become an addiction. Indeed in one form it is possibly the most common type, the erotic type. The other form in which this strategy occurs is mysticism, and this too can be addictive. The love discussed in the previous chapter is agape, or social love: the submission to the seduction of cultural redundancies, so that it is even possible to respond to the ultimate sanctions (particularly torture and execution) as if they were instances of the rhetoric of seduction. This is the source of the conversion so frequently experienced by the condemned on their way to the scaffold and the nobility of demeanor they so often display. A similar attitude seems to have been characteristic of the Aztec sacrificial victims, and it seems equally likely that it is responsible for the strategy of *suttee*. It is also rehearsed in the practice of masochism in sexual encounters, just as the sadist, in applying pain, is rehearsing or practicing (as one practices the piano exercises of Czerny) the application of the ultimate sanctions. Sadism is particularly interesting, because it acts out the terminality of the ultimate sanctions. Sexual encounters, because of their privacy, are particularly suitable for acting out these fundamentals of human behavior; sexual behavior is a social institution of great importance in maintaining the redundancy systems of seduction and force, and of hierarchy, and it is doubtful if any sexual encounter is entirely free of sadism and masochism. Moreover, sexual activity, again because of its privacy and because of its imprecise cultural transmission, particularly in European and American society, is suitable for acting out virtually any interest. One manifestation of that fact is the phenomenon of fetishism: there is no limit to the configurations which, for someone, can be sexually arousing and even consummatory. And this can be turned the other way around, so that, as agape, all sexual activity is fetishistic. The frequency with which sex and religious practices have been used as metaphors for each other suggests, indeed, that in our secularized society, with its extraordinary redundancy about sexual fulfillment, sexual activity is not only analogous to prayer, the acceptance of the control of cultural redundancies, but has almost taken its place.

Sexual behavior as agape, then, sustains the redundancies of both the culture and also of the individual, that is, his interests; in the first of these it is the nonverbal rhetoric of force and submission, of free and controlled aggression; in the second, fetishism, it sustains the individual's persona-stabilizing rhetoric. But sexual behavior also offers the possibility of eros, for it offers orgasm. Up to the moment of orgasm, it is agape as well as the promise of orgasm, though some individuals can extend eros into the pre-orgasmic behavior. Eros resolves the problem of sustaining the persona by simply dissipating it, for it offers the shock of the sudden and total relaxation of tension, the source of which is maintaining semiotic-categorial distinctions. To use old-fashioned terminology, in mystical experiences and in the erotic response to orgasm (and, for some individuals, in all or nearly all of a complete sequence of sexual behavior), the distinction between subject and object is obliterated and disappears. In the terms of the present discourse, that distinction is the unbridgeable abyss between stimulus field and semiotic response, so that the abyss opens up as soon as a figure is distinguished from the ground and a minimal categorization of that configuration is performed. The experience in question is that which Buddhism has named nirvana. Insofar as it is interpreted at all—and it is always said to be ineffable and uninterpretable and that any interpretation is a falsification—the entire stimulus field becomes both figure and ground. (It is not surprising, indeed, that it should be said to be an ineffable experience, for all semiosis depends upon a distinction between figure and ground.) From reports of the experience it occurs in either of two modes. In one the persona evaporates; it is not a figure distinguished from the perceptual ground. In the other, the configurations in the stimulus field are responded to as attributes of the persona. The most general report is that in mystical experience the ego and the world become one. In the sexual mode of the erotic, a term I shall use to subsume both the mystical and the sexual modes, the experience is said to involve the loss of identity, to use the rhetoric most commonly encountered today. If the mystic mode is explained in terms of a religious explanatory regress, the experience is most frequently described as union with the Godhead or, simply, with God. Moreover, since probably the most common mode of the erotic is the sexual—and it certainly is the most violent—the rhetoric of mysticism is often filled with sexual metaphors.

What actually happens is not difficult to understand. As we saw in Chapter II, we appear to be born with the capacity to respond, but we must learn to fixate upon a figure distinguished from its ground. What is learned can be unlearned, or forgotten; or it can disappear under shock. One result can be the dissipation of the persona construct. Another can be the loss of all categorial discrimination in the perceptual field being examined, as when the individual experiences information overload from a semiotic field he is scrutinizing with great intensity. The eroticism of mysticism has developed numerous techniques for reducing to the minimum, even to zero, the capacity to respond. The repetition of a nonsense word, of a *mantra,* or of a prayer is one such technique, but there are many. Steady, rhythmic stroking on any part of the body can be successful. Long-sustained masturbation is particularly effective in arriving at the sexual mode of the erotic experience, for it virtually eliminates the conflict between agape and eros ("virtually," because the behavioral individual is a dyad). But contemplation of a candle flame or listening to the constant repetition of a musical element can do the trick, especially if a drug helps matters along.

The universality of innumerable modes of eros indicates the universality of origin. As suggested above, the ultimate, fundamental source of human tension arises from maintaining the distinction between figure and ground and from maintaining the categorial stability of the figure so distinguished. Hence, eros is the profoundest escape from being human; it is a marvelous vacation. Its duration can last from the moment or two of orgasm to the long withdrawals of mysticism. But, since it is an escape and a vacation, it is always sought for in situations both protected and irresponsible. The institutional establishment of eros, whether sexual or mystic, maintains the redundancy of its availability and, likewise, the redundancy of the burden of being human and the weight of human freedom.

There is, then, in sexual activity a permanent possibility of incoherence; it can be either agape or eros, or both; that is, the individual's primary interest can be one or the other. "Falling in love" is selecting agape as a dominating interest, one which can be fairly temporary or

life-long. Some people are always falling in love, sometimes again and
again with the same individual, sometimes with a series of individuals.
Adolescence and youth are the stage in life during which falling in love
is most common, for it is precisely at these times that self-ascription of
value is most unstable, since the individual is moving from primary
control by learning-schooling institutions (especially the family) to
primary control by other institutions. In the West, eros has an uneasy
place; religious institutions accept it, but they do not encourage it and
grant it a place only grudgingly, as if the sole justification could be that
it derives its explanatory rhetoric from Christian rhetoric. The explanation for this uneasiness is to be found in the long-standing incoherence
in the West between the Judaeo-Christian tradition and the Platonic-
Platonistic. This incoherence has made it more difficult and therefore
more necessary to emphasize agape as a mode for sustaining the persona. In the Orient, eros and agape exist side by side in greater comfort. In China are the Taoist eros and the Confucian agape; in India
Hinduism embraces both. Japan is particularly interesting, for there
agape is to be found in the native religion and eros in the imported
Buddhistic Zen. But since the native religion is itself anti-explanatory,
with remarkable resemblances to sophisticated pragmatism and even to
such philosophers as Wittgenstein, it complements the Zen interpretation of eros, the basic semiotic practice of which is to force the individual out of explanatory behavior.

This antithesis between the West and the Orient is to be observed in
their differing notions of life after death—of heaven. In the Christian
heaven, the soul is saved; and even in the Christian hell the soul is
maintained. Hell is a kind of heaven, in that although the value of the
persona is imprisoned in eternal torture, its existence and its integrity
are eternally preserved. This is why it can be so bafflingly asserted that
the existence of hell and the condemnation of Christians to it is not
incoherent with the omnibenevolence of God. In heaven, of course, the
persona is maintained, but the ultimate sanctions vanish; there is no
possibility of economic deprivation; there is total spontaneous freedom
(there is no incoherence of interests or of redundancy systems); all
response is appropriate; and the value of the individual is never ques-
tioned and eternally asserted. In at least some Oriental religions, however, the persona becomes one with the divine universe after death; it
disappears. In both the West and in the Orient the problem of maintaining the persona is resolved. But in the Orient the analogical equivalent

to hell is the condemnation for one's sins to a return to life, in a different and probably a hierarchically baser form. In one Indian tradition, human life is hell, and who in West or East would entirely commit himself to denying it? Goethe said the *Iliad* convinced him of it. It is therefore not surprising that the West's greatest exploration of eroticism both sexual and mystic, Wagner's *Tristan und Isolde*, should have come into existence partly under the control of Oriental ideology.

As Wagner demonstrates with stunning clarity, in erotic behavior the beloved object becomes the promise of fusion of subject and object, the disappearance of distinction between figure and ground, the release from the struggle to turn figures into categorized configurations, the release from the burden of maintaining the persona. And since the erotic offers relief from what may be the most difficult of the brain's tasks and burdens, the promise of the erotic is responded to with an internal gestural regulatory sign of an almost unendurable yearning. And the music of *Tristan and Isolde* is the most consummate set of regulatory signs ever created of a yearning that can be appeased only by the evaporation of the persona. In Isolde's fate, or persona death, and in Tristan's physical death, Wagner identifies eros and thanatos; and I find it difficult to deny that he is right.

The consummations of both agape and eros are subsumed in verbalizations in which paradise is the central term. To the erotic lover the beloved offers the promise of suspension of all judgmental behavior and the elimination of all destabilizations of the persona. The beloved becomes the sign of such elimination and destabilization. To the social lover—whom we may call the addict of agape—a life after death in heaven, or even in hell, offers the same promise. This structural identity shows the close relation between agape and eros. However, there is a difference. Agape is function of interaction. When consummated, eros eliminates interaction, even interaction with the beloved, as Hemingway so penetratingly points out in *For Whom the Bell Tolls*. Agape sustains life by ascribing value to the persona. Eros, by eliminating the persona, or by eliminating the world as the demand for judgment, sustains the attraction of death. It appears to be the case that for most people, after achieving an acceptance of their own death in the early or middle forties, the fear of death and the desire for death alternate in their response to the predictability of physiological death. But the fear and the desire have not to do with that but with the fear of, and the desire for, the elimination of the unresolvable problem of sustaining the persona.

The secularization of culture has by no means changed the situation. It has simply meant the secularization of agape redemptionism and the increase of ascription of value given to eros redemption. Agape redemption now offers the promise of a life upon earth in which the persona is totally and eternally stabilized; and since any explanatory innovation can invade any explanatory regress within a culture area, it can be said to offer a redemptionism universal for all of mankind. It is thus in support of governmental institutions committed to an unshakably coherent ideology and the enemy of governmental institutions modeled on modern science and moving in the direction of the exploitation of ideological instability. Hence, redemptionism, whether that of agape or that of eros, is the great enemy of that aspect of man I have called *homo scientificus*, and this enmity is directed against the ultimate incoherence of the behavioral individual, the incoherence between the persona and the instability of the behavioral individual, between self-ascription of value and competencies, between maintaining the redundancy of irresolvable tension between subject and object and of maintaining and exploiting that tension, in spite of all the dangers and in spite of the fact that it requires a life of taking risks. (To use a biological rhetoric: for redemptionism the proper aim of man is perfect adaptation of organism to environment; for the antiredemptive, all adaptations are maladaptations, for they limit the range of behavior and therefore of response.) Once again the individual is catch-22, the irreducible surd of behavior, the precipitate of culture. Redemptionism is, to modify Goethe a bit, the vulgar that binds us all.

INDIVIDUAL RANDOMNESS

Yet in spite of the limitation of behavior, which finds its most extreme form in the erotic, the individual is also the source of randomness. It is no accident that explanations of eros, in both its forms, sexual and religious, culminate in an identification of the meaning of eros with such extreme terminations of explanatory regresses as God, Nature, the Unconscious, the Cosmos, *Das Welt-All*, Nirvana, the Buddha. What eros and the regressive termination of explanation have in common is the flight from randomness. Yet, as we have seen, randomness undermines explanation and thus makes possible the modification or destruction of ideologies, which are always inappropriate to an existential situation, since they are derived from previous situations. The response to explanations involves response transfer, and response transfer is possible because of the continuity of perceptual attributes. But that invariably means that some perceptual attributes are neglected. Since it is verbal, explanation can direct response transfer in spite of the total absence of continuity of perceptual attributes. Thus explanation has enormously extended the range of behavior but at the same time has increased the probability of inappropriateness of response. The application of ideologies is thus always uncertain, arguable, moot, and in any case possible only by the neglect of some or even all of the verbal and nonverbal signs to which the explanation was a verbal response. Since randomness is the prime source for undermining ideologies, it is of some moment to understand what its behavioral source is.

Learning amounts to the acquisition by the organism of what in his situation is judged to be the appropriate response to signs, the judgment of appropriateness being produced by others or by himself. However, as we also have seen, learning involves degrees of competence in semiotic response, i.e., semiotic transformation. In learning any response, then, it is possible to learn a response that occupies a point on a continuum between total competence—a matter of cultural judgment, of course—and total incompetence, the extreme of the latter being negation. As we emerge from infancy we learn untold myriads of responses and patterns of response. Two learning continua can intersect at any point or cannot intersect at all. Thus, a child who has not learned very well aggressive competency in interaction may find it difficult to learn to play the piano, a behavior which requires manipulatory aggression, both quantitatively and qualitatively, over his body and the piano mechanism. On the other hand such a child may be perfectly competent, even abnormally competent, in playing the piano. Anna Freud has pointed out that although some homosexuals played with dolls when they were children, there are plenty of men perfectly competent in heterosexuality who also played with dolls when they were children. "As the twig is bent, so grows the tree" is as untrue as it is true. That old adage is merely a normative attempt to control personality formation, just as psychiatry in its effort to find causal relations between childhood and adult behavior is likewise a normative explanatory effort to control behavior. Both are explanatory efforts to provide a pseudo history of such a nature that the individual can disclaim responsibility for his incompetences, stabilize his self-attribution of value, and get on with living. He can correct his incompetencies, if they are sufficiently interesting to him, or it can very frequently be quite enough for him to forget all about them or to ascribe to them supreme unimportance. The actual state of affairs is that randomness in personality formation is so uncontrolled by culture, so totally resistant to explanation, that the personality of every human individual is unique. Behavioral management or social control is thus a desperate effort to accomplish the impossible.

Culture is the effort, at best only partially successful, to control this randomness which is the necessary consequence of learning appropriate responses. Institutions maintain the redundancies which maintain culture. Exactly the same structure can be found in the behavioral individual. Interests are the culture of the individual, and the individual as a dyadic institution maintains the redundancies which maintain his interests. The verbal redundancies of individual behavior maintenance are the explanatory justifications which the individual produces by the behavior of semiotic transformation. Furthermore, what is true of the randomness of the acquisition of response and response patterns is equally true of the acquisition of individual culture, or interests, not only in childhood but throughout the individual's entire life. We cannot say that the interest of a parent is the cause of an interest in a child because siblings develop quite different interests. If in the family culture, redundancies ascribe value to both science and art, there is no way of predicting that one sibling will turn to science and the other to art, nor that the third will turn to neither but rather to pulling the wings off of flies. What has happened is that from an available redundancy, the application of the ultimate sanctions to himself, he has decided—a word used here metaphorically—to specialize in sadism (as the word is loosely used outside the sphere of sexual behavior). Hence, we may say that the source of an interest is not only an interest available in the growing child's immediate interactional environment, but also that it can be any redundancy. In the task of limiting the range of behavior, all interests are of equal effectiveness. For example, most children start playing with language between the ages of four and six. Play is a form of rehearsal, and games can be distinguished from play by the fact that games are temporary institutions, probably best understood as schooling institutions which instruct children in abstractions of adult behavior, while play is rehearsal of interests. Play with language ceases for the vast majority of children after lasting for rarely more than a year and a half, but with some children it remains a life-long interest. If their subsequent experience turns out to be such that they can use that interest within an institution, they might become politicians, philosophers, or poets, all of whom have in common linguistic "talent" (as an interest is called which, ordinarily at any rate, has received social validation). On the other hand, the chances of life might land them permanently in the army, in which linguistic talent is not particularly prized, especially among enlisted men. They might then become guardhouse lawyers, treated with a mixture of mockery and respect—mockery because the talent has no economic recognition and respect because it is after all a competency, a rhetorical overdetermination that rises above the norm of verbal expectancies in that situation.

The problem is complicated by the fact that though interests are rehearsed in play, most of them are abandoned, as most children abandon an interest in language great enough to become a dominating interest for the rest of their lives. By observing the development of adult interests, it is possible to create a model of how a child develops interests. An adult will try out an interest but then abandon it because it has no relation with his existent interests. Why he will try it out is fairly obvious: among cultural redundancies are approved interests, as can be seen by the frequent directions, "You ought to be interested in . . . ," or even more instructively, "I ought to be interested in . . . " Such statements are frequently followed by causal justifications, such as, "Since I am now very wealthy, and since the very wealthy in the past (and my peers in wealth right now) are interested in providing economic support for the arts at a high cultural level, I ought to get interested in one of them." (Such an individual may not be successful in sustaining such an interest, for the personality is less obviously a disjunctive category if the individual's interests, those behaviors which sustain the personality through various situations, are themselves related or at least judged by the individual to be related.) Among children, therefore, at the age of rehearsing an interest in language, that interest may not be relatable to any other interest already established. On the other hand, the social validation of interests is at work here also. If the child has been surrounded by a high level of verbal behavior from infancy, and if he himself is constantly talked to even before he can respond to verbal behavior, the probability is high that he will develop some interest in language and sustain it throughout his lifetime. This appears to be at least one explanation for the fact that an elite, concerned as it is with verbal explanation and needing a high level of competence in ideological manipulation, tends to be a self-perpetuating class. Nevertheless, it is impossible to say that a child growing up in an atmosphere of verbal behavior at a low cultural level in which nonverbal signs are of greater frequency than verbal signs cannot develop an interest in language. There are, indeed, mute inglorious Miltons, children who have developed a linguistic interest but whose education has not been such that that interest was maintained with sufficient frequency for it to become a talent. For such children the mere redundancy of some verbal behavior is enough to establish an interest. Thus, though an interest in verbal behavior may be traced back to the establishment of that interest before the child began to play with language around the age of four, there necessarily comes a point at which, no interests having been established, no new interest is relatable to an established interest.

The initiation of interest seems to be a random process, and even in adults this can be seen, for the establishment of a new interest is the consequence of interaction with redundant systems which have been randomly encountered, having been neither planned for nor predicted. Our newly wealthy man may try out many arts before he meets (quite by accident) someone with an intense interest in music; and this, it turns out, is an interest he can establish. Something like this is what happens to a child in establishing its initial interests. Bentham said that from the utilitarian point of view, poetry was no better than push-pin, and for the purposes of establishing an interest and sustaining the personality he was quite right. Initially it makes no difference what strategy is adopted for limiting the range of behavior, so long as some strategy is adopted. It is possible, for example, for an individual to remember exactly when the persona was established, after its long period of gestation, and from then on his dominating interests began to be assembled. It is by no means uncommon to hear such statements as, "He's a real person, because he has genuine interests." It seems probable, then, that the infant, which is most freely random in its activity during infancy, singles out a redundancy and turns it into an interest and that in infancy such behavior is entirely random. (A selective factor may be intelligence, but that word is one we understand so little about that it can only be suggested as a possibility.) It seems probable, then, that the establishment of interests and the establishment of a personality are either related processes or, more likely, two rhetorics for locating but a single process, two ways of categorizing but one set of behaviors. Certainly, as the individual ages, the interests become better established as a consequence of self-generated redundancy, the range of behavior becomes increasingly limited, and the interests themselves are judged to be more thoroughly relatable, more easily subsumed under a single category, merely by asserting an identity of semiotic attributes. The attributes of that category are then effective in narrowing the behavior within each interest, in making each interest more efficient in limiting the range of behavior, and in selecting and increasing the attributes which are common to all of the individual's interests. An individual may be interested in both painting and physics. Under the influence of the latter he becomes increasingly interested in the theory of painting, and in his fifties may suddenly realize that his "real" interest is in epistemology, since both in some strangely similar way appear to offer "knowledge of the real world," to use for a moment the odd and amusing rhetoric of philosophy. It not infrequently happens, especially among individuals who have penetrated to a high cultural level and are therefore unusually competent in explanatory behavior, that they are well on in life before they discover what their "true," their "real" interest is.

However, what has been presented so far are but extremely neat cases given in order to exemplify the factors at work in the selection and assembling of interest. The actual state of affairs is far different. The man who comes to subsume his interests under epistemology may also be interested in sexual encounters only with strikingly fat women between the ages of thirty and forty. Possibly he also has an interest in baking bread. His interests might very well include a particular way of opening cigarette packs. He may limit his tie-wearing behavior to the purchase of foulards only. And so on, almost infinitely. "Interest," however, remains an explanatory term, though very regressive. What is observable, and what enables us and indeed almost forces us to recognize an interest, is *overdetermination of response as judged by our normal expectancies for that kind of behavior*. For example, it is not uncommon today for individuals to own what are known as high-fidelity stereophonic sound-reproduction systems, and our ordinary expectations are that the quality of the equipment is approximately determined by the income level of the owner. However, if an $8,000 a year clerk has equipment rated as Class A, of which there is very little manufactured, worth thousands of dollars, and otherwise lives barely above the poverty level, this is what I am calling overdetermination of response. It is even more overdetermined if he spends his time not listening to his equipment but fussing with it. What can also be observed is the intensity of response when an individual judges that the behavioral protocol of his interest has been violated, whether that protocol is maintained by widespread cultural redundancies or solely by his own. "Intensity" is a term which can subsume a great variety of behaviors: sudden change in the production of gestural regulatory signs, as when a man turns white with fury if his maid has rearranged the candlesticks on his mantelpiece, as she invariably does, thus giving him the happy opportunity for maintaining that particular redundancy once a week; or perhaps the change can be in the frequency and length of time devoted to production of the signs of his interest, as when a logician, one interested in the procedural overdetermination of verbal behavior, judges that a colleague in his profession has violated logical protocol and responds by spending two weeks writing a scathing article. Thus, he is interested in logic, the procedural overdetermination of verbal behavior, not just to make a living in an academic institution, but for his persona's sake. The high frequency in his article of denigratory rhetoric is a further measure of "intensity," an indication of overdetermination. Likewise, the behavioral change in the individual can be manifested in a refusal even to discuss the interest which he judges to have been violated. Members of academic institutions at a high cultural level do not tend to enter such institutions because they are interested in high-level economic reward, but they do tend to enter because they are interested in the behavior such institutions control and maintain. Except for the nonverbal behavior of the arts and higher mathematics, most academic individuals begin with an interest in verbal behavior, which is then gradually limited to their particular subject or specialty within that subject. The intensity of their interest entails a corresponding intensity of response when they encounter violations of what they believe to be the behavioral protocol of their specialty. Given their verbal interest, developed into a talent by intensive training, it is not surprising that in academic institutions the rhetoric of abuse is more overdetermined than in any other kind of institution, with the possible exception of countergovernmental institutions. But both, after all, are ideological. The abuse at sports events, uttered by people who are not interested in language but in sports, is pallid and unimaginative by comparison. Indeed it is not uncommon for individuals operating in ideological institutions to develop such an interest in the rhetoric of abuse or denigration that the other possibilities of ideological behavior are relatively neglected. In the ideological institution of literature these are the great satirists. Jonathan Swift was not merely interested in the rhetoric of abuse; he was intensely interested in overdetermination of response to the violation of the protocol of *anything* he had an interest in, even not a very intense one. The objects of abuse in *Gulliver's Travels* are consequently extraordinarily miscellaneous, even random, and this is why he sent Gulliver on voyages.

Examples could be multiplied, and the multiplication would be tedious, for writer as well as for reader. It is sufficient to draw a lesson from this: it is impossible on the basis of one interest to predict what the character of another will be. It is thus impossible to say with any degree of predictability, "If he has this interest in x situation, he will necessarily have the same interest in y situation"; or, "If his interest has x attribute, then any other interest must have x attribute." And equally impossible are negative statements of the same sort. Clearly the assemblage of interests in any individual is random. This randomness of interest is not to be confused with the alleged structure of an individual's belief system, maintained by a considerable psychological literature which is, however, to my mind dubious both theoretically and procedurally. Here the term "interest" covers such trivialities as bodily tics, or a man's scratching his behind when he is perplexed by alternative behavioral possibilities. (Indeed, this latter example seems to me a particularly attractive instance of how an interest limits the range of behavior.)

It is also clear that the randomness of interest interferes with the predictability upon which smooth interaction depends. The more unpredictably an individual behaves, the more unpredictable to him will be the responses to his behavior. Two cultural redundancies are strategies that deal with this continuous threat of behavioral dissolution. One is the concealment of interests judged inappropriate to a situation and likewise the concealment of interests which are given a negative valuation by the redundancies at work in that situation (though they might be given a positive valuation in another situation). If civilization is smoothness of interaction combined with high-level ideologies, rich exemplification by ideological institutions, and governmental, economic, and schooling institutions characterized by relatively easy modifiability under the impact of negative feedback, then hypocrisy and insincerity and lying form the very foundations of civilization. The second strategy to counter the threat of behavioral dissolution is the construction of explanations of the persona discussed above. This is why such explanations are both coherent and highly selective—and also a priori. The individual who is most disturbed at the threat of the dissolution of his own behavior is the one who is readiest with explanations, justifications, excuses, and a personal history which constructs a ''causal'' account of his own behavior. (It is what makes the economic institution of psychiatry possible. Psychoanalysis has been a great gift, for it makes rich explanations of absolutely any behavioral dissolution quite easy, and it provides an extraordinary and by now nearly random range of such explanations. Its trouble, as has been said often enough, is not that it explains but that it explains entirely too much. It can even explain negation of itself. It is perfectly solipsistic; hence, the rapidity with which it was exemplified in literature and theater and also the rapidity with which it penetrated cultural levels lower than that at which it originated.)

RANDOMNESS, INTERESTS, AND GOVERNMENT

When this randomly assembled package of interests, of behavioral overdeterminations which are semiotic overdeterminations, this ''individual'' (or persona) is given a place in an institution, all hell breaks loose, and hell is always breaking loose in all institutions. To give but a few examples, the randomness of interests is responsible for favoritism, which is terribly disruptive in institutions and which is absolutely unavoidable, for the response to violation of protocols increases enormously the incidence of contempt from above and resentment from below, both of which, as we have seen, are endemic in institutions. The randomness of interests increases the frequency and intensity of loyalty, which is one of the principal institutional impediments to modification by feedback. And it increases the incidence of vandalism. Randomness of interests, therefore, increases the instability of institutions, for like any randomness it undermines the explanatory structure of institutions and the behavior that structure controls. Its ultimate consequence is that it increases the probability of the application of the ultimate sanctions and the severity of that application.

The effect of this randomization of behaviors and interests in the individual is that any population group is a random collection of personalities. Consequently, the ideology, or explanatory regress, which subsumes a population has the relation to that population that a scientific theory has to its data. From this flow several other consequences. No governmental ideology can successfully subsume all the behavioral attributes or combinations of attributes or interests or combination of interests of the populations under its control. Only populations so small that no governmental institution has emerged are exceptions; for them no explanation has emerged as a result of the effort to stabilize personality interaction by means of subsumption and attempted resolution of incoherence. For this reason subpopulations are formed by individuals who form a nongovernmental or even antigovernmental culture bonded by a commonalty of interests, if those interests are judged not to be adequately subsumed and controlled by the governmental ideology. A subculture of Satanists falls thus into the same category as trade unions did originally. This relation between government and population also provides an explanation for the political activities of governmental institutions, so frequently (and perhaps always) incoherent with their behavioral control and employment of ultimate sanctions. The effort of Russia to solve that incoherence by having the political party control the government does not resolve the incoherence; it merely places a rhetorical mask in front of it. Significantly, such an effort to resolve the incoherence between politics and government and the random character of a population inadequately subsumed by governmental institutions and the government's ideology was made after a revolution. Revolutions occur when the ideology is one in which an ideological stability at any cost is a factor in the ideology. Governmental institutions cannot then respond to population randomization and to the formation of interest subpopulations, both of which emerge as the situation of the government changes economically or as antigovernmental ideology is introduced into the population. The French Revolution was the consequence of both of these factors. On the one hand, an enormous population increase in the course of the preceding century created a new situation for the governmental institutions which was primarily economic in character; while, on the other hand, the Enlightenment, superficially different from the Christian ideology, was introduced by ideological institutions. It is extremely doubtful if the population change (and its economic consequences) was in any way related to the ideological innovations in France in the eighteenth century. Just as scientific instruments undermine a scientific theory by producing more data than the theory can handle (and data of a kind which the theory cannot handle at all), so randomization of personality and interests undermines governmental institutions and their ideologies. It is the peculiar character of the modern age that both personality and interest randomization have increased—the result of the communication revolution which began with the mechanization of paper production in the early nineteenth century and the resultant enormous increase of printed verbal behavior. Innovative subpopulation groups have emerged, and in addition the quadruplication of the population of Europe in the nineteenth century, not to speak of increase since then, has created a situation which by statistical necessity increased the randomization of both. The more recent expansion of communication media throughout the world has resulted, moreover, in a striking increase in what optimists call cultural cross-fertilization and pessimists call cultural disintegration and sterility. Probably both are right. In any case, events of the last several decades show that governmental institutions are steadily losing their control over randomly emerging subpopulations. (Such subpopulations that call themselves Marxists are controlled in fact by a wide range of mutually incoherent ideologies. "Marxism" is rapidly becoming a disjunctive category.)

From all this flows another disagreeable notion. Modern states have accepted as their responsibility the welfare of the population under their control. Even if "welfare" is limited to the simplest, most primitive, and most basic needs of food, clothing, and shelter, it is barely possible for the wealthiest of modern states to carry out that responsibility. However, once anything more than this simplest notion of welfare is attempted, the factor of diverse judgment comes into play. If it is accepted that "welfare" subsumes "happiness" and "personal self-fulfillment" (as, for example, by means of the educational systems), then the randomization of personalities and interests comes into play (that is, the randomization of judgment of what "welfare" in fact means). To give a trivial but revealing example, that portion of the public which does not receive food stamps is indignant when they see luxury or snack foods—at once expensive and nutritionally almost worthless—being bought with food stamps. Yet the extension of the meaning of "welfare" now subsumes the judgment by the food stamp beneficiary that he needs luxury foods and snack foods. This fragmentation of the population into categories self-identified as being badly put-upon by the society (categories that become interest groups) requires an expenditure of the economic resources of a nation very much like pounding money down a rat hole. The attempt to create social stability by satisfying the demands of interest groups merely brings into existence more interest groups and increases the amount of social instability. The effort of a government to satisfy all the randomly created interests of its population, interests which are not economically productive, is precisely the same situation in which a scientific theory attempts to explain with equal validity and explanatory-exemplificatory success all of the data which the theory does in fact subsume. In both cases the effort is futile. Governmental satisfaction of interests, if not selective, destroys its explanatory power, just as a scientific theory must be selective in order to maintain the stability necessary for putting it to use. In short, any government must be selective in responding to the interests of the population under its control, and ultimately that selection can be maintained only by force. The domination of a society by an egalitarian ideology must necessarily be followed by an authoritarian regime. Will Durant is not a great historian, but he has undoubtedly read more history than most professional academic historians. He is worth paying attention to. The conclusion of his studies, he says, is, ''order is the mother of liberty, and liberty is the mother of chaos.'' One may add, ''And chaos is the mother of order.'' It makes little difference whether a new government with a new ideology replaces the undermined one or whether the old government reestablishes its authority. The dynamics of this is that for any institution, not merely governmental, fragmentation or randomization of interest demands emerges if the interests of the population under its control become recognized. The only attributes which all members of the population now have in common is resentment, a word which subsumes noncooperative response to the behavior-controlling hindrances of aggression. Given the reduction of common attributes to resentment, so that it becomes a highly active redundancy system, the result is a greater degree of aggression than the aggression imposing the hindrance. Chaos is the mother of order because the continuity of the attribute of resentment among all or most of the population creates a condition of selection of behavior, the requisite for the reestablishment of an authoritarian regress, capable once again of successfully imposing hindrance.

EMERGENT INNOVATION: CULTURAL TRANSCENDENCE
From that very randomness of the personality package and the randomness of the individual's selection of interests from his total range

of behavior, his strategy for limiting the range of his behavior, emerges innovation. It may be either fruitful or damaging. If it is judged to be the first, it is validated by the word "creativity"; if it is judged to be the second, it is invalidated by the word "error." Whether human innovation is beneficial or harmful to the survival of the human species is impossible to say, for the species is neither extinct nor yet free from the threat of extinction. At the moment it looks very much as if the development of modern science, the "creativity" of modern science, responsible for an ever more rapidly rising rate of innovation during the past couple of hundred years, is increasing the probability of extinction, or at least of the transformation of civilization back into much more primitive conditions. Moreover, it is not only the randomness of the personality package that is responsible for innovation, but the randomness of the occurrence of situations in which innovation is possible. We have already seen something of that principle in the examination of scientific behavior, but scientific institutions are precisely set up to increase the probability of "creativity." They are institutions which have to a certain extent brought creativity under control.

But let us take a more homely example. An army inspector exclaims to the captain of a company that the quality of the company mess is infinitely superior to the usual army food, even though the cooks use only the standard rations issued to all companies at that post. The captain explains that the company's mess had been for a long time perfectly ordinary and frequently worse. One day, however, he happened to overhear a sergeant discussing with evident knowledge the dinner he had had the night before in one of the better restaurants in the neighboring town. It was evident that he was not only knowledgeable about restaurants but took an unusual degree of pleasure in good food. Although he had no experience in cooking or running a mess, he was intelligent. The captain took a chance and appointed him mess sergeant. The result was what the inspector had observed, an extraordinarily good mess. The principle here is clear enough: an interest, hitherto unexploited, coincided with the performance of an institutional routine. The result was innovation. The sergeant, who had shown no signs of creativity before this, suddenly became creative. Nor was it cultural innovation; it was merely the application of an established mode of behavior to a situation in which it had not been hitherto employed. Further, it must not be imagined that the innovation was stabilizing. If the inspector general, as army inspectors will, pointed this out to the other company captains of the post and urged them to go and do likewise, a considerable destabilization of the companies as institutions (and of the whole post) would be the result. One of the most common incoherences is that between the judgment that all innovation is harmful and the judgment that all innovation is fruitful.

Of greater interest and importance than such a minor innovation as our mess sergeant's is the kind of innovation which is a true cultural innovation in that it introduces into a culture a behavior which is unknown not only to that culture but to any culture. I shall call it *emergent innovation,* or *cultural transcendence.* It is always negational or anticultural and depends upon the randomly assembled package of the interests of some individual. It also depends upon an over-determination of aggressive competence (an "interest in" aggressiveness). We may begin by considering one minor manifestation of such aggressiveness, the behavioral phenomenon of adolescent vandalism. Even while I have been writing this chapter, a group of five unusually enterprising adolescents from my city stole from construction and demolition companies large amounts of explosives, together with the equipment needed to set them off. There were several mysterious minor explosions and then came a really quite spectacular one, the destruction of the concrete ticket-office at one of the high school stadiums. Fortunately or unfortunately (it is difficult to decide), the boys were detected and captured within a few days. Such acts take place in situations of impunity. There are consequences, but not, the vandals hope, to themselves. Vandalizing empty houses is particularly popular, especially if the residents of the house are at a higher economic level than that of the vandals. More than once in this book we have encountered the behavioral phenomenon of rehearsal, and adolescent vandalism is the rehearsal of aggressive competence—in situations of impunity. Nevertheless it is designed to destroy or damage property valuable to others. Sometimes the value of the property is quite small; twice in seven years I have had my mail box destroyed, both times very late at night, and obviously with bricks or stones thrown from moving automobiles. On the other hand, a few years ago a nearby expensive house burned to the ground. The point is that the property destroyed is valuable to somebody; otherwise there would no point to the vandalism. But property is a sign, at least minimally a sign of value. The vandals themselves respond to that sign either with little intensity or a great deal. The sign destroyed may elicit from them a powerful response (it may engage an interest), or it may elicit a very weak response. But it can be successfully predicted that it will elicit a powerful response in the vandalized. I am furious when my mailbox is destroyed, although it is worth only a few dollars. Nevertheless, since it is *my* property, the mailbox is an interest which sustains my persona and also my self-ascription of value, particularly since it has my name on it. I am likewise irritated when children cross my property or play in my pond, but I am ashamed of being irritated, and I let them. Children have to play someplace besides home. The man next door, however, has put up a hurricane fence specifically to keep children from treading on his sacred ground. It may not be sacred to them, but it is sacred to him. It sustains his personality. His fence is an act of aggressiveness, masked as defense.

These may seem trivial considerations, but they are not. An act of anticultural innovation entails an act of cultural vandalism, an act of desecrating a sign or sign complex, the value of which is sustained by the redundancies; and that sign is therefore necessarily an interest of some portion of the society's population. If the innovation is a religious statement, one can be sure that an interest of a large portion of the population is attacked. They will judge it to be an act of vandalism, will respond with corresponding intensity, and will find it incomprehensible for the very reason that to them it is an interest. Two deductions may be made at this point. First, an act of cultural vandalism connected with an emergent innovation is designed to destroy, and it is done publicly, not in conditions of impunity. It may begin privately in that the cultural vandal destroys one of his own most cherished beliefs, but it is not fully manifest until others are affected, and affected profoundly, just as with adolescent vandals. Only if others are affected and respond with great intensity can the vandalizing emergent innovator be sure that his innovation is of cultural significance. The second deduction to be made is that here we have an explanation as to why it is that emergent innovation is so passionately resisted. It is the same phenomenon as that already discussed. If the protocol associated with an interest is violated, the interested individual responds with rage; an attempt, he judges, has been made to undermine his personality, to deprive of their validity the interests that sustain it.

We are now equipped to examine the behavioral pattern of emergent innovation. It is actually a pattern first extracted from the matrix of human behavior by a tiny group of Europeans at the beginning of the nineteenth century, a group cultural history knows as the Romantics. What they were responding to was the French Revolution and the Napoleonic tyranny and imperialism that followed it. Their judgment was that specific directions for behavior had been derived from a high-level explanation, but that the predictions made about the consequences of that behavior were so completely incoherent with what in fact happened that the high-level explanation itself must be rejected. Specifically, the high-level Enlightenment position was that the mind is naturally a reproduction of the world. Whenever it is not, then error and tyranny and priestcraft, as the Enlightenment propagandists called it, had interfered. The directions were that if these *interferences* were destroyed, then the *congruence of mind and world* would be established; and a *perfect* congruence of mind, society, and world would be the result. The course of the French Revolution—disastrous in the judgment of a handful of individuals—indicated that the terminating proposition was in error, that the tension between subject and object, between mind and world, was not a consequence of the failures of human history but inherent. What is crucial is the pattern of behavior that unfolded, as well as the establishment of the conditions of the emergent innovation introduced into Europe by the Romantic tradition; initially the innovating Romantic redundancies were on a small scale, but they eventually spread out. Moreover, since they were at the highest level of explanatory regress in European culture, they attracted the attention (and often, and increasingly, the assent) of members of the ideological institutions. No emergent innovation can be culturally established unless a redundancy system is established and maintained institutionally and spread by propaganda.

The effect of the Romantics' judgment on the explanatory termination of the Enlightenment was devastating. Virtually the highest level of the explanatory regress of European culture was undermined. The result was explanatory collapse; and since this epistemology had been an interest of the Romantics when they were still believers in the Enlightenment, there was a corresponding threat to themselves and for some a fairly general collapse of the persona. Wordsworth held himself together for a year and a half by devoting himself to mathematics. That became his sole interest, an example of the extremely common behavior (one which psychiatrists often encounter) of responding to explanatory collapse by limiting the range of one's behavior to concentration upon a single interest—very frequently by taking up a nonverbal activity, usually one concerned with visual or "natural" signs. (A wholehearted interest in sex is often the strategy used.) For Wordsworth, since what had collapsed was so deeply involved with Nature, turning to "natural" signs was not a strategy open to him. For the Romantics, once the explanatory termination had collapsed, everything it subsumed collapsed—that is, virtually the entire explanatory regress of European culture.

The result of explanatory collapse, the first attribute of the behavioral pattern of emergent innovation, was the second: alienation. Since this term has been so widely used in the past decade, a distinction must be made between alienation and polarization. During the 1960s two ideologies of this country became compromised in the judgment of a great many individuals, particularly in the judgment of a large enough segment of the university and college population to make a difference. The Vietnam war was judged to be incoherent with the ideology that ours is a benevolent government; and the ideology that the social usefulness of an economic institution is determined by its production of profit was perceived to be incoherent with the environmental deterioration which was only too obvious throughout the country, especially in the cities. The result, for most of those who responded to these perceived incoherences, was polarization. That is, they turned to an ideology in antithesis to the regnant ideologies, a primarily Enlightenment ideology (or an ideology of the Marxist version of the Enlightenment). "Polarization," then, is the response to explanatory collapse by commitment to a rival explanation. "Alienation" is a response that judges no alternative explanation or ideology to be available. To the alienated, the polarized ideologies are subsumable under a single category. (In the same way, a scientist is alienated from a theory which he judges his experiments to have undermined because he judges that no scientific theory is available which can effectively subsume those experiments.)

Alienation and polarization are easily confused, because the response to them is identical—cultural vandalism. But it is not the kind of vandalism which is a rehearsal and which is done with impunity. It can in fact be extremely dangerous to the individual who undertakes it. An example of cultural vandalism done with the support of governmental institutions is to be found in an affair already mentioned, the destruction during the Chinese Cultural Revolution of artifacts and works of art which exemplified a governmentally rejected ideology. The same kind of vandalism occurred in the pillaging, destruction, and secularization of churches during and after the Russian Revolution. For individuals whose cultural vandalism takes place in conditions of risk, without governmental support, those risks are great, as Solzhenitsyn found out when he vandalized the ideology of the Soviet government. (Servetus made the same discovery when he vandalized the Calvinist ideology and was burned alive.) Such drastic responses from governmental institutions are not always the case, of course, and very little of the sort happened to the Romantics as a consequence of their cultural vandalism, which was as powerful as they could make it. It was usually verbal, however, and when it was pictorial, as with Caspar David Friedrich, it was easily misinterpreted. Furthermore, it was at such a high cultural level that the segment of the population that could even understand it was itself very small. Even so, the Romantics suffered social ostracism, exclusion from ideological schooling institutions (particularly universities) and found publication by no means easy. The ultimate sanction of economic deprivation was principally the one applied to them; and the growth of censorship in the early nineteenth century was a subtle way of applying that sanction. Cultural vandalism, then, is the strategy for attaining and maintaining the high level of aggression required for sustaining alienation.

The next factor in this pattern is social withdrawal. It is very similar to the response of an individual when the protocols of an intensely held interest are violated, except that in this pattern just the reverse happens. Social interaction requires constant exposure to redundant protocols which, to the alienated individual, are infuriating because there is no explanatory justification for them. Great areas of the culture (and almost all of high-level culture, if the alienation is the consequence of highly regressive explanatory collapse) become not only unavailable; they become offensive. Furthermore, when an individual experiences explanatory collapse and engages in cultural vandalism, what he is vandalizing are his own former interests. Thus, cultural vandalism is always self-vandalism and inevitably undermines the persona. Continuous social interaction with the protocols of such rejected interests are necessarily interpreted as a powerful aggression directed against himself, for up to this point his persona is maintained only negatively, by the negation of the validity of his interests. For this reason, since no alternative explanation has yet been constructed, social interaction also involves a temptation to return from alienation to social integration, (putting oneself once more under the control of the rejected redundancies and ideologies), a temptation which is best resisted by the strategy of social withdrawal, by removing oneself from exposure to the redundancy systems which have now become both aggressive and seductive. This is of the greatest possible importance.

A low interaction rate is virtually a necessity for emergent innovation, among both animals and men. John Calhoun has discovered that in both wild and artificial rat populations low-interaction rats innovate patterns of behavior which are sometimes adopted by the successful and sleek high-interaction rats and that such innovations can rapidly become redundant within the population. Low interaction, or social withdrawal, which entails removal from the culture's redundancy systems, separates the individuals from those redundancy systems which maintain learned behavior. In the absence of such maintenance, the brain, which is always as busy as it can be, produces random behavior. This is why scientific laboratories, libraries, high-level executive offices, and such places as art museums permit and demand an extreme reduction of interaction, for only thus can the individual randomize his behavior and select from the products of that randomization a promising and perhaps ultimately fruitful bit. A low-interaction rate also permits another mode of behavior: sustained problem exposure (behavior which is impossible in situations of high interaction, unless the individual has developed techniques of eliminating his responses to most semiotic stimuli). Thus, in low interaction a problem can be concentrated on; an idea can be pursued; intuitive responses to each step in arriving at a solution can be examined and accepted or rejected; and each step accepted can be followed by further randomization. Romantic literature and painting, and even music (noticeably in the behavior of Beethoven) are filled with socially isolated and wandering figures, such isolation being a way of exemplifying randomness. In actual behavior, however, something rather different happens.

The alienated individual, having performed or still performing his cultural vandalism, having withdrawn from interaction into a living style of low interaction, having arrived at virtual social isolation, is now faced with a problem. Culture is sustained by redundancy systems. The redundancy systems generated by an individual when they are in antithesis to the redundancies of his culture and, therefore, to his own redundancies (which the brain continues to produce, in spite of the fact that it has negated them) are rarely sufficient to sustain the culture of alienation and withdrawal if the individual remains totally isolated. As a friend of mine has well said, whenever you have a really new idea, you think you are crazy. The fact that the ordinary behavior in response to a new idea is to talk it over with a sympathetic friend is sufficient to indicate that it is very difficult, and perhaps impossible, to sustain an alienated personality in total isolation, not to speak of sustaining an emergent innovation. Virtually every Romantic of stature surrounded himself with a small group of sympathetic and usually like-minded friends. Tiny clusters of alienated individuals emerged here and there across Europe. Further, ever since the early nineteenth century this "little group" syndrome has been part of the behavioral pattern of generating emergent innovation. Both before and after the individual has arrived at his innovation, he requires a high interaction rate with a small number of individuals who can maintain his redundancies by reiterating them. This has become the behavioral style of innovation even among scientists. It is not that interaction with a little group as a strategy for maintaining behavior had not previously existed. On the contrary, it is the norm of behavior. Rather, like the other factors in the Romantic pattern, it was extracted from the context of human behavior and used to maintain behavior discontinuous from the other behaviors of the culture. It is instructive that without the support of a little group the alienated individual is likely to exhibit bizarre behavior and is much less likely to generate a fruitful innovation.

The emergent innovation having been achieved, the next step is to propagandize it, to establish it as one of the redundancy systems of the culture. The technique here is to introduce it into a context of established redundancies and thus to create for a larger public the incoherence which led to the explanatory collapse and the alienation. Pope Gregory gave a nice example of this strategy when he recommended in his *Pastoral Care* that Christian images be placed upon the altars of heathen temples and that only subsequently should the temple be demolished and a Christian church be built in its place. The use of the same place is of great importance, and the Spaniards in Mexico did exactly the same thing, no doubt having read Pope Gregory. Wordsworth used a poetic tradition which was not only well established but was in some ways more historically regressive than some of his earlier experimental poetry, which was marked by a much higher degree of cultural vandalism. Hugo used the intensely conservative and anti-innovative world of the public theater, vandalizing the Alexandrine poetic line when he did so—a good example of how in propagandizing an emergent innovation, cultural vandalism may be used as a diversionary tactic. It attracts attention; it arouses the fury of the conservative, thereby drawing the sympathy of those who have begun to have their doubts about what the innovator has rejected; and it permits the innovation to enter the culture almost unnoticed. It is a splendid example of seduction.

Explanatory collapse, alienation, cultural vandalism, social withdrawal and a severe reduction of the interaction rate, the support of a little group, and propagandization—these together constitute the pattern, or cluster, or syndrome of behaviors which raise to a high level the probability of generating an emergent innovation and establishing it in the culture. Exactly the pattern that is observable in the first Romantics is observable equally well in the behavior of the early Christians. The difference is the nature of the explanatory collapse, which was only partial, and the nature of the emergent innovation. Christianity was not a full-scale emergent, for it was aimed at establishing a stable and redemptive ideology to which absolute commitment was required. The pattern of emergent innovation can be seen as a pattern of deconversion, and the early Christians responded by offering a new pattern of conversion, and that pattern, at its highest levels of regress and in many of its lower levels and exemplifications, differed little in its structure from the explanatory patterns which preceded it. Romanticism too was a de-conversion, but the conversion it offered was to an explanatory regress marked by instability and antiredemptiveness: *it was a de-conversion that led to a conversion into permanent de-conversion*. It was thus the most fully emergent innovation in European culture since the early Neolithic and, possibly, since the Paleolithic. The number of individuals who are fully converted to it is still very small and possibly will never be very large.

Perhaps that in itself is not important. All that might be useful is the acceptance in high-level government institutions of the explanatory principle of ideological instability and its exploitation (and also at the high cultural level of other institutions, particularly economic and ideological, just as that principle was ultimately accepted by science some seventy or eighty years ago). Yet it must be remembered that it is not a redemptive principle; it does not assure a satisfactory life nor a perfect society. What it does do is to make possible the observation of incoherence, to make possible the modification of ideologies, to facilitate a government's dealing with ideological crisis, and thus to reduce the dependence upon both politics and the ultimate sanctions. It makes it possible, and certainly much easier, to be aware of and to resist those redundancies of the culture which give directions for performances that are unavailing. It instructs us that the only fruitful ideological commitment is a commitment to an ideology of noncommitment. Were that established, then a truly democratic social situation might emerge—not one that is free of hierarchy, for institutional hierarchy is no more than explanatory regression, and that is the condition of human existence—but rather a social situation in which throughout all institutions negative feedback could be fed upward with impunity or at least with greater impunity than is now the circumstance for all of us.

Yet the contemplation of even this modest possibility is too optimistic. The individual, let it be remembered, is an institution, and as an institution he has his own politics—his own strategies for maintaining his stability as an institution within a larger institution. Any innovating instructions from above, and any modifying feedback from below, threaten the institutional stability of the individual. It is always to his interest to modify politically any innovation from either direction. Hence, no institutions work well, whether authoritarian or democratic, for there is always a conflict, an incoherence, between the task or mission of the larger institution and the stability of the individual, for innovation always threatens dissolution of the persona.

CONCLUDING MORAL

And that I hope is the moral of this book, this inquiry into the control of human behavior which has concluded with the presentation of the behavioral pattern necessary for throwing off worn-out controls and imposing upon oneself—there is no choice—controls which, it is to be hoped, are more fruitful. Truly the individual is catch-22, for there is nothing but the individual organism, behaving, and by that device we call semiosis turning behavior into performance. The behavioral individual is the precipitate of semiosis and culture and redundancies and institutions and ultimate sanctions; he is the irreducible surd of existence, the fundamental incoherence of human life, for he cannot but strive with all his might, with all his aggressiveness, for stability; and yet at the same time he is the only source of that randomization from which issue emergent innovations—which if they cannot eliminate can at least modify, and not infrequently for the better, our fictive and normative absurdities of explanation.

Explanation is the ineluctable condition, the defining attribute of human behavior, and in this book I have endeavored to explain human behavior by taking that proposition as the termination of an explanatory regress. Let us take a hint from the incomparable Hegel. To grasp the centrality of explanation and to accept the indeterminability of explanation and therefore of behavior is to enter Golgotha. And Golgotha is the place of skulls and crucifixion.

INDEX

Abstract-concrete distinction, 104-5
Acting as semiosis, 132
Addiction, 255-56
Agape systems. *See* value ascription
Aggression. *See* arts; behavior
Appia, Adolphe, 22
Architecture as semiosis, 123-25
Art and Pornography, 164
Arts: as controlling aggression, 131-34; as ideological institutions, 231-32; perceptual discontinuity in, 232-33; performatory signs in 130-31; regulatory signs in, 121-29; in undermining ideologies, 234-35; as value institutions, 205-6
Attention, 93

Bacon, Francis, 146, 200
Beethoven, Ludwig van, 127-28
Behavior: as aggressive, 119-21, 203 (*see* signs: categories of, regulatory); search and test, 10; subsumes "response," 53-54; uncertainty in, 138
—control of, 3, 153, 161-62; by agape systems, 203; necessity for, 242. *See* force *and* seduction
—erotic, 257-59; persona evaporation, 260; as redemption, 260
—homosexual, 203
—human, 1-2; "homo scientificus,"155-66; indeterminability of, 115; innovation in, 160-61; modification of, 158; rehearsal of, 204; as semiotic transformation, 116; sign as basic unit of, 162-63; termination of explanatory regress of, 166

—linguistic, 89-90; intonation, 121
—nonverbal, 1; dependent on verbal, 115; as distinguished from verbal, 102
—randomization of, 108-10
—semiotic, 96-99; as pre-human, 102; response transfer in, 102
—sexual, 20, 124, 256-57; as agape, 257, 258-59; as eros, *see* behavior, erotic
—verbal, 1, 13, 82; as distinguished from nonverbal,102-3; establishment of, 106; explanation as condition of, 87; opacity of, 116
Belasco, David, 22
Bibbienas, 22
Boltzmann, Ludwig, 143, 145, 147, 156
Brain: randomness of response by, 107, 165-66
Bribery, 172
Bruner, Jerome, 68
Buddhism, 257
Burke, Edmund, 196-97
Burnett, Frances Hodgson, 202
Burroughs, William, 255

Carlyle, Thomas, 100
Categorial regress. *See* explanatory regress
Categories, 68-71; as direction-giving, 69; as fictive and normative, 69-71
Categorization. *See* explanatory regress
Causality, 3-10, 48-49, 104
Cause-effect, 4, 6
Chomsky, Noam, 86
Cinema. *See* psychology, experimental
Clubs. *See* institutions: social, value ritual in